Practical Undergraduate Instrumental Analysis Laboratory Experiments

N. H. Chen
University of Maryland Eastern Shore

First revision: December 20, 2013
Second revision: June 28, 2018

ISBN-10: 0-615-74252-1
ISBN-13: 978-0-615-74252-6

TABLE OF CONTENTS

PREFACE

The aim of this book is to provide a practical and affordable general lab manual for undergraduate Instrumental Analysis (IA) course. After extensive experience in teaching IA laboratory course for a number of years, I have developed this lab manual in what I believe to be an improved version of an IA manual that is both concise and comprehensive. The factors I consider most important for an IA laboratory manual to be effective in teaching are as follows: 1) the instruments covered in the manual should follow ACS guidelines, and reflect new advances in the field of IA, while also addressing industrial needs; 2) experiments in the manual should address the basic principles of the instruments and help the students to understand the fundamental concepts and mechanisms of the instruments; 3) the manual should facilitate the instructor to cover lab processes from both theoretical and operational perspectives; and 4) the lab manual should be affordable, and meet the needs of majority of today's undergraduate chemistry and other multi-disciplinary (e.g. environmental science) programs.

This manual provides the core essentials for the most common instruments recommended by ACS guidelines as well as those used in a traditional chemistry program. They are electrochemistry (Chapter 2), spectroscopy (Chapter 3, 4, 5, 6, 7), separation (Chapter 8, 9, 10) and thermal analysis (Chapter 11). Hyphenated techniques (GC/MS, LC/MS and ICP/MS) are also included in relevant chapters. Traditional mass spectroscopy is not covered in separate experiments, but the basic principles are introduced in the experiments of the hyphenated techniques. A separate chapter covering basic statistics is provided at the beginning of the manual (Chapter 1). I strongly believe that some basic statistical principals and operations (e.g., linear regression) are critical for students to comprehend the course objectives, as it has become an ever-expanding and important aspect for IA courses. This also provides some buffer period for the lecture session to proceed ahead the laboratory session.

In my opinion, most IA instructors would agree that it's more challenging to develop a general IA laboratory manual than for other chemistry courses. This is largely due to the diversity of analytical instruments and availability of instruments in various chemistry programs. There are many manufacturers for almost every type of instrument; the more popular the instrument, the more providers. Even the same manufacturer might offer multiple models for the same type of instrument. In addition, manufacturers keep updating both the hardware and software of the same model. All these make it impossible to generalize the detailed operational procedures for a specific type of instrument. For example, a home-assembled HPLC system may only have one pump, one detector, a manual injector and a selection of columns with an old computer that may only serves as a recorder. An IA instructor may actually prefer such a system for the course as I do, since everything is "visible" and operable by hand. Unfortunately, such simple systems are becoming more difficult to find in chemistry laboratories that have computer-controlled systems being essentially "magic boxes" for students to acquire data. While these newly developed instruments provide more efficient and accurate analyses, they pose more challenges to the IA instructor to effectively teach linkages between chemical processes and automation. In this manual, system-specific procedures are not the focus of the course; the main foci are basic principles and mechanisms of the instruments, which do not change from system to system. Moreover, there are significant gaps in what different universities are capable of providing in terms of instrumentation for IA courses to their students, this manual allows for a more equitable, yet comprehensive approach for all universities to use. The example provided above, using a home-assembled HPLC system or a highly integrated one, the basic questions that can still be effectively addressed are: 1) how the analytes are separated; 2) how to choose column and solvents for an analysis; 3) how the analytes are detected; 4) how the components of the system are generally incorporated; and 5) how the chemical/physical processes are carried out etc. In this manual, I have tried to provide as much such general information as possible, while avoiding system-specific information. This allows instructors to develop their own system-specific instruction for the system used.

All experiments in this manual have been carefully selected and developed to address the factors mentioned earlier with consideration of applicability to research. Unlike other similar manuals, which are simple collection of experiments, I tried to select the most applicable experiments with different level of difficulties. For most chapters, the three experiments (categorized as A, B and C) are chosen to represent three levels of difficulty with experiment A addressing the basic principles and instrumentation, B representing more advanced application and C involving more advanced knowledge of general chemistry.

In addition, the experiments are selected to minimize the use of toxic, flammable, and expensive chemicals. However, training students to handle hazardous materials is one objective of this course, and instructors are expected to address safety issues whenever necessary. In addition, usage of expensive and less commonly available equipment is also minimized in this manual.

I strongly believe that an IA textbook should cover both the theory and instrumentation of analytical techniques, while a general IA lab manual should focus on the basic principles of the instrumentation. In this manual, an introduction of the basic principles and instrumentation are provided for each type of analytical technique. Each introduction aims to bring forward new ideas on the terminology, formula, basic components of instruments etc., which are necessary for implementation of an experiment. The introduction sections are brief and therefore, cannot be used as sole source of theoretical background for any specific analytical technique. This requires students to refer to the textbook or other available hard-copy or electronic (e.g. internet) resources to understand the theory of the instrument for each experiment before attending lab. In addition, by limiting the length of each introduction, the overall volume of the manual remains low, making the manual more affordable.

Finally, I have also tried to include as much online resources in this manual as possible. However, as everyone knows, I must caution all students that reliability and quality of information cannot be guaranteed for all online resources. The future plan is to build an accompanying website which incorporates online resources to facilitate student to study the theory of each type of instrument covered in this manual.

I am very grateful for all help and encouragement from my colleagues at UMES during the development of this manual. I hope this manual will help both instructors and students to pursue their goals of teaching and learning in Instrumental Analysis.

Nianhong Chen, Ph.D
Department of Natural Sciences
University of Maryland Eastern Shore

ABBREVIATIONS

AAS	atomic absorption spectroscopy
ACS	American Chemical Society
AES	atomic emission spectroscopy
APCI	atmospheric pressure chemical ionization
CCD	charge-coupled device
CE	capillary electrophoresis
CV	coefficient of variation
CV	cyclic voltammetry
CW	continuous wave
CZE	capillary zone eletrophoresis
DAD	diode array detector
DSC	differential scanning calorimetry
DTA	differential thermal analysis
DTG	derivative thermogravimetry
ECD	electron capture detector
EI	electron impact
Eqn.	Equation
ESI	electrospray ionization
FID	flame ionization detector
FT	Fourier transform
FTIR	Fourier transform infrared
GC	gas chromatography
GFC	gel-filtration chromatography
GPC	gel permeation chromatography
HDPE	high-density polyethylene
HPLC	high performance liquid chromatography
IA	Instrumental Analysis
IC	ion chromatography
ICP	inductively coupled plasma
IQR	interquartile range
IR	infrared
IUPAC	International Union of Pure and Applied Chemistry
LDPE	low-density polyethylene
MS	mass spectroscopy
MSD	mass spectrometry detector
MWD	molecular weight distribution
NMR	nuclear magnetic resonance
PE	polyethylene
PDA	photodiode array
RSD	relative standard deviation

SD	standard deviation
SEC	size exclusion chromatography
TA	Thermal analysis
TGA	thermogravimetric analysis
TOF	time of flight
UV	ultraviolet
Var	variance
Vis	visible

STATISTICS IN INSTRUMENTAL ANALYSIS

INTRODUCTION

Modern analytical chemistry is concerned with the detection, identification, and measurement of the chemical composition of unknown substances using existing chemical or instrumental methods, and the development or application of new techniques and methods. It is generally a quantitative science, meaning that the desired result is usually numeric. We need to know whether the concentration of lead in a tap water is over 15 μg in one liter, or whether a blood sample contains less than 125 mg of glucose per deciliter.

In instrumental analysis, quantitative results are obtained using devices or instruments that allow us to determine the concentration of a chemical in a sample from an observable signal. There is always some variation in that signal over time due to noise and/or drift within the instrument. We also need to calibrate the response as a function of analyte concentration in order to obtain meaningful quantitative data. As a result, there is always an error, deviation from the true value, inherent in that measurement. One of the uses of statistics in analytical chemistry is therefore to provide an estimate of the likely value of that error; in other words, to establish the uncertainty associated with the measurement.

Even when only a qualitative answer is required, quantitative information might be used to obtain it. In reality, an analyst would try to find out if two groups of measurements of the same sample are different, or a quantitative method capable of detecting arsenic of 1 μg/L level. In the former case, two groups of quantitative results are compared. If the outcome is positive, it would be described as "The two groups of measurement are different"; otherwise, it could be described as "The two groups of measurements are virtually the same". In the latter case, if the outcome is negative, it would be described as "This sample contains less than 1 μg/L arsenic"; otherwise, the sample will be reported to contain at least 1μg/L arsenic.

This chapter introduces some useful approaches to conduct statistical analysis for analytical data including descriptive statistics, correlation analysis, and t-test. An understanding of basic principles in statistics such as sample/population means, standard deviation, linear regression, t-test is assumed. Familiarity with computer operating systems (Windows/Mac) and basic skills in spreadsheet (e.g. MS Excel) is expected.

General Reading

1. Skoog, D. A.; F. J. Holler, and S. R. Crouch, 2007. Principles of Instrumental Analysis. 6th ed. Thomson Brooks/Cole Publishing. Belmont, CA.
2. Miller, N. J. and J. C. Miller, 2010. Statistics and Chemometrics for Analytical Chemistry. Sixth edition. Prentice Hall Pearson. (Online access: **http://gendocs.ru/docs/10/9503/conv_1/file1.pdf**).
3. Van Bramer, E. S., 2007. A Brief Introduction to the Gaussian Distribution, Sample Statistics, and the Student's t Statistic. J. Chem. Educ. 84(7): 1231.
4. Online introduction: **http://en.wikipedia.org/wiki/Statistics**
5. Online introduction: **http://www.fgse.nova.edu/edl/secure/stats/index.htm**

EXERCISE 1A: DESCRIPTIVE STATISTICS

A. Objectives

1. To get familiar with descriptive statistics, measures of central tendency and dispersion.
2. To calculate measures of central tendency and statistical dispersion manually.
3. To derive descriptive statistics with spreadsheet (e.g. MS Excel).

B. Introduction

Descriptive statistics are ways of summarizing large sets of quantitative (numerical) information. The simplest form of quantitative statistical analysis is **univariate analysis**, which involves reporting **frequency distribution** of a single variable, and measures of **central tendency** and statistical **dispersion** of a set of measurements.

Frequency distribution: is a summary of how often different measurements occur within a sample of measurements, usually represented in a graphical or tabular format. In the tabular format, each entry in the table contains the frequency or count of the occurrences of values within a particular group or interval, and in this way, the table summarizes the distribution of values in the sample.

Central tendency: is the degree of clustering of the values of a statistical distribution that is usually measured by the arithmetic **mean**, **mode**, and **median**. Central tendency refers to the idea that there is one number that best summarizes the entire set of measurements, a number that is in some way "central" to the set.

a. **Mode:** is the measurement that occurs the most frequently.
b. **Median**: is the number at which half the measurements are more than that number and half are less than that number.
c. **Mean:** or the average, is the sum of all your measurements, divided by the number of measurements. When the mean refers to the whole population, it is called **population mean** (μ). When it's calculated from a finite set of samples, it is called **sample mean** ($\bar{x}$).

Statistical dispersion: refers to the idea that there is a second number which tells us how "spread out" all the measurements are from that central number. The following are measures of statistical dispersion:

a. **The range**: is the measure from the smallest to the largest measurement.
b. **Interquartile range (IQR)**: also called the **midspread** or **middle fifty**, is a measure between the upper and lower quartiles, IQR = $Q_3 - Q_1$.
c. **Variance (Var)**: a measure of the amount by which each value deviates from the mean. It's obtained by taking the mean of the squared deviations of the observed values from their mean in a frequency distribution. It is called **population variance** (σ^2) when it refers to the whole population, and **sample variance** (s^2) if only finite number of samples is involved.
d. **Standard deviation (SD)**: a measure of the amount by which each value deviates from the mean; equal to the square root of the variance. It is called **population standard deviation** (σ) when it refers to the whole population, and **sample standard deviation** (s) when only finite number of samples is involved.
e. **Relative standard deviation (RSD) and coefficient of variation (CV)**: RSD is the ratio of standard deviation to the mean. When RSD is given as a percent, it is called coefficient of variation. Again, there are population RSD and CV and sample RSD and CV.

Table 1-1 summarizes notations for describing samples and populations, and formulas for calculating sample statistics and population parameters.

Table 1-1 *Symbols and formulas of sample statistics and population parameters.*

	Sample statistics	**Population parameters**
Mean	$\bar{x} = \dfrac{\sum_{i=1}^{n} x_i}{n}$	$\mu = \dfrac{\sum_{i=1}^{N} x_i}{N}$
Variance	$s^2 = \dfrac{\sum_{i=1}^{n}(x_i - \bar{x})^2}{n-1}$	$\sigma^2 = \dfrac{\sum_{i=1}^{N}(x_i - \mu)^2}{N}$
Standard deviation	$s = \sqrt{\dfrac{\sum_{i=1}^{n}(x_i - \bar{x})^2}{n-1}}$	$\sigma = \sqrt{\dfrac{\sum_{i=1}^{N}(x_i - \mu)^2}{N}}$
Relative standard deviation (RSD)	$RSD = \dfrac{s}{\bar{x}}$	$RSD = \dfrac{\sigma}{\mu}$
Coefficient of variance	$CV = \dfrac{s}{\bar{x}} \times 100\%$	$CV = \dfrac{\sigma}{\mu} \times 100\%$

C. Procedure

Problem: A student conducted 5 replicates of measurements of lead content in a blood sample with atomic emission spectrometry (AES). The result (x_i) is listed in Table 1-2. Follow the procedure to calculate the mean and standard deviation of the measurements.

Part I. Hand calculation of central tendency and dispersion

Exercise 1A-I: Hand calculate central tendency and dispersion parameters or with help of a calculator using data in Table 1-2. Don't use Excel functions in this exercise.

1. Sum all 5 ($n = 5$) measurements: $\sum x_i$.
2. Determine the mean: $\bar{x} = \sum x_i / n$.
3. Determine the median and mode.
4. Calculate the difference between each measurement and the mean: $x_i - \bar{x}$.
5. Calculate the square of $(x_i - \bar{x})$: $(x_i - \bar{x})^2$.
6. Calculate the sum of $(x_i - \bar{x})^2$: $\sum (x_i - \bar{x})^2$ (= variance s^2).
7. Calculate standard deviation s.
8. Calculate relative standard deviation: $RSD = s/\bar{x}$.
9. Calculate coefficient of variance (CV): $CV = s/\bar{x} * 100\%$.

Table 1-2 *Manual calculation of descriptive statistics.*

	A	B	C	D
1	**Sample**	x_i	$x_i - \bar{x}$	$(x_i - \bar{x})^2$
2	1	0.752		
3	2	0.756		
4	3	0.752		
5	4	0.751		
6	5	0.760		
7	Sum ($\sum x_i$)		Sum ($\sum (x_i - \bar{x})^2$)	
8	Mean ($\bar{x}$)		Variance (s^2)	
9	Median		Standard Deviation (s)	
10	Mode		Relative SD	$s/\bar{x}$

Part II. Calculation of descriptive statistics with Excel functions

Exercise 1A-II: Calculate descriptive statistics with Excel spreadsheet using built-in functions.

1. In an Excel spreadsheet, copy the same data in Part I.
2. Use Excel functions to calculate mean in cell B7, type "= AVERAGE(B2:B6)"; variance in cell B9, type "=VAR(B2:B6)"; standard deviation in cell B13, type "=STDEV(B2:B6)". And other functions such as maximum ("=MAX()"), minimum ("=MIN()") in the same way.
3. Document all formulas in cell C7-C20. Your final spreadsheet should looks like Table 1-3.
4. Compare variance and standard deviation derived from this exercise with the result in Part I. Are they the same?

Table 1-3 *Calculation of descriptive statistics with MS Excel functions.*

	A	B	C
1	**Sample**	x_i	
2	1	752	
3	2	756	
4	3	752	
5	4	751	
6	5	760	**Documentation**
7	Sum	3771	Cell B7 = SUM(B2:B6)
8	**Central tendency**		
9	Mean	754.2	Cell B9 = AVERAGE(B2:B6)
10	Median	754	Cell B10 = MEDIAN(B2:B6)
11	Mode	752	Cell B11 = MODE(B2:B6)
12	**Statistical dispersion**		
13	Variance	14.2	Cell B13 = VAR(B2:B6)
14	Standard Deviation	3.768288736	Cell B14 = STDEV(B2:B6)
15	**Other descriptive statistics**		
16	Maximum	760	Cell B16 = MAX(B2:B6)
17	Minimum	751	Cell B17=MIN(B2:B6)
18	Count	5	Cell B18=COUNT(B2:B6)
19	Kurt	0.020829201	Cell B19=KURT(B2:B6)
20	Skewness	1.143717867	Cell B20=SKEW(B2:B6)

D. Post-laboratory exercise

A student conducted measurement of absorbance of a solution at a certain wavelength, and made 5 readings: 0.249, 0.253, 0.247, 0.250 and 0.252. Follow the procedures in the exercise to calculate standard deviation for the above data both manually and with Excel functions. Attach the Excel work sheet as shown in the exercise in your final lab report.

EXERCISE 1B: ASSOCIATION STATISTICS

A. Objectives

1. To understand the application of linear regression analysis in instrumental analysis.
2. To manually calculate the slope and intercept of simple linear correlation between two variables.
3. To conduct correlation analysis with a spreadsheet (e.g. MS Excel).

B. Introduction

Almost every quantitative analytical instrument used in chemical analysis can be characterized by a specific **calibration function** – an equation relating the **instrument output signal** (S) to the **analyte concentration** (C). The exact form of this response function depends on the system being measured and the measurement process itself. For a specific system, the calibration function may be known theoretically; however, a separate calibration is still necessary for each instrument for a specific analyte under specific measurement conditions. This is because various factors (such as the specific analyte being measured, interference effects caused by other components of the sample matrix, or random experimental errors) might cause significant deviation of the real calibration relation from the theoretical one. Hence, a calibration that directly relates analyte concentration to instrumental response is necessary. Figure 1-1 illustrates the relationship between calibration function, $S = f(C)$, and instrumental measurement.

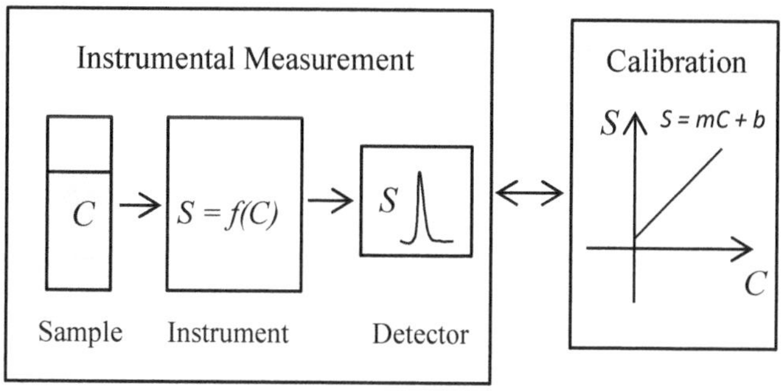

Figure 1-1 Instrumental analysis and calibration function.

The **calibration curve** is obtained by fitting an appropriate equation to a set of experimental data (calibration data) consisting of the measured responses to known concentrations of analyte. This response function may be linear or nonlinear. However, the nonlinear calibration is rarely used in practical analysis. For example, in molecular absorption spectroscopy, we expect the instrument response to follow the Beer-Lambert equation, $A = \varepsilon bC$, so we would fit a linear equation with zero intercept to the data.

The calibration is achieved through least-square regression analysis. The theory of least-square regression is out of the scope of this manual. Three commonly used standard calibration approaches in instrumental analysis are **external standard calibration**, **internal standard calibration** and **standard addition calibration**. In this exercise, you will practice a few approaches of linear correlation analysis used in external standard calibration. Standard addition calibration is introduced in Experiment 3B. Internal standard calibration method is covered in several other experiments.

C. Procedure

Problem: In Table 1-4, the concentrations of the 5 standards (x_i) and the instrument responses for each standard (y_i) from an experiment are given. Calculate the slope and intercept of the calibration curve manually and with MS Excel spreadsheet.

Part I. Hand calculation of simple linear regression formula

Exercise 1B-I: Follow the procedures below to calculate simple linear regression parameters for a set of external standard calibration data (Table 1-4).

1. Calculate x_i^2, y_i^2 and x_iy_i for each pair of data in appropriate columns (D, E and F).
2. In row 7, find five sums (Σx_i, Σy_i, Σx_i^2, Σy_i^2 and Σx_iy_i).
3. In row 8, find the mean of concentrations ($\bar{x}$) and response ($\bar{y}$).
4. Find S_{xx} (row 9), S_{xy} (row 10) and S_{xy} (row 11) using the formula given in the table. N ($= 5$) is the number of measurements.
5. Find slope (m, row 12), intercept (b, row 13) and R square (R^2, row 14) using the formula given.
6. Find the standard deviation of the regression (s_r, row 15), the slope (s_m, row 16) and the intercept (s_b, row 17) using the formula given.
7. Write the calibration equation by plugging in m and b values (row 19).

Table 1-4 *Hand calculation of simple linear regression parameters.*

	A	B	C	D	E	F
1	#	Conc. (x_i)	Response (y_i)	x_i^2	y_i^2	x_iy_i
2	1	0	0.06			
3	2	5	1.48			
4	3	10	2.28			
5	4	15	3.98			
6	5	20	4.61			
7	**Sum**					
8	**Mean**					
9	$S_{xx} = \Sigma(x_i - \bar{x})^2 = \Sigma x_i^2 - (\Sigma x_i)^2/N =$					
10	$S_{yy} = \Sigma(y_i - \bar{y})^2 = \Sigma y_i^2 - (\Sigma y_i)^2/N =$					
11	$S_{xy} = \Sigma(x_i - \bar{x})(y_i - \bar{y}) = \Sigma x_iy_i - (\Sigma x_i\Sigma y_i)/N =$					
12	**Slope:**		$m = S_{xy} / S_{xx} =$			
13	**Intercept:**		$b = \bar{y} - m\bar{x} =$			
14	**R square:**		$R^2 = \dfrac{(N \sum x_iy_i - \sum x_i \sum y_i)^2}{[N \sum x_i^2 - (\sum x_i)^2][N \sum y_i^2 - (\sum y_i)^2]} =$			
15	**SD of Regression:**		$S_r = \sqrt{[(S_{yy} - m^2 S_{xx})/(N-2)]} =$			
16	**SD of the Slop:**		$S_m = \sqrt{(s_r^2/S_{xx})} =$			
17	**SD of the intercept:**		$S_b = S_r/\sqrt{[N - (\sum x_i)^2/\sum x_i^2)]} =$			
18	**The calibration equation:** $y = \underline{\quad} x + \underline{\quad}$					

Part II. Calculation of linear regression parameters with built-in Excel functions

Exercise 1B-II: Construct a calibration curve fitting with Excel spreadsheet for the same data in Part I following the procedures below (Table 1-5).

1. In an Excel spreadsheet, type "Conc. (x_i)" in cell A1, and "Response (y_i)" in cell B1.
2. Type concentrations of standard in cells A2-A6, and responses in cells B2-B6.
3. Type formulas to calculate slope, intercept and R square of simple linear regression.

    Slope: in cell B9, type "= SLOPE(B2:B6, A2:A6)".
    Intercept: in cell B10, type "= INTERCEPT(B2:B6, A2:A6)".
    R square: in cell B11, type "=RSQ(B2:B6, A2:A6)".

4. Calculate errors of regression analysis: in cell B13, type "=STEYX(B2:B6,A2:A6)".
5. Document all formulas in cells A15-A18. The final spreadsheet should look like Table 1-5 (the trendline will be added in Part III).

Table 1-5 *Correlation analysis with Excel spreadsheet.*

	A	B	C	D	E	F
1	Conc. (x_i)	Response (y_i)				
2	0.00	0.01				
3	5.00	0.71				
4	10.00	1.11				
5	15.00	1.99				
6	20.00	2.33				
7						
8	**Regression Equation**					
9	Slope					
10	Intercept					
11	R Square					
12	**Error analysis**					
13	Standard error in y					
14	**Spreadsheet Documentation**					
15	Cell B9=SLOPE(B2:B6, A2:A6)					
16	Cell B10=INTERCEPT(B2:B6,A2:A6)					
17	Cell B11=RSQ(B2:B6,A2:A6)					
18	Cell B13=STEYX(B2:B6,A2:A6)					

Part III. Excel scatter plot and simple linear regression fitting

Exercise 1B-III: Use Excel GRAPH function to conduct linear regression fitting for the data used in Part I and II. Follow the procedures below.

1. Open the spreadsheet from exercise Part II. Highlight the calibration data (A2-B6). Note that the values for the x axis (concentration) are on the *left* (column A), while the values for the y axis (responses) are on the *right* (column B).
2. Select **Insert→Chart** on the main menu. The **Chart Wizard** dialog box will appear.

3. There are many types of charts to choose from. Select the XY (**Scatter**) plot and click the **Next** button. Click on the **Next** button again to continue. A graph showing the scatter plot between x (concentrations) and y (responses) appears.

4. If the linear regression formula and trendline are not shown on the graph, right click any data point on the scatter plot, click **Format Trendline**. In the Format Trendline dialog window, check "**Display Equation on Chart**" and "**Display R-square on Chart**". Click **OK**.

5. You can add chart titles, axis labels, and other features on the chart. The final chart should look like the graph in Table 1-5.

6. Compare the slope and intercept values from all three methods. Are they the same?

Watch online tutorial: **http://www.youtube.com/watch?v=dCF4Cwx-WXo**

D. Post-laboratory exercise

The following is external standard calibration data obtained from an experiment. Use the different methods in Exercise 1B to construct standard calibration curve for the data given.

Concentration (ppb)	Analytical Signal
0	0.002
5	0.259
10	0.489
25	1.284
50	2.407
100	4.903

An unknown sample gives a signal of 0.833. Use the calibration curve you have constructed to calculate the concentration of the unknown sample. Calculate the standard deviation of the measurement.

E. Reference

1. Skoog, D. A.; F. J. Holler, and S. R. Crouch, 2007. Principles of Instrumental Analysis. 6th ed. Thomson Brooks/Cole Publishing. Belmont, CA.

2. Miller, N. J. and J. C. Miller. (2010). Statistics and Chemometrics for Analytical Chemistry. Sixth edition. Prentice Hall Pearson. (Online access: **http://gendocs.ru/docs/10/9503/conv_1/file1.pdf**).

3. Harvey, D., 1999. Modern Analytical Chemistry. MaGraw-Hill. (Online access: **http://www.cntq.gob.ve/cdb/documentos/quimica/210.pdf**).

EXERCISE 1C: COMPARATIVE STATISTICS

A. Objectives

1. To understand the basic principle of hypothesis testing.
2. To demonstrate the statistical comparison and its application in instrumental analysis.
3. To practice hypothesis testing (t-test) for comparing means.

B. Introduction

Hypothesis analysis: A **statistical hypothesis** is an assumption about a population parameter. This assumption may or may not be true. **Hypothesis testing** refers to the formal procedures used to accept or reject statistical hypotheses. In instrumental analysis, hypothesis test can be used to explain experimental result. The first step is to formulate a **null hypothesis**, which typically corresponds to a general or default position. The hypothesis test then determines whether or not the null hypothesis is supported by the data.

For example, experimental result might not agree with the predicted from a theoretical model. It's necessary to examine if the difference is a result of the random errors, or a systematic errors. In this example, the null hypothesis (H_0) can be stated as "the experimental result is the same as the predicted from a theoretical model". The outcome of the hypothesis test on the null hypothesis could be either positive or negative. The negative outcome results in rejection of the null hypothesis and favors the opposite situation, which is represented as **alternate hypothesis** (H_a). One way to state the alternate hypothesis is "the experimental result is different from the predicted".

The statistical analysis to compare whether two means are statistically different is t-test (also called student t-test). The formula for the t-test is the ratio of the difference between the two means to the measure of the variability or dispersion of the scores.

$$t = \frac{m_1 - m_2}{SD} \quad (1C-1)$$

where m_1 and m_2 are two means ($\bar{x}$ for sample mean and μ for population mean) to be compared, and SD is combined standard deviation of the two set of samples. Large t value indicates the two means are significantly different, and vice versa. The way in which the SD is computed depends on details of the structure of the data. There are two types of t-test, paired and unpaired t-tests, and they differ by the way they compute the SD. An important assumption of t-test is the two sets of samples are **normally distributed**.

Paired and unpaired t-test: Paired t-test is used when each data point in one group corresponds to a matching data point in the other group, or one group of measurements that has been tested twice (repeated measurement). Unpaired t-test is used when two groups of data are independent to each other but identically distributed. In both cases, normal distribution is assumed.

1- and 2-Tailed t-test: In case that two means are compared to examine if they are significantly different, the null hypothesis (H_0) could be "they are the same". The alternate hypothesis (H_a) would be "they are different". This is a **2-tailed t-test**. In case that two means are compared to examine if one is significantly greater than the other, the null hypothesis (H_0) could be "one mean is less than another". The alternate hypothesis (H_a) would be "one mean is greater than or equal to another mean". This is a **1-tailed t-test**.

In this exercise, you will practice two types of unpaired t-test commonly used in Instrumental Analysis. One is to compare if a sample mean is significantly different from the population mean. The formula for calculating the t value is given as

$$t = \frac{\bar{x} - \mu_0}{s/\sqrt{n}} \qquad (1C\text{-}2)$$

where $\bar{x}$ and μ_0 are sample and population means respectively, s is sample deviation, n is sample size.

Another type of t-test is to compare if two sets of samples are significantly different from each other. The formula for calculating the t value is given as

$$t = \frac{\bar{x}_2 - \bar{x}_1}{\sqrt{\frac{s_2^2}{n_2} + \frac{s_1^2}{n_1}}} \qquad (1C\text{-}3)$$

where $\bar{x}_1$ and $\bar{x}_2$ are sample means of two sets independent data, s_1 and s_2 are sample standard deviations of the two set of data, n_1 and n_2 are sample sizes of the two sets of data.

The following examples show how the two types of t-test are used in hypothesis testing and help you to understand the difference between 1- and 2-tailed t-test.

Example 1. The pH of a stream water was monitored, where six samples were taken each time. In the first year, the mean pH reading was 6.5 ($\bar{x}_1$) with standard deviation $s_1 = 0.2$; and in the second year, the mean pH reading was 6.8 ($\bar{x}_2$) with standard deviation $s_2 = 0.1$. Did the pH of the stream water significantly changed from first to second year?

1. Define the hypothesis

    The null hypothesis can be stated as "the pH of the stream does not change in two years", and written as

    H_0: $\bar{x}_1 = \bar{x}_2$

    The alternate hypothesis, H_A, that the pH value had changed significantly from first to second year, is written as

    H_A: $\bar{x}_1 \neq \bar{x}_2$

    P = 0.90

    P = 0.05   P = 0.05

2. Calculate t value using Formula 1C-3

    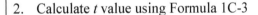
    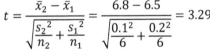

    $$t = \frac{\bar{x}_2 - \bar{x}_1}{\sqrt{\frac{s_2^2}{n_2} + \frac{s_1^2}{n_1}}} = \frac{6.8 - 6.5}{\sqrt{\frac{0.1^2}{6} + \frac{0.2^2}{6}}} = 3.29$$

3. Look up tabulated t-values for significance level (95%) and degrees of freedom (df = $n_1 + n_2 - 2$ = 10). Referring to t-table for a 95% confidence limit for a 2-tailed t-test, we find $t_{v=0.95\%} = 2.228$.

4. We are now ready to accept or reject the null hypothesis. If the $t_{calc} > t_{tab}$, we reject the null hypothesis. In our case, $t_{calc}=3.29 > t_{tab} = 2.228$, so we reject the null hypothesis, and say that the pH did change significantly from first to second year.

Example 2. Consider the analysis of a soil sample for arsenic content. Suppose a set of 7 (n) replicate measurements on a soil sample returned a mean concentration of 4.0 ppm ($\bar{x}$) with standard deviation $s = 0.9$ ppm, and that the maximum allowable concentration (MAC) was 2.0 ppm (μ_0). In such a situation, we might want to know whether the experimental value exceeds MAC.

1. Define the hypothesis

    The null hypothesis (H_0) can be stated as "the mean arsenic concentration is equal to the MAC within experimental error", and written as

    H_0: $\bar{x} = 2.0$ ppm

The alternate hypothesis (H_A) that the mean arsenic concentration is greater than the MAC is

H_A: $\bar{x} > 2.0$ ppm

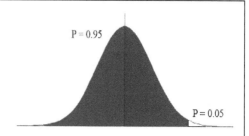

2. Calculation t value using Formula 1C-2

$$t = \frac{\bar{x} - \mu_0}{s/\sqrt{n}} = \frac{4.0 - 2.0}{0.9/\sqrt{7}} = 5.88$$

3. Look up tabulated t-values for significance level (95%) and degrees of freedom (df = n - 1 = 6). Referring to t-table for a 95% confidence limit for a 1-tailed t-test, we find $t_{v=0.95\%} = 1.943$.

4. We are now ready to accept or reject the null hypothesis. If the $t_{calc} > t_{tab}$, we reject the null hypothesis. In our case, $t_{calc}=5.88 > t_{tab}= 1.943$, so we reject the null hypothesis, and say that our sample mean is indeed larger than the accepted limit, and not due to random chance. Thus, we can say that the soil is indeed contaminated.

C. Procedure

Part I. Student t-test: comparison of two sample means

Problem: Two students conduct measurement of iron in tap water three times each with UV/Vis spectrophotometry under the same condition. The results from student A are 0.344, 0.351, 0.385 ppm, and the results from student B are 0.532, 0.443, 0.489 ppm. Are the results from the two students significantly different?

1. State the null and alternate hypotheses.

Null hypothesis H_0: _____

Alternate hypothesis H_a: _____

2. Calculate means and standard deviations (Stdev) of two sets of measurements.

Student	1	2	3	Mean	Stdev
A	0.344	0.351	0.385		
B	0.532	0.443	0.489		

3. Calculate t value

$$t = \frac{\bar{x}_1 - \bar{x}_2}{\sqrt{\frac{s_1^2}{n_1} + \frac{s_2^2}{n_2}}} = \frac{(\quad\quad) - (\quad\quad)}{\sqrt{\frac{(\quad\quad)^2}{(\quad)} + \frac{(\quad\quad)^2}{(\quad)}}} = \underline{\quad\quad}$$

4. Look up the t-table (**Appendix F**) for the critical value of t for 4 degree of freedom and the 95% confidence level, $t_{0.95}$, compare the calculated t value and $t_{0.95}$.

$t_{0.95} =$ _____

5. Accept or reject null hypothesis. What conclusion you can draw on whether the two sets of measurements are significantly different?

Conclusion: _____

Part II: Student *t*-test: comparison of sample and population means

> **Problem**: The certified concentration of silver in a NIST soil reference sample is 5.9 mg/Kg with standard deviation of 0.2 mg/Kg. A new ICP/MS has been purchased and the professor run a series parallel measurements to determine the silver concentration in the NIST reference sample. His results are: 5.74, 4.98, 5.53, 5.88, 5.12 mg/Kg. Assuming the measurement result is normally distributed, using a 0.05 level of significance, is there sufficient evidence to conclude that the professor's measurement is too low?

1. Write the null and alternate hypothesis:

   Null hypothesis H_0: _____

   Alternate hypothesis H_a: _____

2. Calculate mean and standard deviation of the measured values

   Mean: $\bar{x} =$ _____

   Standard deviation: $s\; =$ _____

3. Calculate *t* value

   $$t = \frac{\bar{x} - \mu_0}{s/\sqrt{n}} = \text{_____}$$

4. Look up the *t*-table (Appendix F) for the critical value of *t* for 4 degrees of freedom and the 95% confidence level, $t_{0.95}$, compare the calculated t value and $t_{0.95}$.

   $t_{0.95} =$ _____

5. Accept or reject null hypothesis. What conclusion you can draw on whether the professor's measurement is lower than the NIST certified value?

   Conclusion: _____

D. Post-laboratory exercise

1. A new spectrofluorometer has just been purchased. The lab technician wants to test if the new instrument gives the same result with the old machine. He conducted an experiment to measure concentration of quinine in tonic water 4 times each on both fluorometers. The result from the old machine is 37.9, 40.8, 38.4, 41.7 µg/L; and the result from the new machine is 42.4, 45.3, 43.5, 46.8 µg/L. Is the result from the new machine is significantly higher than that from the old machine ($\alpha = 0.05$)?

2. A 1.3270 g sample of an iron ore known to contain 53.51% (w/w) Fe is dissolved in a small portion of concentrated HCl and diluted to volume in a 250-mL volumetric flask. A spectrophotometric method is used to determine the concentration of Fe in this solution, yielding results of 2920, 2885, 2825, and 2830 ppm. Determine whether there is a significant difference between the experimental mean and the expected value at $\alpha = 0.05$.

E. Reference

1. Miller, N. J. and J. C. Miller, 2010. Statistics and Chemometrics for Analytical Chemistry. Sixth edition. Prentice Hall Pearson. (Online access: **http://gendocs.ru/docs/10/9503/conv_1/file1.pdf**).
2. Harvey, D., 1999. Modern Analytical Chemistry. MaGraw-Hill. (Online access: **http://www.cntq.gob.ve/cdb/documentos/quimica/210.pdf**).
3. Online introduction: **http://en.wikipedia.org/wiki/Student's_t-test**

ELECTROANALYTICAL CHEMISTRY

INTRODUCTION

In **electrochemical analysis,** the potential (volts) and/or current (amperes) are measured in an electrochemical cell containing the analyte (Figure 2-1). Based on how the cells are controlled and which parameter is measured, the electroanalytical methods are categorized to **potentiometry, coulometry** and **voltammetry.**

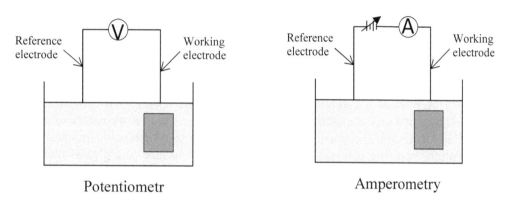

Potentiometr   Amperometry

Figure 2-1 Schematic diagrams for two-electrode electrochemical experiments. Left: potentiometry. Right: amperometry

In potentiometry, the potential of a solution between two electrodes is passively measured. The potential is then related to the concentration of analyte. The cell, often referred as an electrode, contains two electrodes: an **indicator electrode** and a **reference electrode.** Potentiometry usually uses electrodes made selectively sensitive to the ion of interest, such as a fluoride-selective electrode. The most common potentiometric electrode is the glass-membrane electrode used in a **pH meter.**

In coulometry, a current or potential is applied to completely convert an analyte from one oxidation state to another. The total current passed is measured directly or indirectly to determine the number of electrons passed, which indicate the concentration of the analyte.

In voltammetry, a constant and/or varying potential is applies at an electrode's surface in a three electrode system and the resulting current is measured. This method can reveal the reduction potential of an analyte and its electrochemical reactivity.

Electroanalytical chemistry encompasses a wide range of qualitative and quantitative analytical methods. The three experiments in this chapter address basic principles and instrumentations of each technique described above.

General Reading

1. Skoog, D. A., F. J. Holler, and S. R. Crouch, 2007. Principles of Instrumental Analysis. 6th ed. Thomson Brooks/Cole Publishing. Belmont, CA.
2. Sawyer, D. T., W. R. Heineman and J. M. Beebe, 1984. Chemistry Experiments for Instrumental Methods. Wiley.
3. Scholz, F., 2002. Electroanalytical Methods: Guide to Experiments and Applications. Springer.
4. Bard, A. J. and L. R. Faulkne, 2000. Electrochemical Methods: Fundamentals and Applications. Wiley.

EXPERIMENT 2A: pH TITRATION OF PHOSPHORIC ACID

A. Objectives

1. To demonstrate the principles of pH measurement and acid/base titration.
2. To titrate triprotic acid (phosphoric acid) with strong base.
3. To determine equilibrium constant of acid/base conjugates.

B. Introduction

pH *measurement*: Measuring pH involves comparing the potential of solutions with unknown [H⁺] to a known reference potential. pH meters convert the voltage ratio between a **reference half-cell** and a **sensing half-cell** to pH values which is defined as the negative logarithm of hydrogen activity. A standard pH measuring system consists of a **reference electrode**, an **indicator electrode** (glass electrode), and a current meter which measures the resistance of the circuit in a great small potential difference.

The reference half-cell contains a conductor (usually silver with a silver chloride coating, Figure 2-2A) immersed in a solution with known [H⁺]. The potential between this internal conductor and the known solution is constant, providing a stable reference potential. The sensing half-cell (measuring half-cell, Figure 2-2B) is made of a non-conducting glass (or epoxy) tube sealed to a conductive glass membrane. Like the reference half-cell, the sensing half-cell also contains a conductor immersed in a buffered electrolyte solution, ensuring constant voltages on the inner surface of the glass membrane and the sensing conductor.

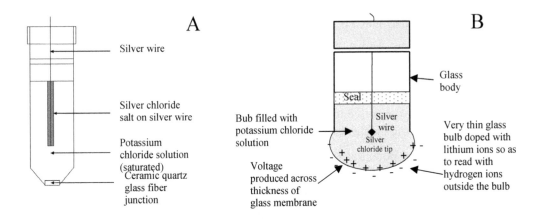

Figure 2-2 A: silver/silver chloride electrode; B: glass indicator electrode.

When the pH electrode is immersed in the solution to be measured, a potential is established on the surface of the sensing glass membrane. The pH meter detects the change in potential and determines [H⁺] of the unknown by the Nernst equation

$$E = E^0 - \frac{RT}{nF}\log[H^+] = E^0 - 0.0592\log[H^+] = E^0 + 0.0592pH \qquad (2A\text{-}1)$$

where E = total potential difference (measured in mV), T = temperature in Kelvin (room temperature ~298°K), n = number of electrons (= 1), E° = reference potential, F = Faraday's constant, R = gas constant, [H⁺] = hydrogen ion concentration (activity).

pH *titration of phosphoric acid*: Acids that contain more than one acidic (ionizable) hydrogen (proton) are called polyprotic or polybasic acids. The dissociation of polyprotic acids occurs in a stepwise fashion, one proton is lost at a time. For example, the generic triprotic acid will dissociate as shown in Reactions (2A-2) through (2A-4). The equilibrium constants for these reactions are symbolized by K_a. The trailing subscript "a" indicates that the equilibrium constant describes an acid dissociation reaction. The trailing subscript "n" is written as a number and indicates which proton is being dissociated.

$$H_3A + H_2O \leftrightarrow H_3O^+ + H_2A^- \quad K_{a1} = [H_3O^+][H_2A^-]/[H_3A] \quad (2A\text{-}2)$$
$$H_2A^- + H_2O \leftrightarrow H_3O^+ + HA^{2-} \quad K_{a2} = [H_3O^+][HA^{2-}]/[H_2A^-] \quad (2A\text{-}3)$$
$$HA^{2-} + H_2O \leftrightarrow H_3O^+ + A^{3-} \quad K_{a3} = [H_3O^+][A^{3-}]/[HA^{2-}] \quad (2A\text{-}4)$$

When a strong base is added to a solution of a polyprotic acid such as phosphoric acid, the protons of the acid are neutralized in a stepwise fashion. That is, the neutralization reaction will proceed in the order from 2A-5 to 2A-7. Therefore, there are three titration end points (point c, e, g in Figure 2-3).

$$H_3A + OH^- \leftrightarrow H_2A^- + H_2O \quad (2A\text{-}5)$$
$$H_2A^- + OH^- \leftrightarrow HA^{2-} + H_2O \quad (2A\text{-}6)$$
$$HA^{2-} + OH^- \leftrightarrow A^{3-} + H_2O \quad (2A\text{-}7)$$

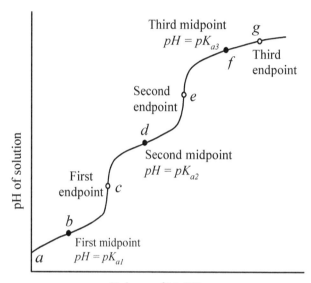

Figure 2-3 Titration curve of phosphoric acid with sodium hydroxide. Point a is the initial point. The pH of the solution equals pK_{a1}, pK_{a2}, and pK_{a3} at midpoints b, d, and f, respectively. Points c, e, and g are the first, second, and third endpoints, respectively.

Theoretically, equilibrium constant can be calculated if the concentrations of conjugate acid/ base and proton at any point on the titration curve are known with general formula

$$K_a = \frac{[B^-][H^+]}{[A]} \quad (2A\text{-}8)$$

It can also be established that the pH value at each titration midpoint equals to equilibrium constant of an equilibrium reaction (point b, d, f in Figure 2-3). Consult general electrochemistry textbooks for details on how to determine endpoint and midpoint of mono- and multi-protic acid titration (Sawyer et al., 1984; Skoog et al., 2004).

C. Chemicals

1. Sodium hydroxide (NaOH, ACS grade, >97%).
2. Phosphoric acid (H_3PO_4, ACS grade, Conc. >85%).
3. Sodium phosphate, monobasic, monohydrate ($NaH_2PO_4 \bullet H_2O$, ACS grade, >98%).
4. Buffer solutions, pH = 7 and pH = 4.

D. Apparatus

1. pH meter and electrodes (pH electrode and reference electrode).
2. Magnetic stirrer and stirring bar.
3. Erlenmeyer flasks, 250 mL.
4. Volumetric flasks, 1000 mL.
5. Buret and buret stand.

E. Procedure

> **Safety Precautions:** Concentrated H_3PO_4 and NaOH solution are highly corrosive and irritating to skin. Wear gloves and goggles when handling any concentrated acid and/or base.

1. Preparation of solutions

    a. *Preparation of 0.1 M of NaOH*: Weigh 4 g NaOH into 1000 mL volumetric flask, dilute to mark with deionized water.

    b. *Preparation of 0.1 M H_3PO_4*: Pipet 6.83 mL concentrated phosphoric acid into 1000 mL volumetric flask, dilute to mark with deionized water.

    c. *Preparation of 0.1 M NaH_2PO_4*: Weigh 13.8 g $NaH_2PO_4 \cdot H_2O$ into 1000 mL volumetric flask, dilute to mark with deionized water.

2. Titration of H_3PO_4

    a. Set up a titration assembly as shown in Figure 2-4.

    b. Standardize the pH meter with two buffers, pH = 4 and 7, following the procedures provided by the manufacturer. Rinse the electrode with deionized water, and keep the electrode immersed in deionized water until titration.

    c. Clean the electrode thoroughly with deionized water; drying is not necessary.

    d. In a 250 mL Erlenmeyer flask, add 25 mL 0.1 M H_3PO_4 solution and 75 mL deionized water.

    e. Fill the buret to the 0.00 mL level with titrant (0.1 M NaOH).

    f. Immerse the electrodes in the solution to be titrated; the electrodes should not touch each other, the bottom of the beaker and the stirring bar.

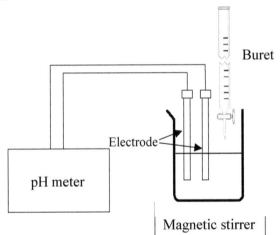

Figure 2-4 Schematic representation of the pH titration system.

    g. Start the magnetic stirrer.

    h. Set the mode of the meter to pH and begin the titration.

    i. Watch for the region where the pH begins to change rapidly with each added portion of titrant. The first few additions of titrant could be large, 3-4 mL. Read pH and titrant volume after each addition. When the pH begins to change rapidly, reduce the size of addition to 0.1 mL when pH approaching the end point. Continue titration until pH reaches 12.

    j. Record pH and number of mL of titrant added on the Data Record and Processing Table.

    k. Rinse and store the electrodes.

3. Titration of NaH_2PO_4

    Titrate 0.1 M NaH_2PO_4 with 0.1 M NaOH following the procedures above.

Data Entry and Processing Table

Titration #	pH	V_{NaOH}	V_{total}	M_{H3PO4}	M_{NaOH}
1					
2					
3					
4					
5					
6					
7					
8					
9					
10					
11					
12					
13					
15					
16					
17					
18					
19					
20					

F. Result report

1. Tabulate your raw data on a spreadsheet. Calculate molarity of H_3PO_4 (or NaH_2PO_4), NaOH present in your sample. Be sure to take into account the increase of volumes due to titration when calculating concentrations at all points on the curve.
2. Plot pH vs. volume of NaOH solution added on a spreadsheet.
3. Determine the end points for both titrations.
4. Determine K_{a1}, K_{a2} and K_{a3}. Compare your result with the published ones.

G. Questions for discussion

1. Explain how pH responds to the volume of titrant on a pH titration curve.
2. Why pH changes more rapidly when the titration nears the titration endpoint? Explain why the third endpoint of the H_3PO_4 does not follow this pattern (Figure 2-3).
3. Compare the titration curves of H_3PO_4 and NaH_2PO_4. Discuss the differences.
4. Explain why a buffer is mixture of a conjugate acid and base.

H. Reference

1. Sawyer, T. D., W. R. Heineman and J. M. Beebe, 1984. Chemistry experiments for instrumental methods. John Wiley & Sons.
2. Skoog, D. A, D. M. West, F. J. Holler and S. R. Crouch, 2004. Fundamentals of Analytical Chemistry. 8th Ed. Brooks/Cole, Belmont, CA.
3. Murphy, J., 1983. Determination of phosphoric acid in cola beverages: a colorimetric and pH titration experiment for general chemistry. J. Chem. Educ. 60(5): 420-421.

EXPERIMENT 2B: COULOMETRIC TITRATION OF ARSENIC

A. Objectives

1. To learn the basic principles of coulometry and basic instrumentation of coulometric titration.
2. To determine concentration of arsenic in unknown sample with coulometric titration.

B. Introduction

Coulometry is the technique that determines the amount of matter transformed during an electrolysis reaction by measuring the amount of electricity (in coulombs) consumed or produced. There are two basic categories of coulometric techniques.

In **potentiostatic (controlled-potential) coulometry**, the electric potential is held constant during the reaction. The charge required to convert the analyte to its reaction product is then determined by integrating the current-versus-time curve during the electrolysis.

In **coulometric titration** or **amperostatic coulometry**, a constant current generates the titrant electrolytically. The current is applied to the unknown solution until all of the unknown species are either oxidized or reduced to a new state, at which point the potential of the working electrode shifts dramatically. This shift in potential indicates the endpoint. The magnitude of the current (in amperes) and the duration of the current (in seconds) can be used to determine the moles of the unknown species in solution. When the volume of the solution is known, the molarity of the unknown species can be determined.

Figure 2-5 illustrates a typical electrochemical cell for coulometric titration. The cell consists of a **platinum generator electrode** with a large surface area and a second electrode to complete the electrochemical cell. The second electrode is usually a coiled platinum wire that is isolated in a separate solution from the sample solution by a sintered glass disk, which prevents the products that are formed at this electrode from interfering with the titration reaction in the main cell. The cell is positioned on a stirring motor to enable stirring during titration.

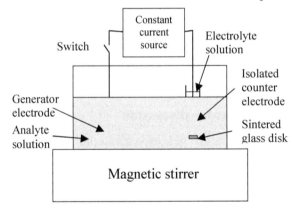

Figure 2-5 Schematic representation of the coulometric titration system.

Coulometric titration of arsenic: In this experiment, a platinum generating electrode is placed in a solution of iodide (I^-). Iodine (I_2) is generated by the following reaction

Anode reaction: $2I^- \rightarrow I_2 + 2e$ (2B-1)

If an unknown quantity of As(III) is present in the same solution, it will be oxidized by the electrochemically generated I_2 to As(V) in a manner analogous to a conventional redox titration. Under the pH conditions in this experiment, the titration reaction is:

Solution reaction: $I_2 + H_3As(III)O_3 + H_2O \leftrightarrow 2I^- + H_3As(V)O_4 + 2H^+$ (2B-2)

When all of the As(III) has reacted, an excess of I_2 appears which then reacts with a starch indicator, turning the solution purple. It is necessary that the actual amount of iodine generated be known. This can be calculated from Faraday's Law if the number of coulombs consumed is known. The most convenient method of measuring this value is to employ a constant generating current and simply measure the time needed to reach the starch endpoint. The number of coulombs (ampere-second, A·s) can be converted to the number of mole of substance oxidized or reduced at an electrode

$$mol = \frac{Q}{nF} \qquad (2B\text{-}3)$$

where *mol* = mole number of substance oxidized or reduced; Q = number of coulombs passed through the cell (C); F = Faraday constant (96,485, C/mole); n = number of equivalents per mole.

C. Chemicals

1. Starch indicator, 1%, freshly prepared or purchased commercially.
2. 0.05 M sodium arsenite stock solution, commercially available; or prepared from arsenic trioxide.
3. Potassium iodide (KI, ACS grade, ≥99.0%).
4. Sodium bicarbonate ($NaHCO_3$, ACS grade, >99.7%).
5. 0.5 M H_2SO_4 solution.

D. Apparatus

1. Constant current coulometer.
2. Analytical balance.
3. Pipets, 1, 20, 25 mL.
4. Beakers, 250 mL.
5. Volumetric flasks, 100, 1000 mL.
6. Magnetic stirrer and stirring bar.
7. Large foil platinum electrode (1x2 cm)
8. Platinum wire electrode.
9. Electrochemical cell.

E. Procedure

1. Preparation of solutions

> **Safety Precautions**: Arsenic containing compounds are poisonous. Wear gloves, lab coat and goggles during entire period of experiment. Wash hands thoroughly when leaving the lab.

   a. *Preparation of 0.005 M sodium arsenite standard solution*: Transfer 10 mL 0.05 M sodium arsenite stock solution into 100 mL volumetric flask, bring to mark with deionized water.
   b. *Preparation of composite 0.1 M KI and 0.1 M $NaHCO_3$ buffer solution*: Weigh 16.6 g KI and 8.4 g $NaHCO_3$, transfer to 1 L volumetric flask. Add approximately 250 mL deionized water to dissolve the KI and $NaHCO_3$. Add 250 µL 0.005 M sodium arsenite standard solution. Bring to mark with deionized water. (**Note**: The optimal pH range for performing the reaction is 7-9. The bicarbonate used in this experiment has the ability to restrict the pH in this range).
   c. Prepare a sample with unknown concentration of sodium arsenite in 0.1 M KI/$NaHCO_3$ solution, or obtained from the instructor.

2. Pretitration

   a. Set up the apparatus as shown in Figure 2-5. Clean the electrodes with 0.5 M H_2SO_4. Make sure that the large platinum foil (generator) electrode is connected to the positive terminal and the small platinum-wire (reference) electrode is connected to the negative terminal.
   b. Into the 250 mL beaker, transfer 75 mL of 0.1 M KI/ $NaHCO_3$ solution and 10 drops of starch indicator solution. Place the stirring bar in the beaker and set the beaker on the stirrer.
   c. Start the stirrer and cautiously lower the electrodes into the beaker, being careful to avoid the large platinum foil hitting the bottom of the beaker or the stirrer.
   d. See the instructor for any special instructions for adjusting or calibrating the instrument. Turn the control switch to ON position, the counter should begin to run. The solution should turn blue when excess I_2 generated on anodic electrode. Then turn the control switch to OFF.
   e. Add small amount of 0.005 M sodium arsenite standard solution drop-wise until the blue color disappears. Then turn the switch ON and back to OFF until a light blue color develops in the

entire solution. This color will be taken as the endpoint for the titration. Set the counter back to zero.

3. Titration of arsenite standard solution

   a. Pipet 25 mL of 0.005 M sodium arsenite standard solution into 100 mL volumetric flask, bring to mark with deionized water.

   b. Pipet 20 mL of diluted sodium arsenite solution above into the titration beaker and turn the control switch ON. Let the titration continue with rapid stirring until the light blue color develops; then stop the titration and record the time (T) in seconds using data table below. (**Note**: During titration, turn the titration switch OFF and let the iodine diffuse off the electrode every 2 minutes of titration. When the entire solution develops a permanent light blue color, turn the titration switch OFF and see if the color persists and matches the endpoint color in Step **2.e**).

   c. Return the timer to zero. Pipet 20 mL more of the diluted arsenite solution and repeat the coulometric titration. There is no need to replace the KI solution although it might be necessary to discard some of it if the beaker fills up. Repeat this until T values agree to within 1 second.

   d. Calculate number of mole and concentration of arsenite in each aliquot using Eqn. 2B-3. Compare the calculated value with the known concentration.

Replicate	$V_{arsenite}$ (*mL*)	Current (*A*)	T (*s*)	Mole	C (*mM*)
1	20				
2	20				
3	20				
4	20				

4. Titration of unknown sample

   a. Pipet 25 mL of unknown sample into 100 mL volumetric flask, bring to mark with deionized water.

   b. Titrate 20 mL of the diluted unknown sample as in Step **3.b**. Repeat the titration 3-4 times. Record titration time (T) in second for each replicate.

   c. Calculate number of mole and concentration of arsenite in each aliquot.

Replicate	V_{sample} (*mL*)	Current (*A*)	T (*s*)	Mole	C (*mM*)
1	20				
2	20				
3	20				
4	20				

5. Cleanup and waste disposal: Arsenic containing compounds are considered poisonous, dispose the waste generated in this experiment under supervision of the instructor.

F. Result report

1. Calculate molarity of arsenite in the standard solution based on titration result. Is it the same as the known concentration?
2. Calculate concentration of arsenite in the unknown sample based on the titration result.
3. Tabulate your raw data and processed results and include them in your lab report.

G. Questions for discussion

1. What is the purpose of the KI? (Hint: where do the electrons go first, and ultimately?)
2. What is the purpose of the bicarbonate buffer solution?

3. Why is the anode a large platinum foil and the cathode a small platinum wire?
4. Why use platinum electrodes instead of copper, zinc, or mercury electrodes?
5. Why doesn't the cathodic process counteract the anodic process?
6. What is the fundamental requirement for a coulometric titration?
7. Why should a coulometric titration be intrinsically more accurate than a corresponding volume-tric titration?

H. Supplementary experiment: Coulometric Acid-Base Titration

Summary

Acid (H^+) is titrated with base (OH^-) generated by cathodic process. Endpoint is indicated by an acid/base indicator.

Chemicals

1. 0.1 M KNO_3
2. 0.05 M KBr
3. 5.0 mM HCl
4. 0.1% bromothymol blue or methyl red solution

Apparatus

1. Coulometric titration system similar to the one described in the main experiment.
2. Electrodes: generating - platinum (~0.3 cm^2 area); counter (isolated) - platinum.

Electrode reactions

1. Cathode: $H_2O + e \rightarrow OH^- + \frac{1}{2} H_2$
2. Anode: $H_2O \rightarrow \frac{1}{2} O_2 + 2H^+ + 2e$

Procedure

1. Add to the coulometric cell a few drops of 5.0 mM HCl, 2 drops of the indicator solution and enough of 0.1 M KNO_3 to cover the electrodes. Insert the generating electrodes into the solution. Check that the counter-electrode compartment is filled with electrolyte (1 M KNO_3). Titrate until a color change is observed. This change of color will be taken as the endpoint of the titration.
2. Set the timer back to zero. Pipet 1.00 mL of 5.0 mM HCl into the vessel. Let the titration continue until the same color is reached. Several runs may be made in the same solution.
3. Follow the same procedures above to titrate an unknown acid sample.

I. Reference

1. Sawyer, D. T., W. R. Heineman and J. M. Beebe, 1984. Chemistry Experiments for Instrumental Methods. Wiley.
2. Harris, D. C., 2010. Quantitative Chemical Analysis, 8th Ed. Freeman, New York.
3. Bard, A. J. and L. R. Faulkne, 2000. Electrochemical Methods: Fundamentals and Applications. Wiley.
4. Scholz, F., 2002. Electroanalytical Methods: Guide to Experiments and Applications. Springer.
5. Ramsey, J. W., P. S. Farrington and E. H. Swift, 1950. Coulometric Titrations with Iodine. Anal. Chem. 22(2): 332–335.
6. James, S., E. Edward, R. M. Laura and P. David, 1996. Constant-current coulometric titration of hydro-chloric acid. J. Chem. Edu. 73(7): 679.
7. Pastor, J. T., V. J. Vajgand, V. V. Antonijević, 1980. Coulometric titrations of arsenic(III) and antimony(III) with electrically generated bromine in acetic acid. Analytica Chimica Acta. 120:357-360.
8. Online introduction: **http://en.wikipedia.org/wiki/Coulometry**

EXPERIMENT 2C: CYCLIC VOLTAMMETRY OF Fe(III)(CN)$_6^{3-}$/Fe(II)(CN)$_6^{4-}$

A. Objectives

1. To demonstrate the use of cyclic voltammetry to characterize electrochemical systems.
2. To determine the reduction potential, $E^{0\prime}$, and electron transfer number, n, of the Fe(III)(CN)$_6^{3-}$/Fe(II)(CN)$_6^{4-}$ couple.
3. To explore the effect of scan rate and analyte concentration on electrochemical process.

B. Introduction

*C*yclic voltammetry (CV) is perhaps the most effective and versatile electroanalytical technique available for the mechanistic study of redox systems. The effectiveness of CV results from its capability for rapidly observing redox behavior over a wide range of potential. The resulting **voltammogram** conveys information as a function of an energy scan. Thus, CV is often the first experiment performed in an electrochemical study.

*B*asic instrumentation: A basic CV system is consisted of a **waveform generator** to produce the excitation signal, a **potentiostat** to apply this signal to an **electrochemical cell**, a **current to voltage converter** to measure the resulting current and an **X-Y recorder** or **oscilloscope** to display the **voltammogram** (Figure 2-6). The first three components are normally incorporated into a single electronic device called an **epsilon** (Figure 2.7).

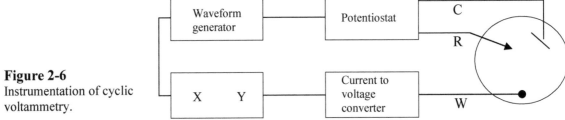

Figure 2-6
Instrumentation of cyclic voltammetry.

A **potentiostat** is the electronic hardware required to control a three-electrode cell and run most electroanalytical experiments as shown in Figure 2-7.

Figure 2-7 A typical electrochemical cell for cyclic voltammetry. The potential is applied through working electrode (W), and maintained at a constant level with respect to the reference electrode (R) by adjusting the current at a counter electrode (C). The reference electrode circuit contains a large resistance such that no current is present in the electrode, therefore, providing a stable, reproducible voltage to which the working electrode potential may be referenced. Inert gas (e.g. nitrogen) is purged before and during experiment to keep oxygen being dissolved in the electrolyte.

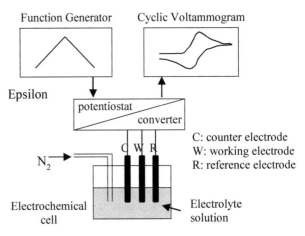

*C*yclic voltammetry of Fe(III)(CN)$_6^{3-}$/Fe(II)(CN)$_6^{4-}$ couple: In this experiment, potential is applied to the ferricyanide (Fe(III)(CN)$_6^{3-}$) solution through working electrode (W) and the reference electrode

(R), and the current response is measured using the working electrode and a counter electrode (C). The waveform used is triangular (Figure 2-8A), and a typical current-voltage curve for ferricyanide/ ferrocyanide couple is shown in Figure 2-8B.

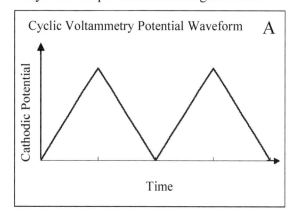

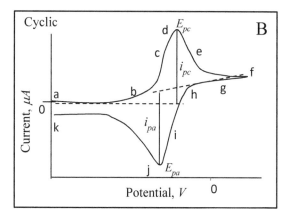

Figure 2-8. Triangular waveform (A) and cyclic voltammogram (B) for the CV of ferricyanide/ferrocyanide couple.

Referring to the voltammogram shown in Figure 2-8B, upon the start of the experiment (point *a*), a potential applied to the working electrode increases with time. When the cathodic potential is sufficiently negative to reduce $Fe(III)(CN)_6^{3-}$, cathodic current start to increase (point *b*) due to the electrode process

$$Fe(III)(CN)_6^{3-} + e \rightarrow Fe(II)(CN)_6^{4-} \qquad (2C\text{-}1)$$

With further increase in the potential, the cathodic current increases rapidly ($b{\rightarrow}d$) until $Fe(III)(CN)_6^{3-}$ is depleted, and the current decreases ($d{\rightarrow}g$). The scan direction is then switched to positive for the reverse scan. When the electrode becomes a sufficiently strong oxidant (positive), $Fe(II)(CN)_6^{4-}$ accumulated in the early process starts to be oxidized by the electrode process

$$Fe(II)(CN)_6^{4-} \rightarrow Fe(III)(CN)_6^{3-} + e \qquad (2C\text{-}2)$$

This causes anodic current ($i{\rightarrow}k$). The anodic current rapidly increases until $Fe(II)(CN)_6^{4-}$ is depleted. Therefore, CV is capable of rapidly generating a new oxidation state during the forward scan and then probing its fate on the reverse scan.

The formal reduction potential, $E^{0\prime}$, of $Fe^{III}(CN)_6^{3-}/Fe^{II}(CN)_6^{4-}$ couple is calculated to be 356 mV (Kolthoff and Tomsicek, 1935). However, this value varies with concentration of potassium and pH (Papp and Mohai, 1962).

The important parameters of a cyclic voltammogram are the magnitude of the anodic peak current (i_{pa}), cathodic peak current (i_{pc}), anodic peak potential (E_{pa}), and cathodic peak potential (E_{pc}). The i_{pa} and i_{pc} are estimated by extrapolating the base-line current as shown in Figure 2-8B.

A redox couple in which both species rapidly exchange electrons with the working electrode is termed an **electrochemically reversible couple**. The formal **reduction potential** $E^{0\prime}$ for a reversible couple is centered between E_{pa} and E_{pc}

$$E^{0\prime} = (E_{pa} + E_{pc})/2 \qquad (2C\text{-}3)$$

The number (*n*) of electrons transferred in the electrode reaction for a reversible couple can be determined from the separation between the peak potentials

$$\Delta E_p = E_{pa} - E_{pc} \approx 0.059/n \qquad (2C\text{-}4)$$

Thus, an one-electron process such as reduction of $Fe(III)(CN)_6^{3-}$ to $Fe(II)(CN)_6^{4-}$ exhibits a ΔE_p of approximately 0.059 V. Slow electron transfer at the electrode surface, "irreversibility", causes this peak separation to increase.

The peak current for a reversible system is described by the Randles-Sevcik equation for the forward sweep of the first cycle

$$i_p = 2.69 \times 10^5 n^{3/2} A D^{1/2} C v^{1/2} \qquad (2C\text{-}5)$$

where i_p = peak current (mA); n = electron stoichiometry; A = electrode area (cm^2); C = concentration (mol/mL); v = scan rate (V/s).

Accordingly, i_p increases with $v^{1/2}$ and is directly proportional to concentration, C. The relationship to concentration is particularly important in analytical application and in studies of electrode mechanisms. The value of i_{pa} and i_{pc} should be close for a simple reversible (first) couple. However, the ratio of peak currents (i_{pa}/i_{pc}) can be significantly influenced by chemical reactions coupled to the electrode process.

C. Chemicals

1. Potassium nitrate (KNO$_3$, ACS grade, >99.0%).
2. Potassium ferricyanide (K$_3$Fe(CN)$_6$, ACS grade, >99.0%).
3. Powdered alumina.

D. Apparatus

1. A basic cyclic voltammetry system.
2. One two-piece glass CV cell.
3. One platinum working electrode.
4. One platinum auxiliary electrode.
5. One saturated calomel electrode (SCE) or Ag/AgCl reference electrode.
6. Analytical balance (0.001 g).
7. Volumetric flasks, 100, 1000 mL.
8. Pipet, 1 mL, 5 mL.
9. Ultrasonic bath.

E. Procedure

1. Preparation of solutions

   a. *Preparation of 1.0 M KNO$_3$ solution*: Add 101.1 g of KNO$_3$ into 1000 mL volumetric flask. Bring to mark with deionized water.

   b. *Preparation of 100 mM K$_3$Fe(CN)$_6$ in 1.0 M KNO$_3$ stock solution*: Add 10.11 g of KNO$_3$ and 3.292 g of K$_3$Fe(CN)$_6$ into 100 mL volumetric flask. Bring to mark with deionized water.

   c. *Preparation of concentration series of K$_3$Fe(CN)$_6$ solutions*: Into five 100 mL volumetric flasks, transfer 2, 4, 6, 8 and 10 mL 100 mM K$_3$Fe(CN)$_6$ solution. Bring to mark with 1.0 M KNO$_3$ solution. This yields K$_3$Fe(CN)$_6$ solutions of 2, 4, 6, 8, 10 mM in 1.0 M KNO$_3$ solution.

2. Preparation of the instrument

   a. Pretreat the electrodes as specified by the manufacturer or under supervision of instructor. Polish the surface of platinum working electrode with powdered alumina, and rinse thoroughly with deionized water. Sonicate the electrode in an ultrasonic bath.

   b. *Deoxygenation*: Assemble and fill the cell with 1.0 M KNO$_3$ so that the ends of the electrodes are immersed. Purge the cell with N$_2$ for approximately 10 minutes. The N$_2$ is then redirected over the solution to prevent oxygen reenter the solution during experiment.

   c. *Set the scan parameter*: Switch off or disconnect the working electrode. Set initial potential at 0.80 V (or specified by instructor, same for other parameters) and scan limit at 0.80 and -0.12 V. All scans are initiated in the negative direction with a scan rate of 20 mV/s.

3. Cyclic voltammetric scanning of $Fe(III)(CN)_6^{3-}$ /$Fe(II)(CN)_6^{4-}$

a. *Scan background CV*: Switch on the working electrode. After allowing the current to attain a constant value (~10 s), the potential scan is initiated and the background CV of the support-ing electrolyte solution is obtained.

b. *Scan the working solution*: Turn off the working electrode. Clean the cell and refill with 4 mM $K_3Fe(CN)_6$ in 1M KNO_3. Follow the same procedure in Step **3.a** to scan a CV voltammogram for the working solution.

c. *The effect of the scan rate on the voltammogram*: Following the same procedure to scan CV voltammogram for the same solution at different rates: 50, 100, 150, and 200 mV/s. Between each scan, initial conditions at the electrode surface are restored by moving the working electrode gently up and down without removing out from the solution or by activating a stirring bar. Make sure there is no bubble on the electrodes. Allow one or two minutes after stirring for the solution to rest before the next CV scan.

d. *The effect of concentration on the voltammogram*: Set scan rate at 20 mV/s, scan CV voltammograms on 2, 6, 8, and 10 mM $K_3Fe(CN)_6$ following the same procedure above.

e. *Measuring unknown sample*: A voltammogram of a sample with unknown concentration of $K_3Fe(CN)_6$ is measured as above.

4. Clean up and waste disposal: no hazardous chemicals are used in this experiment. All solution prepared can be vacated to the drain.

F. Result report

1. Determination of $E^{0\prime}$ and n of $Fe(III)(CN)_6^{3-}$ /$Fe(II)(CN)_6^{4-}$ couple.

a. Include the CV voltammogram of 4 mM $K_3Fe(III)(CN)_6$ in 1.0 M KNO_3 (Step **3.b** in Procedure).

b. Determine E_{pc} and E_{pa} based on the CV voltammongram as shown in Figure 2-8B.

c. Determine $E^{0\prime}$ and n for the $Fe(III)(CN)_6^{3-}$ /$Fe(II)(CN)_6^{4-}$ couple with Eqn. 2C-3 and 2C-4.

d. Compare your values with the ones reported in literature (see Introduction).

v (mV/s)	C (mM)	i_{pc}	i_{pa}	E_{pc}	E_{pa}	ΔE_p	$E^{0\prime}$	n
20	4							

2. Determine the effect of scan rate on peak height (current).

a. Combine all CV voltammograms of 4 mM $K_3Fe(III)(CN)_6$ in 1.0 M KNO_3 at different scan rates (Step **3.b** and **3.c** in Procedure). Visually check how scan rate affect the shape of CV voltammogram, and the currents (i_{pc} and i_{pa}).

b. Determine i_{pc} and i_{pa} for each scan rate. Calculate square root of the scan rate ($v^{1/2}$).

c. Plot i_{pc} and i_{pa} vs. $v^{1/2}$.

v (mV/s)	C (mM)	$v^{1/2}$	i_{pc}	i_{pa}
20	4			
50	4			
100	4			
150	4			
200	4			

3. Determine the effect of scan rate on ΔE_p.

a. Use the combined CV voltammograms above, check how scan rate affect the peak potentials (E_{pc} and E_{pa}) visually.

b. Determine E_{pc} and E_{pa} for each scan rate (Figure 2-8B). Calculate ΔE_p (Eqn. 2C-4).

c.   Plot ΔE_p vs. v.

v (mV/s)	C (mM)	E_{pc}	E_{pa}	ΔE_p
20	4			
50	4			
100	4			
150	4			
200	4			

4.   Determine the effect of concentration on currents.

a.   Combine all CV voltammograms of different concentrations of $K_3Fe(III)(CN)_6$ in 1.0 M KNO_3 (Step **3.d** of Procedure). Visually check how concentration of $K_3Fe(III)(CN)_6$ affect the shape of CV voltammogram, and the currents (i_{pc} and i_{pa}).

b.   Determine i_{pc} and i_{pa} for each concentration (Figure 2-8B).

c.   Plot i_{pc} and i_{pa} vs. C.

C (mM)	v (mV/s)	i_{pc}	i_{pa}
2	20		
4	20		
6	20		
8	20		
10	20		

G. Questions for discussion

1.   Referring to Figure 2-8B, explain why the current increase rapidly from b to d, and then reach maximum (d) and decays during forward scan (f to j).

2.   Discuss how scan rate affect the currents, and explain why larger peak currents are obtained for faster scan rates.

3.   Explain how scan rate affect the ΔE_p.

4.   Explain how concentration affects the currents.

H. Reference

1.   Sawyer, D. T., W. R. Heineman and J. M. Beebe, 1984. Chemistry Experiments for Instrumental Methods. Wiley.

2.   Kissinger, P. T., and W. R., Heineman, 1983. Cyclic Voltammetry. J. Chem. Educ. 60: 702-706.

3.   Van Benschoten, J. J., J. Y. Lewis, W. R. Heineman, D. A. Roston and P. T. Kissinger. 1983. Cyclic voltammetry experiment. J. Chem. Educ. 60(9): 772-775.

4.   Maloy, J. T., 1983. Factors affecting the shape of current-potential curves. J. Chem. Educ. 60(4): 285-288.

5.   Kolthoff, I. M. and W. J. Tomsicek, 1935. The oxidation potential of the system potassium ferrocyanide-potassium ferricyanide at various ionic strengths. J. Phys. Chem. 39(7): 945–954.

6.   Papp. S. and B. Mohai, 1962. The oxidation-reduction potential of the $K_3(Fe(CN)_6)$-$K_4(Fe(CN)_6)$ system in the presence of various potassium compounds. Veszprem. Vegyip. Egyct. Kozlemen. 6: 165-172.

UV/VIS MOLECULAR ABSORPTION SPECTROSCOPY

CHAPTER

3

I. BASIC PRINCIPLES

Quantitative UV/Vis spectroscopy: Molecules containing π-electrons or non-bonding electrons (*n*-electrons) can absorb the electromagnetic energy in **ultraviolet (UV)** and/or **visible (Vis)** region (200-800 nm) to excite these electrons to higher anti-bonding molecular orbits. When a beam of UV/Vis radiation passes through a medium with absorbing molecules, the intensity of radiation is attenuated due to absorption by the absorbing molecules and other processes such as reflection and scattering. The attenuation of radiation intensity is expressed by **transmittance** (*T*), which is the fraction of electromagnetic radiation passing through the medium (Figure 3-1)

$$T = \frac{I}{I_0} \qquad (3\text{-}1)$$

where I_0 is the intensity of incoming (**incident**) radiation, and *I* is the intensity of radiation which passes through the medium.

Transmittance is related to **absorbance** (*A*) by

$$A = -log(T) = -log\frac{I}{I_0} \qquad (3\text{-}2)$$

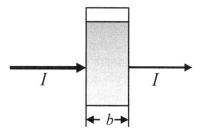

Figure 3-1 Absorption of radiant energy.

The relation between absorbance and concentration of absorbing molecules (*c*) is defined by **Beer's law**

$$A = abc \qquad (3\text{-}3)$$

where *a* is a constant of proportionality, called **absorptivity**, *b* is the path length of radiation. When molar concentration is used for concentration *c*, the absorptivity is called **molar absorptivity**, and assigned a different letter, ε. Formula 3-3 is then rewritten as

$$A = \varepsilon bc \qquad (3\text{-}4)$$

Qualitative UV/Vis spectroscopy: The molecules do not absorb all lights (differentiated by **wave-length**) equally. An UV/Vis **spectrum** is a plot of absorbance vs. wavelength. The absorption bands shown on a UV/Vis spectrum can be correlated with the types of bonds in a given molecule and are valuable in determining the functional groups (**chromophores**) within a molecule. As an example, Figure 3-2 illustrates the relationship between UV/Vis spectrum and molecular structure of tetraphenyl-cyclopentadienone. The nonbonding electrons ("**n**" electrons) are located on the oxygen of carbonyl

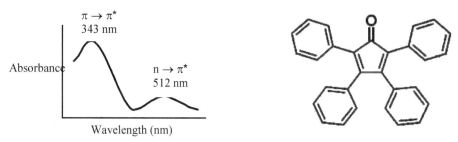

Figure 3-2. UV/Vis spectrum (right) and molecular structure (left) of tetraphenyclopentadienone.

group of tetraphenylcyclopentadienone. Thus, the **n to π*** transition corresponds to the excitation of an electron from one of the unshared pair to the π* orbital indicated by absorption peak around 512 nm.

II. BASIC INSTRUMENTATION

A basic UV/Vis photometer/spectrophotometer has **light source** to provide incident radiation, a **monochromator** to separate/filter source light to obtain monochromatic light beam with a narrow range of wavelength, a **transducer** (detector) to convert radiation signal to electrical signal, and a readout device (recorder) for recording the signal (Figure 3-3).

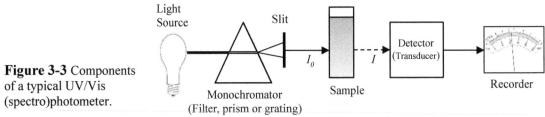

Figure 3-3 Components of a typical UV/Vis (spectro)photometer.

1. Light sources: Both **deuterium** and **hydrogen lamps** are common source of UV radiation in the range of 160-375 nm. The **tungsten filament lamp** is commonly employed as a source of visible radiation in the wavelength range of 350-2500 nm.

2. Filters and monochromators: Filters can only provide radiation at a few fixed wavelength bands. Instruments quipped with filters do not support spectrum scanning. This type of instruments is called **photometer** (or **colorimeter** when only visible light is used). In **spectrophotometers**, monochromator (prism or grating) is used to provide selection of radiations of variable wavelengths. Therefore, spectrophotometer support UV/Vis absorption spectrum scanning, but can also be operated as a photometer at fixed wavelength.

3. Sample container: **Quartz** and **fused silica** cell (cuvette) can be used in entire (UV/Vis) range, but they are very expensive. If only visible lights are involved, glass and plastic cuvettes provide inexpensive options. A rule of thumb in all spectroscopic analysis is that the sample container should not interfere with the light band used for the analysis.

4. Detectors (transducer): **Phototube, photomultiplier, photodiode, photodiode array (PDA), charge-coupled device (CCD)** are commonly used transducers in UV-Vis spectroscopy. Photo-multipliers are very sensitive to UV and visible radiation, limited to measuring low power radiation (more suitable for fluorometer). PDA and CCD array provide options for recording absorbance at multiple wavelengths at the same time.

General Reading

1. Skoog, D. A., F. J. Holler and S. R. Crouch, 2007. Principles of Instrumental Analysis. 6th ed. Thomson Brooks/Cole Publishing. Belmont, CA.
2. Sawyer, D. T., W. R. Heineman and J. M. Beebe, 1984. Chemistry Experiments for Instrumental Methods. Wiley.
3. Harris, D. C., 2010. Quantitative Chemical Analysis, 8th Ed. Freeman, New York.
4. James W. R., E. M. Skelly Frame, G. M. Frame II, 2004. Undergraduate Instrumental Analysis, Sixth Edition, CRC Press.
5. Online introduction: **http://teaching.shu.ac.uk/hwb/chemistry/tutorials/molspec/uvvisab1.htm**
6. Online introduction: **http://en.wikipedia.org/wiki/UV/VIS_spectroscopy**

EXPERIMENT 3A: QUALITATIVE AND QUANTITATIVE ANALYSIS OF QUININE IN TONIC WATER

A. Objectives

1. To learn basic principles of quantitative and qualitative UV/Vis absorption (spectro)photometry.
2. To construct external standard calibration for quantitative UV/Vis analysis of quinine.
3. To conduct measurement of quinine in tonic water, and determine detection limit of the analysis.
4. To draw UV/Vis absorption spectrum of quinine.

B. Chemicals

1. Quinine ($C_{20}H_{24}N_2O_2$, anhydrous, >98%).
2. Sulfuric acid (H_2SO_4, ACS grade, conc. 98%).
3. Unknown: tonic water.

C. Apparatus:

1. Basic UV/Vis (spectro)photometer.
2. Analytical balance (0.001 g).
3. Volumetric flasks, 100, 500, 1000 mL.
4. Capped test tubes, 15 mL.
5. Pipets, 1, 5, 10 mL.
6. Cuvette, 1 cm standard cuvette cells.

D. Procedure

Part I Quantitative analysis

1. Preparation of quinine standard solutions

> **Safety Precautions:** Concentrated H_2SO_4 are highly corrosive. Wear gloves and goggles when handling any concentrated acid and/or base. When concentrated H_2SO_4 and water mix, large amount of heat is released, and the heat can cause the water to boil. Thus, always mix concentrated H_2SO_4 to large volume of water slowly to allow the heat to be dissipated.

   a. *Preparation of 1M stock H_2SO_4 solution*: In a 1000 mL volumetric flask with about 500 mL deionized water, slowly and carefully add 56 mL concentrated H_2SO_4 with stirring. Bring to mark with deionized water.
   b. *Preparation 0.05 M H_2SO_4 solution*: Transfer 50mL 1 M H_2SO_4 solution to 1000 mL volumetric flask. Bring to mark with deionized water.
   c. *Preparation of 1000 ppm quinine stock solution*: Weigh exactly 0.100 g of quinine, and transfer into a 100 mL volumetric flask, followed by 5.00 mL 1 M H_2SO_4. Dissolve all the quinine by swirling before diluting to volume with deionized water.
   d. *Preparation of quinine standard solutions*: Pipet 100, 300, 500, 750, and 1000 μL of 1000 ppm stock solution into five 100 mL volumetric flasks. Dilute to volume with 0.05 M H_2SO_4.

2. *Preparation of instrument*: depending on the instrument used, the instructor should prepare detailed operational procedures for the instrument used. For a basic photometer, the following are general procedures of operation.

   a. Turn on the instrument main power.
   b. Leave the instrument to warm up for 20 minutes.
   c. Adjust the wavelength to 350 nm.
   d. Zero the instrument with blank (0.05 M H_2SO_4).
   e. Measure transmittance and/or absorbance of standards/samples.

For a scanning UV/Vis spectrophotometer connected to a computer, the following are general procedures of operation.

    a. Turn the instrument main power and the computer power on. Start the computer program.

    b. Turn on the lamp if it's controlled by the software.

    c. Choose between fixed wavelength mode and spectrum scanning mode. In the first part of the experiment, choose fixed wavelength mode.

    d. Set up the measurement parameters. In this experiment, set wavelength (350 nm) at which absorbance is measured.

3. If you are using a scanning spectrophotometer, pick one quinine standard, scan the UV/Vis spectrum from 300 to 450 nm. What is the wavelength of the maximum absorbance (λ_{max})?

4. Standard calibration

    a. Pipet 2-3 mL 0.05 M H_2SO_4 (blank) to a standard 1 cm cuvette. Insert the cuvette into cell holder. Zero the instrument.

    b. Pipet 2-3 mL of each standard solution to a standard 1 cm cuvette. Insert the cuvette into cell holder. Read absorbance and/or transmittance. Record your result in data table below.

    c. Repeat this procedure for all standard solutions.

Standard	C (ppm)	T (%)	A	Note
1	1			
2	3			
3	5			
4	7.5			
5	10			

5. Measurement of samples

    a. Measure transmittance/absorbance for the unknown sample (tonic water). If the absorbance reading of tonic water is higher than that of the highest standard concentration (10 ppm), dilute the tonic water with 0.05 M H_2SO_4 to let the absorbance reading fall within the calibration range (1-10 ppm).

    b. Record the dilution factor for the diluted sample. Record the absorbance/transmittance reading on the data table for both original and diluted sample.

Samples	Dilution factor	T (%)	A	Calculated C (ppm)	Sample C (ppm)
Undiluted Tonic water	1				
Diluted Tonic Water					

Part II Qualitative analysis

If a scanning spectrophotometer is used, simply scan a UV/Vis spectrum by choosing the scanning mode. However, it's recommended that students conduct the following experiment (steps 1-4), which help to understand the basic concepts of UV/Vis absorption spectrometry.

1. Follow the same procedure described in Part I to prepare the instrument. Choose fixed wave-length mode.

2. Pipet 2-3 mL any quinine standard solution prepared in Part I to a clean 1 cm cuvette. Load onto spectrophotometer.

3. Measure absorbance at wavelengths in a range from 250 to 400 nm at interval of 5-10 nm. Record the wavelength and absorbance readings to the data table below.

4. For your lab report, plot the absorbance readings vs. wavelength. This is your UV/Vis absorption spectrum of quinine.
5. Compare your spectrum with published one.
6. If you are using a scanning spectrophotometer, scan spectrum for both quinine standard and tonic water. Include the spectra in your lab report and compare them.

	λ (nm)	T (%)	A	Note
1				
2				
3				
4				
5				
6				
7				
8				
9				
10				
11				
12				
13				
14				
15				

E. Result report

1. Tabulate concentration, transmittance/absorbance of standards. Construct external standard calibration curve following procedure depicted in Experiment 2B.
2. Calculate concentration of quinine in tonic water (undiluted or diluted) using the calibration curve obtained.
3. Calculate absorptivity of quinine at 350 nm using the result obtained from the standards. Convert the unit from ppm to molar concentration, and calculate molar absorptivity of quinine at 350 nm.
4. Plot absorbance vs. wavelength to get your own spectrum of quinine (Part II). Compare your spectrum with the published one.

F. Questions for discussion

1. Is your calibration curve linear and pass the origin? If not, discuss why. Why is an ideal external standard calibration curve linear?
2. Discuss why blank correction is necessary for both quantitative and qualitative analysis.
3. Quinine has two absorption bands with maximum absorption wavelength at ca. 250 and 350 nm. Based on the molecular structure of quinine, discuss the chromophores in quinine molecule.
4. Discuss sources of system and random errors in your measurements.
5. Are the spectra of quinine standard and tonic water significantly different? What information you can infer from this comparison?

G. Supplementary experiments

Many inorganic ions, organic compounds and complexes absorb radiation in UV/Vis region, and can be used as analyte in this experiment. Table 3-1 lists some chemicals commonly found in chemistry laboratory and their spectral properties.

Table 3-1 *Chemicals can be used in UV/Vis spectrometry experiment and their properties.*

Compound	Solvent	Absorption band (nm)	Suggested Concentration
$Ni(NO_3)_2$	H_2O	400	0.15 M
$Cr(NO_3)_3$	H_2O	410 or 575	0.1 M
$Co(NO_3)_2$	H_2O	510	0.15 M
$K_2Cr_2O_7$	$0.5\ M\ H_2SO_4$	440	0.02 M
$KMnO_4$	$0.5\ M\ H_2SO_4$	545	0.02 M
$Fe(SCN)$	H_2O	450	0.005 M
$Fe(phen)_3^{2+}$	H_2O	530	0.002 M
Caffeine	H_2O	274	0.05 M

H. Reference

1. Skoog, D. A., F. J. Holler and S. R. Crouch, 2007. Principles of Instrumental Analysis. 6th ed. Thomson Brooks/Cole Publishing. Belmont, CA.
2. Sawyer, D. T., W. R. Heineman and J. M. Beebe, 1984. Chemistry Experiments for Instrumental Methods. Wiley.
3. Harris, D. C., 2010. Quantitative Chemical Analysis, 8th Ed., Freeman, New York.
4. Online video tutorial: **http://www.youtube.com/watch?v=O39avevqndU**
5. Online introduction: **http://teaching.shu.ac.uk/hwb/chemistry/tutorials/molspec/uvvisab1.htm**

EXPERIMENT 3B: DETERMINATION OF CAFFEINE IN BEVERAGE USING STANDARD ADDITION CALIBRATION

A. Objectives

1. To learn basic principles and instrumentation of UV/Vis absorption (spectro)photometry.
2. To demonstrate the method of standard addition calibration.
3. To conduct measurement of caffeine in beverages with UV/Vis absorption (spectro)photometer.

B. Introduction

In standard addition calibration method, known amount of analyte standard is added to unknown sample (called **spiking** the sample). The change in instrument response between the sample and the spiked samples is assumed to be due only to change in analyte concentration, and their relationship is used to calculate the concentration of analyte in unknown sample. Standard addition method is effective in suppressing **matrix effect**, which is the impact of all interfering components in the sample (matrix) on the response of analyte. Matrix effect is more severe in complex samples such as biological fluids, soil samples etc.

The first step of standard addition calibration is to spike the sample. The sample is split to several aliquots with volume of V_x, which are spiked with different amount of standard (V_s). When standard is added, the sample is diluted; so it's important that all the aliquots (spiked and unspiked) are diluted in the same way. Thus, all aliquots are diluted to a final volume of V_t.

The second step is to conduct the measurement, and the instrument response is plotted vs. amount of standard added. Linear regression is performed to get the slope (m) and y-intercept (b) (Figure 3-4).

The last step is to calculate the analyte in unknown sample. The linear regression is represented as

$$S = mV_S + b \qquad (3B\text{-}1)$$

where S is instrument response (Figure 3-4).

Extrapolate the curve to intercept the x (Vs) axis, the intercept ($(V_s)_0$, a negative value) represents zero instrument response, and therefore, the zero concentration of analyte; while the origin ($V_s = 0$) represents the instrument response of the sample. The absolute value of $(V_s)_0$ represents equivalent volume of standard in which the amount of analyte equals to the amount of analyte present in the unknown sample. Therefore

$$V_x c_x = |(V_S)_0| c_s \qquad (3B\text{-}2)$$

where c_x is original concentration of analyte in the sample, c_s is concentration of analyte in the standard.

Combining Eqn. 3B-1 and 3B-2 and solving for c_x give

$$c_x = \frac{bc_s}{mV_x} \qquad (3B\text{-}3)$$

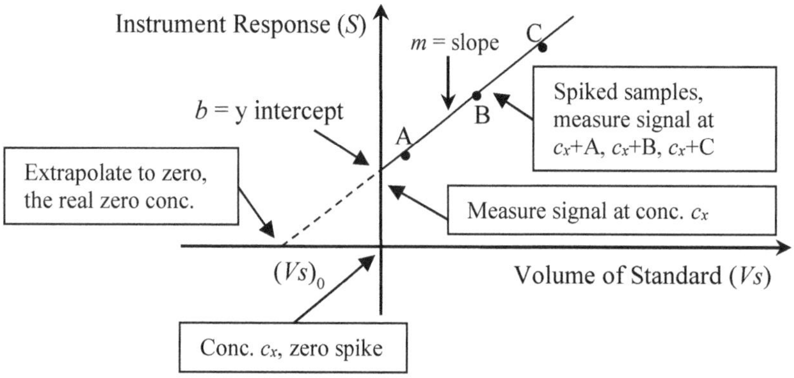

Figure 3-4 Standard addition calibration.

C. Chemicals

1. Caffeine ($C_8H_{10}N_4O_2$, ACS grade, >98%).
2. Tea, Coca Cola or other caffeinated beverage.

D. Apparatus

1. Basic (spectro)photometer.
2. Analytical balance (0.001 g).
3. Volumetric flasks, 1000 mL.
4. Syringe filter.
5. Pipets: 1, 5 mL.
6. Cuvette: 1 cm standard cuvette cells.

E. Procedure

1. *Preparation of 100 ppm caffeine stock solution*: Weigh exactly 0.100 g of caffeine. Transfer into a 1000 mL volumetric flask. Dilute to volume with deionized water and mix thoroughly.

2. *Preparation of spiked samples with standard*

   a. Tea sample can be prepared through brewing any kind of tea in warm water. For carbonated beverage, it's necessary to degas the beverage before proceeding to next step.
   b. Filter all samples with a suitable device such as a syringe filter.
   c. Pipette 5 mL sample (V_x) to each of five 15 mL tubes. Pipette 0, 1, 2, 3, 4 mL of 100 ppm caffeine stock solution (V_s), and 5, 4, 3, 2, 1 mL of deionized water to five tubes (V_{DI}) respectively, so that each tube has total volume of 10 mL.

Aliquots #	1	2	3	4	5
V_x (mL)	5	5	5	5	5
V_s (mL)	0	1	2	3	4
V_{DI} (mL)	5	4	3	2	1

3. *Measurement of samples*: Follow the similar procedures described in Experiment 3A to prepare the instrument and conduct the measurements for each sample:

   a. Turn on the instrument main power.
   b. Leave the instrument to warm up for at least 20 minutes.
   c. Set wavelength at 274 nm.
   d. Blank the instrument with deionized water.
   e. Measure absorbance of each unspiked/spiked aliquot of tea sample.
   f. Record your results to the data entry and processing sheet attached.
   g. Repeat the procedure to conduct experiment for coffee and other samples.

4. *Hardware shutdown and cleanup*: After all experiments are completed, switch off the main power of the instrument and turn off the computer. There is no hazardous wastes are generated in this experiment. Dispose all solutions to lab sink or consult your instructor.

F. Result report

1. Plot the absorbance vs. standard volume addition for each sample. Conduct correlation analysis with a spreadsheet to obtain *m* and *b* for regression equation: $S = mV_{spike} + b$
2. Calculate caffeine concentration in samples with Eqn. 3B-3. Make sure you use correct values for c_s and V_x.

G. Questions for discussion

1. Discuss the advantages of standard addition method over external standard calibration method.

2. Discuss how standard addition method is capable of correcting the matrix effect? Does the standard addition calibration method suppress interfering signal?

3. Discuss the main sources of error in standard addition method.

H. Reference

1. Skoog, D. A., F. J. Holler, and S. R. Crouch, 2007. Principles of Instrumental Analysis. 6th ed. Thomson Brooks/Cole Publishing. Belmont, CA.

2. Miller, N. J. and J. C. Miller, 2010. Statistics and Chemometrics for Analytical Chemistry. 6th Ed. Prentice Hall Pearson. (Online access: **http://gendocs.ru/docs/10/9503/conv_1/file1.pdf**).

3. Harris, D. C., 2010. Quantitative Chemical Analysis, 8th Ed., Freeman, New York.

4. Video introduction to standard addition calibration: **http://www.youtube.com/watch?v=eg4A9PHA9Ps**

Data entry and processing sheet

Sample #1:			Dilution ratio:		
Volume of unknown:			Conc. of standard:		
Aliquot #	V_s	V_{DI}	Transmittance	Absorbance	Note
1	0	5			
2	1	4			
3	2	3			
4	3	2			
5	4	1			
Regression result:		$m =$		$b =$	
Calculated concentration of caffeine in sample:					

Sample #2:			Dilution ratio:		
Volume of unknown:			Conc. of standard:		
Aliquot #	V_s	V_{DI}	Transmittance	Absorbance	Note
1	0	5			
2	1	4			
3	2	3			
4	3	2			
5	4	1			
Regression result:		$m =$		$b =$	
Calculated concentration of caffeine in sample:					

EXPERIMENT 3C: SPECTROPHOTOMETRIC DETERMINATION OF EQUILIBRIUM CONSTANT OF pH INDICATOR

A. Objectives

1. To demonstrate the use of spectrophotometry for simultaneous analysis of a mixture.
2. To demonstrate the use of spectrophotometry for the evaluation of pK_a of an acid/base indicator.

B. Introduction

Equilibrium constant of weak acid and base: Most acid-base indicators are weak acids or bases whose acid and base conjugates have different colors in solution. When the titration proceeds (pH increases or decreases), a shift between the acid and base conjugates occurs, causing change in color of the solution. The acid and base conjugates of an indicator are commonly represented by *HIn* and *In⁻* respectively. The equilibrium between acid/base conjugates can be represented as

$$HIn \leftrightarrow H^+ + In^-$$

The acid dissociation equilibrium constant (K_a) for this equilibrium (without considering the ion strength) is given by

$$K_a = \frac{[H^+][In^-]}{[HIn]} \qquad (3C\text{-}1)$$

where $[H^+]$, $[In^-]$, $[HIn]$ are concentrations of H^+, In^- and HIn, respectively. Convert Eqn. 3C-1 to logarithmic terms

$$-log(K_a) = -log([H^+]) - log\frac{[In^-]}{[HIn]} \qquad (3C\text{-}2)$$

Eqn. 3C-2 can be further rewritten as

$$pK_a = pH - log\frac{[In^-]}{[HIn]} \qquad (3C\text{-}3)$$

Therefore, if pH, $[In^-]$ and $[HIn]$ (or the $[In^-]/[HIn]$ ratio) are known, pK_a can be calculated.

Alternatively, Eqn. 3C-3 can be rearranged to

$$pH = log\frac{[In^-]}{[HIn]} + pK_a \qquad (3C\text{-}4)$$

Therefore, the plot of pH vs. $log([In^-]/[HIn])$ should be a straight line with a slope of 1. And the intercept of the line with y-axis (at which $[In^-]=[HIn]$) equals to pK_a (Figure 3-4).

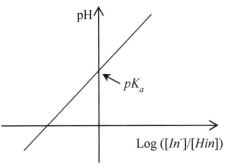

Figure 3-4 A plot of pH vs. $log\frac{[In^-]}{[HIn]}$ for a pH indicator.

Simultaneous analysis of a two-component mixture: One application of UV/Vis spectroscopy is simultaneous measurement of two components in a solution by measuring absorbance at more than one wavelengths. To do this, the absorptivities of the two components at two wavelengths must be known and sufficiently different (Figure 3-5).

36

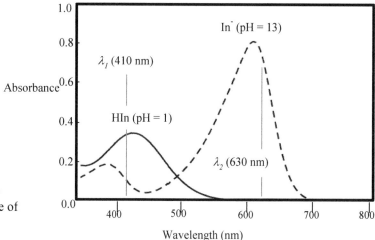

Figure 3-5 UV/Vis spectra of the acid (*HIn*) and base (*In⁻*) conjugate of pH indicator bromothymol blue.

Assuming the concentration of two components are C_a and C_b respectively. Absorptivities of component 1 at wavelength 1 (λ_1) and wavelength 2 (λ_2) are $\varepsilon_{a\lambda1}$ and $\varepsilon_{a\lambda2}$ respectively; and absorptivities of component 2 at λ_1 and λ_2 are $\varepsilon_{b\lambda1}$ and $\varepsilon_{b\lambda2}$ respectively. The total absorbance at λ_1 and λ_2 are

$$A_{\lambda1} = \varepsilon_{a\lambda1}\, b\, C_a + \varepsilon_{b\lambda1}\, b\, C_b \quad \text{(3C-5)} \quad \text{and} \quad A_{\lambda2} = \varepsilon_{a\lambda2}\, b\, C_a + \varepsilon_{b\lambda2}\, b\, C_b \quad \text{(3C-6)}$$

If $\varepsilon_{a\lambda1}$, $\varepsilon_{a\lambda2}$, $\varepsilon_{b\lambda1}$ and $\varepsilon_{b\lambda2}$ are known, and b (pathlength of the cell) is considered known, C_a and C_b can be solved from Eqns. 3C-5 and 3C-6

$$C_a = \frac{\varepsilon_{b\lambda2}A_{\lambda1} - \varepsilon_{a\lambda2}A_{\lambda2}}{\varepsilon_{a\lambda1}\varepsilon_{b\lambda2} - \varepsilon_{a\lambda2}\varepsilon_{b\lambda1}} \quad \text{(3C-7)} \quad \text{and} \quad C_b = \frac{\varepsilon_{a\lambda1}A_{\lambda2} - \varepsilon_{b\lambda1}A_{\lambda1}}{\varepsilon_{a\lambda1}\varepsilon_{b\lambda2} - \varepsilon_{a\lambda2}\varepsilon_{b\lambda1}} \quad \text{(3C-8)}$$

$A_{\lambda1}$ and $A_{\lambda2}$ can be measured with a photometer. Therefore, Eqns. 3C-7 and 3C-8 can be used for simultaneous determination of two components in a mixture with UV/Vis spectrophotometer.

D*etermination of equilibrium constant of acid/base indicator*: In the case of acid/base indicators such as bromothymol blue, there is a way to determine K_a without measuring the concentrations of the chemical species in the equilibrium.

First, based on Eqn. 3C-4, $[In^-]/[HIn]$ (i.e. C_b/C_a) ratio is needed to determine K_a at different *pH*s.

Divide Eqn. 3C-8 by Eqn. 3C-7

$$\frac{C_b}{C_a} = \frac{\varepsilon_{a\lambda1}A_{\lambda2} - \varepsilon_{b\lambda1}A_{\lambda1}}{\varepsilon_{b\lambda2}A_{\lambda1} - \varepsilon_{a\lambda2}A_{\lambda2}} \quad \text{(3C-9)}$$

Second, since acid/base indicators are themselves weak acid/base, their relative abundance is governed by *pH*. At low *pH*, the acid form dominates; at high *pH*, the basic form dominates. Therefore, at very low *pH* value (e.g. *pH* = 1), $[In^-]$ (C_b) is very low (≈ 0) compared to $[HIn]$ (C_a); therefore, $C_{TOT} = C_a + C_b \approx C_a$. Eqns. 3C-5 and 3C-6 are reduced to

At *pH* = 1: $A_{\lambda1(pH=1)} = \varepsilon_{a\lambda1}\, b\, C_a$ (3C-5') and $A_{\lambda2(pH=1)} = \varepsilon_{a\lambda2}\, b\, C_a$ (3C-6')

In contrast, at high pH (e.g. pH = 13), $C_a \approx 0$, and $C_{TOT} \approx C_b$. Eqns. 3C-5 and 3C-6 reduced to

At *pH* = 13: $A_{\lambda1(pH=13)} = \varepsilon_{b\lambda1}\, b\, C_b$ (3C-5") and $A_{\lambda2(pH=13)} = \varepsilon_{b\lambda2}\, b\, C_b$ (3C-6")

Combine Eqns. 3C-9, 3C-5', 3C-6', 3C-5" and 3C-6",

$$\frac{C_b}{C_a} = \frac{A_{\lambda1(pH=1)}A_{\lambda2} - A_{\lambda1(pH=13)}A_{\lambda1}}{A_{\lambda2(pH=13)}A_{\lambda1} - A_{\lambda2(pH=1)}A_{\lambda2}} \quad \text{(3C-10)}$$

Based on Eqn. 3C-10, the ratio of $[In^-] / [HIn]$ (C_b/C_a) at any *pH* can be obtained by the following procedures:

1. Measure absorbance of a solution at λ_1 and λ_2 at both $pH = 1$ ($A_{\lambda1(pH=1)}$, $A_{\lambda2(pH=1)}$) and 13 ($A_{\lambda1(pH=13)}$, $A_{\lambda2(pH=13)}$).
2. Measure absorbance at both λ_1 and λ_2 ($A_{\lambda1}$ and $A_{\lambda2}$) at a series of *pH*s. The ratio of base to acid conjugate ($[In^-]/[HIn]$) at each *pH* can be calculated from Eqn. 3C-10.
3. Determine pK_a by plotting *pH* vs. $log([In^-]/[HIn])$.

C. Chemicals

1. Sodium hydroxide (NaOH, ACS grade, >97%).
2. Sodium phosphate, monobasic, monohydrate ($NaH_2PO_4 \cdot H_2O$, ACS grade, >98.0%).
3. Sodium phosphate, dibasic (Na_2HPO_4, ACS grade, >99%).
4. Hydrochloric acid (HCl, ACS grade, concd, 37%).
5. Bromothymol blue (BTB, $C_{27}H_{28}Br_2O_5S$, ACS grade, 95%).
6. Ethanol (C_2H_6O, ACS grade, 99.7%).

D. Apparatus

1. (Spectro)Photometer.
2. Standard cuvettes, 1cm.
3. Volumetric flasks, 25, 100, 1000 mL.
4. Pipet: 1, 5, 10 mL.
5. Beakers, 100 mL.
6. pH meter (optional).

E. Procedure

1. Preparation of stock solutions

    a. *Preparation of 4 M NaOH stock solution*: Weigh 16.0 g NaOH into 100 mL volumetric flask. Bring to mark with deionized water and dissolve the solid thoroughly.
    b. *Preparation of 0.10 M NaH₂PO₄ stock solution*: Weigh 13.8 g $NaH_2PO_4 \cdot H_2O$ into 1000 mL volumetric flask. Bring to mark with deionized water and dissolve the solid thoroughly.
    c. *Preparation of 0.10 M Na₂HPO₄ stock solution*: Weigh 14.2 g Na_2HPO_4 into 1000 mL volumetric flask. Bring to mark with deionized water and dissolve the solid thoroughly.
    d. *Preparation of 0.1% BTB stock solution*: Weigh 400 mg NaOH into 1000 mL volumetric flask. Add ca. 10 mL deionized water to dissolve the NaOH. Weigh 100 mg BTB to the flask, followed by 20 ml ethanol. Bring to mark with deionized water.

2. Pipet 1.00 mL BTB stock solution into each of two 25 mL volumetric flasks. To one of the flasks add 5 mL deionized water and 4 drops of concentrated HCl. Dilute the solution to mark with deionized water. Label this flask as "Flask 1". The resulting solution should have a pH of approximately 1. To the second flask add 12 drops of 4 M sodium hydroxide solution and fill the flask to the mark with deionized water; label this flask "Flask 9". The solution should have a pH of about 13.

Flask #	pH	$A_{\lambda1}$ (410 nm)	$A_{\lambda2}$ (630 nm)
1	~1		
9	~13		

3. Prepare the (spectro)photometer to measure absorbance of the two solutions in Flask #1 and 9 at wavelength 410 nm and 630 nm. Record your result on the data table above. The absorbance of solution 1 (pH = 1) at 630 nm should be close to zero.

4. Prepare 7 buffer solutions in 25 mL flasks by pipetting 1.00 mL bromothymol blue stock, 0.10 M KH_2PO_4 and K_2HPO_4 stock solutions, and bring to mark with deionized. The table below lists volume of 0.1 M KH_2PO_4 and K_2HPO_4 solution (mL) needed to prepare the pH series. The calculated pH values are listed in the table. Alternatively, if you have a well calibrated pH meter, measure pH for each solution and recorded in the last column.

Flask #	V(KH₂PO₄)	V(K₂HPO₄)	pH	pH (measured)
2	10	0	4.6	
3	9.75	0.25	5.6	
4	8	2	6.6	
5	5	5	7.2	
6	2	8	7.8	
7	0.25	9.75	8.8	
8	0	10	9.8	

5.   Measure absorbance for above solutions at 410 nm (λ_1) and 630 nm (λ_2). Record your result on the data table below.

Flask #	pH	$A_{\lambda 1}$ (410 nm)	$A_{\lambda 2}$ (630 nm)	$[In^-]/[HIn]$	$log([In^-]/[HIn])$	pK_a
2	4.6					
3	5.8					
4	6.6					
5	7.2					
6	7.8					
7	8.6					
8	9.8					

6.   If you are using a scanning spectrophotometer, scan UV/Vis spectrum at range of 300–700 nm for solution 1 and 9. Combine the two spectra, and include it in your lab report.

F.   Result report

1.   Calculate $[In^-]/[HIn]$ value for solutions 2-8 using Eqn. 3C-10. Calculate $log([In^-]/[HIn])$. Calculate pK_a for each solution with Eqn. 3C-3. Use data table in Step **5**.
2.   Plot pH vs. $log([In^-]/[HIn])$ on a spreadsheet. Conduct linear regression and the intercept with y (pH) axis equals pK_a.
3.   The intercept of the two spectra you obtained from solution 1 and 9 is called isobestic point, which is the wavelength at which the absorptivities of two conjugates are equal. What's the isobestic point for bromothymol blue?

G.   Questions for discussion

1.   The accuracy of pK_a determination in this experiment depends on how accurately you can determine pH and $[In^-]/[HIn]$. Discuss factors affecting the accuracy of pH and $[In^-]/[HIn]$ determinations.
2.   To conduct equilibrium constant determination using method in this experiment, it's very important to choose the right pair of wavelengths. Discuss why the two wavelengths chosen in this experiment are appropriate.
3.   Explain why you should not choose isobestic point to conduct simultaneous determination of two components mixture.

H.   Supplementary experiment 3C-1: Equilibrium Constant of pH Indicators

The procedure described in this experiment for determining equilibrium constant of pH indicator can be applied to many other pH indicators. Table 3-2 lists some indicators with suitable pH range and water solubility, and can be easily adapted to the procedure in this experiment.

Table 3-2 *pH indicators can be used in this experiment.*

Indicator	Color		pKₐ	pH range	Suggested Concentration
	Acid	Base	pK_a		
Methyl orange	red	yellow	3.47	3.1-4.4	0.00005%
Bromocresol Green	yellow	blue	4.7	3.8 - 5.4	0.04%
Methyl Red	yellow	red	5.1	4.8 - 6.0	0.04%
Bromocresol purple	yellow	puple	6.3	5.2-6.8	0.04%
Phenol Red	yellow	red	7.9	6.8 - 8.4	0.04%

I. Supplementary experiment 3C-2: Determination of Two-Components Mixture

A classic experiment in UV/Vis spectrophotometry is determination of two-component mixture described in the **Introduction** of the main experiment (the acid and base conjugates of an indicator can be considered as two components). Table 3-3 lists some pairs of compounds which are suitable for this experiment, and useful spectral information is given.

Generally, the experiment involves the following steps:

1. Prepare standard solutions for both components.
2. Scan both components, and choose two wavelengths.
3. Calculate absorptivity of each component at chosen wavelengths by measuring standard of known concentration.
4. Measure absorbance of an unknown sample at two wavelengths.
5. Calculate concentration of two components using Eqns. 3C-7 and 3C-8 in the Introduction.

Table 3-3 *Pairs of components for multi-components UV/Vis experiment.*

No.	Component	Solvent (blank)	Concentration (M)	Wavelength (nm)
1	$Cr(NO_3)_3$	H_2O	0.02	575
	$Co(NO_3)_2$	H_2O	0.0752	510
2	$Co(NO_3)_3$	H_2O	0.04 - 0.12	510
	$Ni(NO_3)_2$	H_2O	0.04 - 0.13	395 or 660
3	$KMnO_4$	0.5M H_2SO_4	0.0008 - 0.0040	545
	$K_2Cr_2O_7$	0.5M H_2SO_4	0.0008 - 0.0040	440
4	Fe(II)	2.0×10^{-4} M 1,10-phenanthroline	5.0×10^{-5}	350 - 700
	Fe(III)	2.0×10^{-4} M 1,10-phenanthroline	5.0×10^{-5}	350 - 700

J. Reference

1. Skoog, D. A., F. J. Holler and S. R. Crouch, 2007. Principles of Instrumental Analysis. 6th ed. Thomson Brooks/Cole Publishing. Belmont, CA.
2. Sawyer, D. T., W. R. Heineman and J. M. Beebe, 1984. Chemistry Experiments for Instrumental Methods. Wiley.
3. Tobey, S. W., 1958. The acid dissociation constant of methyl red. A spectrophotometric measurement. J. Chem. Educ. 35(10): 514.
4. Ramett, R. W., 1967. Equilibrium Constants from Spectrophotometric Data. J. Chem. Educ. 44: 647.
5. Brown, C. W. and R. J. Obremski, 1984. Multicomponent Quantitative Analysis. Appl. Spectrosc. Rev. 20: 373–418.
6. Dado, G. and J. Rosenthal, 1990. Simultaneous Determination of Cobalt, Copper, and Nickel by Multi-variate Linear Regression. J. Chem. Educ. 67: 797–800.

MOLECULAR FLUORESCENCE SPECTROSCOPY

CHAPTER

4

I. BASIC PRINCIPLES

Qualitative fluorescence spectroscopic analysis: Molecules have various electronic states called **energy levels**. The lowest energy level is referred as **ground state** (S_0), the higher energy level is referred as the **excited state** (single excited states S_1 and S_2 and triple excited state T_0). Within ground and excited electronic states are various **vibrational states** (Figure 4-1).

When molecules at ground state (S_0) absorb radiation energy, they are excited to higher energy levels (S_1 and S_2). The molecules at excited states can lose energy and return to ground state (a process called **deactivation)** in three ways: 1) **vibrational relaxation** occurs when molecules at excited states (S_1 or S_2) return to ground state without emitting radiation; 2) convert from S_1 excited state to S_0 and emit radiation, called **fluorescence**; and 3) convert from triple T_1 to S_0 ground state through emit radiation, called **phosphorescence**. These processes are visualized with **Jablonski diagram** (Figure 4-1).

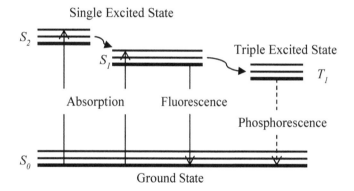

Figure 4-1 Pathways for production and de-excitation of an excited state.

Just like the molecules do not absorb all light equally, the excited molecules do not emit fluorescence equally at all wavelengths. A typical spectrofluorometer allows one to scan spectrum of emitted fluorescence radiation with fixed excitation wavelength, this spectrum is called **emission spectrum**. The spectrofluorometer may also allow to scan the excitation wavelength, and record emitted fluorescence at a fixed wavelength, this is called **excitation spectrum**.

The excitation spectrum of a fluorescent molecule is similar to its absorption spectrum, since the excitation and absorption virtually refer to the same process. Just like absorption (or excitation) spectrum, the emission spectrum of a fluorescent molecule is determined by its molecular structure, and can be used to identify the molecule. As an example, the molecular structure and excitation/ emission spectra of quinine are shown in Figure 4-2.

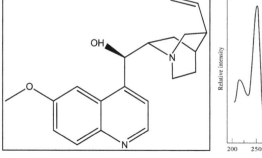 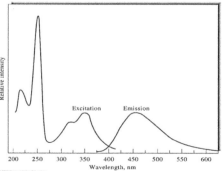

Figure 4-2 Molecular structure (left) and excitation/emission spectra of quinine (right).

Quantitative fluorometric analysis: The quantitative fluorometric analysis is based on the fact that the intensity of fluorescence emission for a specific analyte (at specific excitation and emission wavelengths) has a linear relationship with concentration of the analyte. The relationship is defined as

$$F = 2.303\ K'\varepsilon bc I_o \qquad (4\text{-}1)$$

where F is the power of fluorescence emission, K' is a constant, ε is molar absorptivity, b is the path length, c is the concentration of analyte, I_o is the incident radiant power.

For a specific analyte (such as quinine), if the excitation and emission wavelengths are specified, ε is a constant. If we know the light path length (b), and the incident radiant power (I_o) remains constant, Eqn. 4-1 is reduced to

$$F = Kc \qquad (4\text{-}2)$$

where $K = 2.303\ K'\varepsilon b I_o$. This relationship forms the basis of quantitative fluorescence spectroscopic analysis.

II BASIC INSTRUMENTATION

A basic fluorometer/spectrofluorometer has **light source** to provide incident radiation, a **monochromator** to separate/filter source light to obtain monochromatic light beam. Emitted radiation passes through a second filter or monochromator to filter/separate emitted radiation (fluorescence). A **transducer** (detector) converts radiation signal to electrical signal, and a readout device (recorder) for recording the signal (Figure 4-3). The fluorescent emission is usually measured at **right angle** to the incident light beam.

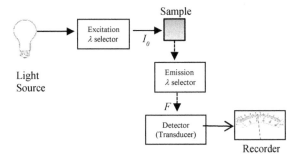

Figure 4-3 Schematic diagram of fluorescence spectrometer.

1. Light Sources: Generally, the source of (spectro)fluorometer must be more intense than that is required for UV-Vis absorption spectroscopy. The most common source for filter fluorometer is **low-pressure mercury lamp**, which provides lines at 254, 302, 313, 546, 578 nm. Spectrofluorometers are often equipped with a high-pressure **xenon arc lamp**, which provides a continuum from 300 nm to 800 nm. Lasers, photodiodes are also used in some specialized fluorometers.
2. Wavelength Selector: Fluorometers use either **interference** or **absorption filters** for both excitation and emission wavelength selectors. **Spectrofluorometers** are usually fitted with at least one (usually two) **grating monochromators**.
3. Sample Container: **Quartz** or **fused silica** cells (cuvettes) are commonly used for (spectro)-fluorometer.
4. Detectors (Transducer): Fluorescence signals are usually low in intensity. More sensitive transducers are required. **Photomultiplier tubes** are the most common transducer for (spectro)fluorometer. **Diode-array detectors** (DAD) and charge-transfer devices such as **charge-coupled devices** (CCDs) are used in some spectrofluorometric instruments.

General Reading

1. Skoog, D. A., F. J. Holler and S. R. Crouch, 2007. Principles of Instrumental Analysis. 6th ed. Thomson Brooks/Cole Publishing. Belmont, CA.
2. Sawyer, D. T., W. R. Heineman and J. M. Beebe, 1984. Chemistry Experiments for Instrumental Methods. Wiley.
3. Lakowicz, R. J., 2006. Principles of Fluorescence Spectroscopy. 3rd ed. Springer.
4. Harris, D. C., 2010. Quantitative Chemical Analysis, 8th Ed., Freeman, New York.

EXPERIMENT 4A: FLUORESCENCE SPECTROSCOPY OF QUININE IN TONIC WATER

A. Objectives

1. To understand the basic principle and basic instrumentation of (spectro)fluorometry.
2. To establish external standard calibration for quinine analysis with (spectro)fluorometer.
3. To conduct measurement of quinine in tonic water with (spectro)fluorometer.
4. To measure excitation/emission spectra of quinine.

B. Chemicals

1. Quinine ($C_{20}H_{24}N_2O_2$, >98%).
2. Sulfuric acid (H_2SO_4, ACS grade, conc. 98%).
3. Unknown: tonic water.

C. Apparatus

1. Basic (spectro)fluorometer.
2. Analytical balance (0.001 g).
3. Volumetric flasks: 100, 1000 mL.
4. Pipets: 100 µL, 1, 5 mL.
5. Quartz or fused silica cells (cuvettes).

D. Procedure

1. Preparation of quinine standard solutions

    > **Safety Precautions:** Concentrated H_2SO_4 are highly corrosive. Wear gloves and goggles when handling any concentrated acid and/or base. When concentrated H_2SO_4 and water mix, large amount of heat is released, and the heat can cause the water to boil. Thus, always mix concentrated H_2SO_4 to large volume of water slowly to allow the heat to be dissipated.

    a. *Preparation of 1M stock H_2SO_4 solution*: In a 1000 mL volumetric flask with about 500 mL deionized water, slowly and carefully add 56 mL concentrated H_2SO_4 with stirring. Bring to mark with deionized water.
    b. *Preparation 0.05 M H_2SO_4 solution*: Transfer 50mL 1 M H_2SO_4 solution to 1000 mL volumetric flask. Bring to mark with deionized water.
    c. *Preparation of 1000 ppm quinine stock solution*: Weigh exactly 0.100 g of quinine, and transfer into a 100 mL volumetric flask. Dilute to mark with 0.05 M H_2SO_4 solution. Dissolve all the quinine and mix thoroughly.
    d. *Preparation of quinine standard solutions*: Pipet 100, 300, 500, 750, and 1000 µL of the 1000 ppm quinine stock solution into five 100 mL volumetric flasks. Dilute to volume with 0.05 M H_2SO_4 for each flask.

2. Preparation of instrument: depending on the instrument used, the instructor should prepare detailed operational procedures for this experiment. For a basic filter fluorometer, the following are general operational procedures

    a. Turn on the instrument main power.
    b. Leave the instrument to warm up for 20 minutes.
    c. Set excitation wavelength at 350 nm, and emission wavelength at 450 nm.
    d. Use 0.05 M H_2SO_4 solution as blank to zero the instrument.
    e. Pipet 2-3 mL of each standard solution to a standard 1 cm cuvette. Insert the cuvette into cell holder.
    f. Record the fluorescence intensity.

For a scanning spectrofluorometer connected to a computer, the following are general operational procedures

a. Turn the instrument main power and the computer power on.
b. Start the computer program.
c. Turn on the lamps if it's controlled by the software.
d. Choose between fixed wavelength mode and spectrum scanning mode.
e. Set the instrumental parameters for the analysis.
f. Pipet 2-3 ml blank into 1 cm cuvette and insert the cell holder. Zero the instrument with 0.05 M H_2SO_4.
g. Load standard/sample onto the instrument, record the fluorescence intensity.

Part I Quantitative analysis

1. Standard calibration

a. Choose fixed wavelength mode. Set excitation wavelength at 350 nm, and emission wavelength at 450 nm.
b. Use 0.05 M H_2SO_4 solution as blank to zero the instrument.
c. Pipet 2-3 mL of each standard solution to a standard 1 cm cuvette. Insert the cuvette into cell holder. Record the fluorescence intensity onto data table below.

Standard	C (ppm)	F
1	1.0	
2	3.0	
3	5.0	
4	7.5	
5	10	

2. Measurement of samples.

a. Measure fluorescence of the unknown sample (tonic water). If the fluorescence reading of tonic water is higher than that of the highest standard concentration (10 ppm), dilute the tonic water with 0.05 M H_2SO_4 to allow the reading fall within the calibration range.
b. Record the fluorescence reading on the data table for both original and diluted sample. Record the dilution factor for the diluted sample.

Samples	Dilution factor	F	Diluted C (ppm)	Original C (ppm)
Undiluted tonic water	1			
Diluted tonic water				

Part II Qualitative analysis

If a scanning spectrofluorometer is used, scan excitation/emission spectra as follow.

1. Choose one quinine standard solution, transfer 2-3 mL into a cuvette. Load it to the cell holder.
2. Choose scanning mode. First, choose excitation scanning mode, set excitation wavelength at a range between 200 and 450 nm, and the emission wavelength at 450 nm.
3. Scan excitation spectrum. Save the spectrum.
4. Change the scanning mode to emission scanning mode. Set excitation wavelength at 250 nm, and emission wavelength range between 375 and 650 nm.
5. Scan emission spectrum. Save your spectrum.
6. Combine the excitation and emission spectra. Attach the combined spectra with your lab report.

7. Scan excitation and emission spectra for tonic water. Attach the combine excitation and emission spectra of tonic water in your lab report.

E. Result report

1. Construct external standard calibration curve in a spreadsheet.
2. Calculate concentration of quinine in tonic water based on the calibration curve.
3. If you used a scanning spectrofluorometer, attach your excitation/emission spectra in your report. Compare your spectra with the published one (Figure 4-2).
4. Compare excitation/emission spectra of the standard with that of tonic water.

F. Questions for discussion

1. Explain why the fluorescence radiation is measured at right angle from the incident light source?
2. Describe how excitation and emission spectra are measured.
3. Compare the excitation spectrum obtained in this experiment with the absorption spectrum obtained in Experiment 3A. Are they similar? Explain why.
4. Referring to the Jablonski Diagram, discuss why there is only one emission band (450 nm), while there are two excitation bands (250 and 350 nm).
5. The emission band has longer wavelength than the excitation bands. Discuss why.

G. Supplementary Experiment

Quantitative analysis of many fluorescent organic compounds can be determined fluorometrically. The following is a list of such compounds and their chemical and fluorometric properties (Table 4-1).

Table 4-1 *Compounds can be used in (spectro)fluorometry experiment.*

	Solvent	Excitation (nm)	Emission (nm)	Suggested C (ppm)	Found in
Acetylsalicylic Acid	0.08 M NaOH	275	340	10	Aspirin
Salicylic acid	0.08 M NaOH	310	440	10	Aspirin
Riboflavin	H_2O	370	440	0.1	Food/vegetable
Fluorescein	0.1 M NaOH	492	516	1	Synthetic

H. Reference

1. Skoog, D. A., F. J. Holler and S. R. Crouch, 2007. Principles of Instrumental Analysis. 6th ed. Thomson Brooks/Cole Publishing. Belmont, CA.
2. Sawyer, D. T., W. R. Heineman and J. M. Beebe, 1984. Chemistry Experiments for Instrumental Methods. Wiley.
3. Harris, D. C., 2010. Quantitative Chemical Analysis, 8th Ed., Freeman, New York.
4. Lakowicz, R. J., 2006. Principles of Fluorescence Spectroscopy. 3rd ed. Springer.
5. O'Reilly, J. E., 1975. Fluorescence experiments with quinine. J. Chem. Educ. 52(9): 610.

EXPERIMENT 4B: FLUOROMETRIC DETERMINATION OF ALUMINUM IN AQUEOUS SAMPLE

A. Objectives

1. To practice sample preparation with separatory funnel liquid-liquid extraction.
2. To learn the application of metal-ligand complexes in fluorescence spectroscopy.
3. To determine aluminum in water sample with (spectro)fluorometry.

B. Introduction

Fluorometric methods are not commonly used directly for analysis of inorganic species since inorganic molecules are usually not fluorescent. However, some inorganic species can form fluorescent complex with ligands, and can be measured photometrically or fluorometrically. A good example is the use of 8-hydroxyquinoline as fluorescent chelate in analysis of aluminum in water.

$$Al^{3+} + 3C_9H_6NOH \rightarrow Al(C_9H_6NO)_3 + 3H^+ \quad (4B-1)$$

The fluorescence of the complex does not vary significantly with time, pH, or amount of fluorophores used. The complex is extracted into solvents such as methylene chloride and analyzed with (spectro)-fluorometer. The presence of iron in amounts equivalent to the aluminum concentration does not seriously interfere with the analysis.

C. Chemicals

1. 8-Hydroxyquinoline (C_9H_7NOH, ACS grade, 99%).
2. Aluminum potassium sulfate dodecahydrate ($KAl(SO_4)_2 \cdot 12H_2O$, ACS grade, >98%).
3. Glacial acetic acid (CH_3CO_2H, ACS grade, >99%)
4. Ammonium hydroxide solution (ammonia, NH_4OH, ACS grade, 28% (w/w))
5. Methylene chloride (CH_2Cl_2, ACS grade, 99.5%)

D. Apparatus

1. Basic (spectro)fluorometer.
2. Analytical balance (0.001 g).
3. Pipet, 1, 5 mL.
4. Flurescence cuvettes.
5. Separatory funnels, 250 mL.
6. Volumetric flasks, 50, 250, 1000 mL.

E. Procedure

1. Preparation of solutions

   a. *Preparation of 100 ppm aluminum stock solution*: Accurately weigh 441 mg potassium aluminum sulfate dodecahydrate to a 250 mL volumetric flask, bring to mark with deionized water. Dissolve thoroughly.

   b. *Preparation of 2 ppm aluminum working solution*: Pipet 20 mL 100 ppm aluminum stock solution to a 1000 mL volumetric flask. Bring to mark with deionized water.

   c. *Preparation of 2% 8-hydroxyquinoline stock solution*: In a 100 mL volumetric flask with about 50 mL of deionized water, add 6 mL glacial acetic acid. Weigh 2 g 8-hydroxyquinoline, and transfer to the flask. Bring to mark with deionized water, and mix thoroughly.

   d. *Preparation of ammonium acetate buffer solution*: Add 45 g of ammonium acetate to a 1000 mL volumetric flask. Add 15 mL 28% (w/w) ammonia. Bring to mark with deionized water. Dissolve the solid and mix thoroughly.

   e. *Preparation of blank*: Add 100 mL deionized water to a 250 mL separatory funnel followed by 2 mL 2% 8-hydroxyquinoline stock solution and 2 mL of the ammonium acetate buffer. The pH of the mixture should be 8.0 ± 1.5. Add 15.0 mL of methylene chloride to the mixture, shake for 5 minutes. Transfer the organic phase to a 50 mL volumetric flask. Repeat this process and combine the methylene chloride. Bring to mark with extra methylene chloride. See the inset below for more details on separatory funnel extraction.

f. *Preparation of aluminum standard solutions*: In four 100 mL volumetric flasks, add 1, 2, 4, 8 mL of 2 ppm aluminum stock solution. Bring to mark with deionized water. This yields 20, 40, 80, 160 ppb of aluminum standards. Follow the same procedure in **1.e** to extract aluminum complex to methylene chloride.

Separatory funnel separation

1. Place the separatory funnel in an iron ring. Remove the stopper and make sure that the stopcock is closed.
2. Add sample to be extracted. Do not fill the funnel more than half. Add the extraction solution (CH_2Cl_2) and place the stopper. The organic phase is on the bottom (why?). There should still be some space on top of the liquid.
3. Take the separatory funnel out of the ring and hold it tightly at the stopper and the stopcock. Invert slowly and open the stopcock towards the back of the hood to release the pressure. You will hear whistling noise when the pressure is being released.
4. Close the stopcock and shake the funnel gently, watching out for emulsions. Vent it again. Repeat this step until no more pressure built up.
5. Place the separatory funnel back in the iron ring. Allow the layers to separate. Remove the stopper and drain the bottom layer (CH_2Cl_2) into a clean flask.
6. Add more extraction solution, and repeat the procedure above. Combine the extractant.

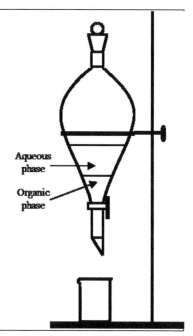

Aqueous phase

Organic phase

---

2. External standard calibration

    a. Prepare the instrument as described in Experiment 4A. Set excitation wavelength at 365 nm and emission wavelength at 520 nm.
    b. Measure the fluorescence of the aluminum standard solutions. Remember to zero the instrument with blank prepared in Step **1.e**. Record the fluorescence intensity (F).

Standard #	C_{Al} (ppb)	F
1	20	
2	40	
3	80	
4	160	

3. Measurement of unknown sample

    Follow the same procedure in Step **1.e** to extract aluminum complex in unknown samples. Measure fluorescence of the extracted samples. Record the fluorescence reading in the data table.

Sample #	F	C_{Al} (ppb)
1		
2		
3		

4. Cleanup and waste disposal: dispose the organic and aqueous waste in properly labeled waste container.

F. Result report

1. Construct external standard calibration curve in a spreadsheet.
2. Calculate concentration of aluminum in unknown sample, report result in ppb of aluminum.

G. Questions for discussion

1. High level aluminum in drinking water has been linked to Alzheimer's disease (AD; Rondeau et al., 2000). The maximum contaminant level (MCL) is set at 200 ppb by USEPA (National Primary Drinking Water Regulations). Is the concentration of aluminum in your sample higher than the MCL?
2. Discuss possible interference of aluminum in this experiment.
3. Discuss main sources of error.

H. Supplementary experiment

Significant effort has been made to find chelates which can be used for determination of inorganic species by forming metal-ligand complexes. Table 4-2 lists some inorganic species and ligands with spectral information of the metal-ligands complexes.

Table 4-2 *Inorganic species which can be analyzed with (spectro)fluorometery through chelating.*

Metal Ion	Chelating Reagent	LOD (ppm)	λ_{ex} (nm)	λ_{em} (nm)
Aluminum	Lumogallion	0.001	465	555
Beryllium	Morin	0.01	420	525
Calcium	Calcein	0.2	410	490
Gallium	Lumogallion	0.001	490	570
Lead	4 NH$_2$ Ph-EDTA	0.08	360	450
Magnesium	8-Hydroxyquinoline	0.01	420	530
Manganese	Carminic acid	0.9	467	556
Zinc	8-Quinolinol	0.5	375	517

I. References

1. White, C. E., 1951. The use of fluorescence in qualitative analysis. J. Chem. Educ. 28(7): 369.
2. Rondeau, V., D. Commenges, H. Jacqmin-Gadda and J. F. Dartigues, 2000. Relation between aluminum concentrations in drinking water and Alzheimer's disease: an 8-year follow-up study. Am. J. Epidemiol. 152: 59–66.
3. Zhang, J., H. Xu, J. L. Ren, 200. Fluorimetric determination of dissolved aluminium in natural waters after liquid–liquid extraction into n-hexanol. Analytica Chimica Acta. 405: 31–42.
4. Online introduction: **http://www.perkinelmer.co.kr/files/fluorescence_inorganic.pdf**

EXPERIMENT 4C: DETERMINATION OF CHLORIDE IN DRINKING WATER BY FLUORESCENCE QUENCHING

A. Objectives

1. To understand the application of fluorescence quenching in spectrofluorometry.
2. To measure concentration of chloride by fluorescence quenching.

B. Introduction

Fluorescence quenching refers to the process that a molecule at excited state transfers energy to other molecules (**quencher**) without emit fluorescence. **Dynamic quenching**, also called **collisional quenching**, occurs when an excited molecule collides with the quencher. In dynamic quenching, the efficiency of quenching is a function of the concentration of quenching agent (Q). The **Stern-Volmer equation** defines the relationship between the reduction of fluorescence and the concentration of quencher

$$\frac{f_0}{f} = 1 + K_{SV}[Q] \qquad (4C\text{-}1)$$

where f_0 and f are the fluorescence signals in the absence and in the presence of quencher respectively, K_{SV} is **Stern-Vilmer constant** and $[Q]$ is concentration of the quencher. Thus, to estimate the Stern-Volmer constant, one can plot f_0/f ratios vs. concentration of quencher, the slope of the plot is K_{SV}.

The constant K_{SV} is related to the lifetime of the excited state, τ_0, as follows,

$$K_{SV} = k_q \tau_0 \qquad (4C\text{-}2)$$

where k_q is the quencher rate coefficient.

In this experiment, you will use Stern-Volmer equation to quantify the concentration of chloride, which serves as quencher (Q) of quinine fluorescence. Since the fluorescence efficiency is strongly affected by other factors (e.g. ion strength), all solutions (standards, samples) are prepared in a way to minimize the impact of variability of other factors.

C. Chemicals

1. Sulfuric acid (H_2SO_4, ACS grade, 98%).
2. Quinine ($C_{20}H_{24}N_2O_2$, anhydrous, >98%).
3. Sodium chloride (NaCl, ACS grade, >99.0%).

D. Apparatus

1. Basic (spectro)Fluorometer.
2. Fluorescence cuvettes.
3. Volumetric flasks, 100, 500, 1000 mL.
4. Pipet, 1, 5, 10 mL.

E. Procedure

Part I Quantitative analysis of chloride in water

1. Preparation of solutions

   a. *Preparation of 1M stock H_2SO_4 solution*: In a 1000 mL volumetric flask with about 500 mL deionized water, slowly and carefully add 56 mL concentrated H_2SO_4 with stirring. Bring to mark with deionized water.

   b. *Preparation 0.05 M H_2SO_4 solution*: Transfer 50mL 1 M H_2SO_4 solution to 1000 mL volumetric flask. Bring to mark with deionized water.

c. *Preparation of 1000 ppm quinine stock solution*: Carefully weigh 0.10 g of quinine to a 100 mL volumetric flask. Pipet 5.00 mL of 1 M H_2SO_4 into the flask. Carefully dissolve all the quinine by swirling before diluting to volume.

d. *Preparation of 40 ppm quinine stock solution*: Pipet 20 mL of 1000 ppm quinine stock solution into a 500 mL volumetric flask. Add 25.0 mL of 1 M H_2SO_4, dilute to volume with deionized water.

e. *Preparation of 0.012 M NaCl stock solution*: Weigh 0.175 g NaCl and transfer to a 250 mL volumetric flask, add 12.5 mL 1 M H_2SO_4, fill to mark with deionized water.

f. *Preparation of working standard solutions*: In five 10 mL test tubes, add 1 mL 40 ppm quinine, 0.012 M NaCl solution, and 0.05 M H_2SO_4 sequentially with volumes of each solution as listed in following table. This should give you standard solutions with 0, 1.2, 2.4, 3.6, 4.8 mM of Cl^- and the same concentration of quinine (4 ppm).

Standard #	1	2	3	4	5
$V_{quinine}$ (mL)	1	1	1	1	1
V_{NaCl} (mL)	0	1	2	3	4
V_{H2SO4} (mL)	9	8	7	6	5

a. *Preparation of sample*: In a 10 mL test tube, add 1 mL 40 ppm quinine, 0.5 mL 1 M H_2SO_4 and 8.5 mL sample (drinking water). Mix thoroughly.

2. Measurement of standard solutions

   a. Turn on the (spectro)fluorometer. Leave it to warm up for 20 minutes. Set excitation wavelength at 350 nm and emission wavelength at 450 nm.

   b. Measure the fluorescence of the working standard solutions. Remember to zero the instru-ment with 0.05 M H_2SO_4 solution. Record the fluorescence readings on data table below.

   c. Calculate f_0/f for each concentration of chloride. Plot f_0/f vs. concentration of chloride (Stern–Volmer plots) on spreadsheet.

   d. Conduct linear regression analysis to obtain the Stern-Vilmer equation. Record the slope (Stern-Vilmer constant) and intercept (close to 1).

Standard #	C_{Cl} (mM)	F (f)	f_0/f
1	0	f_0	1
2	1.2		
3	2.4		
4	3.6		
5	4.8		

3. Quantification of chloride in unknown sample

   a. Measure the fluorescence of unknown sample.

   b. Calculate concentration of chloride in samples with Stern-Vilmer equation obtained in Step 2.

Sample #	F (f)	f_0/f	C_{Cl} (mM)
1			
2			
3			

Part II Effect of ion strength on fluorescence quenching

1. *Preparation of 1 M NaNO₃*: Weigh 8.5 g NaNO₃ into 100 volumetric flask, add 5 ml 1.0 M sulfuric acid. Bring to mark with deionized water.
2. *Preparation of ion strength series solutions*: Prepare 3 sets of solutions with different concentration of NaNO₃. For each set of solution, add 1 ml 40 ppm quinine stock solution to each of 10 mL capped test tube, 0, 1, 2, 3 ml of 0.012 mM NaCl, and 1M NaNO₃. Add 0.05 M sulfuric acid to make the total volume of 10 mL. The following tables help you to prepare all solutions.

C_{Cl} (mM)			0	1.2	2.4	3.6
C_{NaNO3} (M)	0.01	$V_{quinine}$ (mL)	1	1	1	1
		V_{NaCl} (mL)	0	1	2	3
		V_{NaNO3} (mL)	0.1	0.1	0.1	0.1
		V_{H2SO4} (mL)	8.9	7.9	6.9	5.9
	0.05	$V_{quinine}$ (mL)	1	1	1	1
		V_{NaCl} (mL)	0	1	2	3
		V_{NaNO3} (mL)	0.5	0.5	0.5	0.5
		V_{H2SO4} (mL)	8.5	7.5	6.5	5.5
	0.20	$V_{quinine}$ (mL)	1	1	1	1
		V_{NaCl} (mL)	0	1	2	3
		V_{NaNO3} (mL)	2	2	2	2
		V_{H2SO4} (mL)	7	6	5	4

3. Measure fluorescence for each solution. Record data in the following data table.

C_{Cl} (mM)		0		1.2		2.4		3.6	
		f	f_0/f	f	f_0/f	f	f_0/f	f	f_0/f
C_{NaNO3} (M)	0.01	f_0	1						
	0.05	f_0	1						
	0.20	f_0	1						
K_{SV}									

4. For each ion strength level (NaNO₃ concentrations), calculate f_0/f for all samples with different concentration of chlorides. Plot f_0/f vs. concentration of chloride in a spreadsheet. Put all three plots of the ion strength series on one graph. Run linear regression to determine Stern-Vilmer constant, K_{SV}, for each level of ion strength.

F. Result report

1. Tabulate the Cl⁻ concentration, fluorescence, and the quenching ratio (f_0/f) for standards. Plot f_0/f vs. Cl⁻ concentration. Run linear regression to derive the linear correlation equations.
2. Calculate concentration of chloride in unknown sample.
3. Tabulate fluorescence data for the ion strength series experiment. Plot f_0/f vs. Cl⁻ concentration for each level of NaNO₃ concentration (ion strength).
4. Run linear regression to derive the linear equations, the slope is Stern-Vilmer constant, K_{SV}.
5. Plot K_{SV} vs. C_{NaNO3}.

G. Questions for discussion

1. What's the y intercept on f_0/f vs. [Q] plot supposed to be?

2. Discuss how ion strength affect Stern-Vilmer constant, K_{SV}.

H. Reference

1. Skoog, D. A., F. J. Holler and S. R. Crouch, 2007. Principles of Instrumental Analysis. 6th ed. Thomson Brooks/Cole Publishing. Belmont, CA.
2. Sawyer, D. T., W. R. Heineman and J. M. Beebe, 1984. Chemistry Experiments for Instrumental Methods. Wiley.
3. Joseph R. Lakowicz, J. R., 2010. Principles of Fluorescence Spectroscopy. 3rd ed. Springer.
4. Bigger, W. S., P. J. Watkins, 2003. A Fluorimetric Approach to Studying the Effects of Ionic Strength on Reaction Rates. J. Chem. Educ. 80(10): 1191.

CHAPTER 5

INFRARED SPECTROSCOPY

I. BASIC PRINCIPLES

Qualitative IR spectroscopy: **Infrared (IR) spectroscopy** deals with the infrared region of the electromagnetic spectrum. IR radiation has a longer wavelength (0.78 to 1000 μm) and lower frequency than UV and visible light (180-780 nm). For convenience, **wave-number** (ν, cm^{-1}, reciprocal of wavelength) instead of wavelength (λ, nm) is used to distinguish IR radiations.

The IR region of the electromagnetic spectrum is divided into three regions. The high energy **near-IR** region (4000 to 14,000 cm^{-1}) finds application in quantitative analysis for certain species; the **mid-IR** (670 to 4000 cm^{-1}) is the most widely used region, commonly used for illustrating structure of organic compounds; the low energy **far-IR** has relatively limited application.

The IR absorption and emission correspond to the changes of **vibrational** and **rotational state** within a molecule. Qualitative IR spectroscopy is based on the fact that molecules absorb at specific frequencies that are characteristic of their structure. In mid-IR region, an absorption band on IR spectrum is usually associated with vibrational movement of certain bonds. For example, a strong band at 2850-2970 cm^{-1} is caused by the stretch vibration of C-H bond, and indicates the presence of C-H bond. A strong and broad band around 3600 cm^{-1} is an indication of presence of O-H bond. Figure 5-1 shows IR spectrum of pure water, the two bands corresponding to O-H stretch (3000-3600 cm^{-1}) and H-O-H scissoring (1700 cm^{-1}).

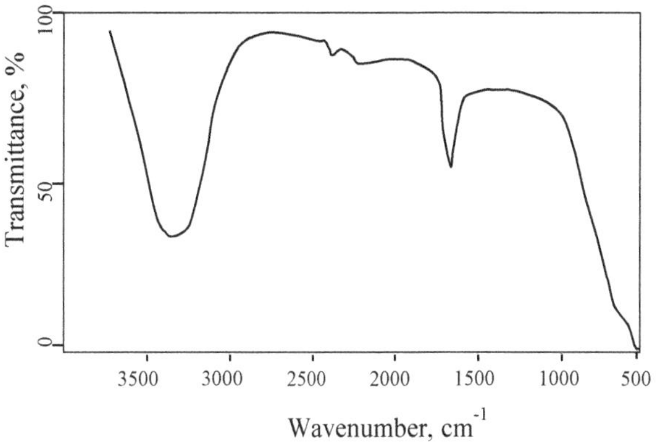

Figure 5-1 Infrared spectrum of pure water. Two absorption bands, O-H stretch (3000-3600 cm^{-1}) and H-O-H scissoring (1700 cm^{-1}), are present.

Quantitative IR spectroscopy: Like UV/Vis spectroscopy, the absorption of the incident beam in IR region follows **Beer's law**.

However, the application of Beer's law in quantitative IR absorption method is different from UV/Vis absorption methods due to the complexity of IR spectra, narrowness of the absorption band and limitation of IR instrumentation. Quantitative data obtained with **dispersive IR** instruments generally has low quality. With development of modern **FTIR** (Fourier Transform IR), precision and accuracy of quantitative FTIR method have been significantly improved. There is a more detailed introduction on the quantitative analysis of IR spectrometry in Experiment 3C.

II. BASIC INSTRUMENTATION

There are three types of IR instrument, 1) the dispersive IR spectrophotometer with a grating mono-chromator; 2) FTIR spectrophotometer with **interferometer**; and 3) nondispersive IR photometer with special design for analysis of atmospheric gases.

Dispersive IR spectrophotometer: The dispersive IR (spectro)photometer is designed based on same concept of UV/Vis absorption method, and therefore, the components are similar: a **radiation source**, **monochromator**, and **detector**. The common IR radiation sources are inert solids that are heated electrically to emit radiation in the infrared region. The grating monochromator disperse or separate IR radiation into narrow IR band. An **IR transducer** convert optical signal to electrical signal and recorded by a **recorder**. Figure 5-2 is schematic representation of a typical double-beamed dispersive IR instrument, which is similar to an UV/Vis absorption spectrophotometer.

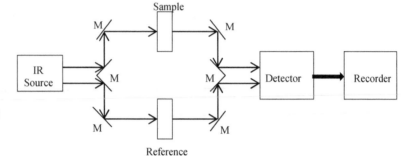

Figure 5-2 Schematic representation of dispersive IR.

Fourier transform IR spectrometer: A key component of FTIR is an **interferometer**, which play the role similar with monochromator of a dispersive IR spectrophotometer. FTIR significantly improve the signal-to-noise ratio and the sensitivity compared to dispersive IR instruments. The technical details of interferometer is out of scope of this manual. Figure 5-3 is schematic representation of a single beamed FTIR spectrometer with an interferometer.

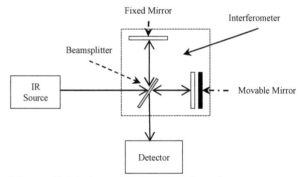

Figure 5-3 Schematic representation of FTIR.

Non-dispersive IR instrument: A specially designed IR photometer suitable for analysis of atmospheric gases (e.g. water vapor and carbon dioxide) has increasing application due to global warming. It's not discussed in this manual.

Sample container for IR instruments: Due to absorption of the IR radiation, glass or quartz cells are not suitable in the most important mid IR region. Sample preparation in IR spectrometry is more challenging than UV/Vis spectrometry. Sample preparation methods are addressed in Exp. 5A.

General Reading

1. Skoog, D. A., F. J. Holler and S. R. Crouch, 2007. Principles of Instrumental Analysis. 6th Ed. Thomson Brooks/Cole Publishing, Belmont, CA.
2. Sawyer, D. T., W. R. Heineman and J. M. Beebe, 1984. Chemistry Experiments for Instrumental Methods. Wiley.
3. Hendra, P., C. Jones, and G. Warnes, 1990. Fourier Transform Raman Spectroscopy: Instrumentation and Chemical Applications. Ellis Horwood, NY.
4. Larkin, P., 2011. Infrared and Raman Spectroscopy: Principles and Spectral Interpretation. Elsevier.
5. Online introduction: **http://en.wikipedia.org/wiki/Infrared_spectroscopy**
6. Online book chapter: **http://www.prenhall.com/settle/chapters/ch15.pdf**

EXPERIMENT 5A: INFRARED ABSORPTION SPECTROMETRY OF ORGANIC COMPOUNDS

A. Objectives

1. To learn the basic principles of infrared spectroscopy.
2. To practice preparing liquid and solid samples for infrared spectrophotometry.
3. To acquire infrared spectra of organic compounds.

B. Introduction

Sample preparation in IR spectrophotometry: IR spectroscopy can be used for the characterization of solid, liquid or gas samples. Material containing sample must be transparent to the IR radiation; thus, the salts like NaCl, KBr rather than quartz and glass are commonly used. The following is a brief introduction of common sample preparation methods used for liquid and solid samples in IR spectrophotometry.

1. Sample preparation of liquids

Liquid sample can be sandwiched between two highly purified alkali halides (e.g. NaCl and KBr) to forms a thin liquid membrane between the two aperture plates. Aqueous solvents cannot be used because they can dissolve alkali halides. Anhydrous organic solvents like chloroform can be used. The sample thickness should be selected so that the transmittance lies between 15-20%. For most liquids, the sample cell thickness is 0.01-0.05 mm. The most commonly used sample cell for liquid samples are **sealed cell** and **demountable cell**. Figure 5-4 shows a sealed cell and an expanded view of a demountable cell.

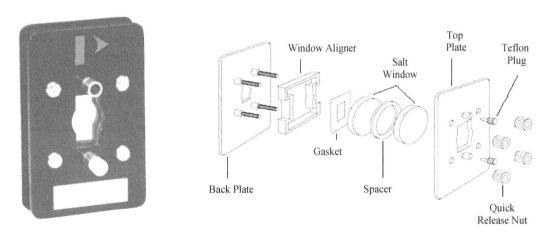

Figure 5-4. A sealed cell (A, Perkin-Elmer) and an expanded view of a demountable IR cell for liquid samples. The sealed cell has two injection ports for introducing liquid sample. In the demountable cell (B), the liquid sample is applied between the two salt windows; the teflon spacer is used to define pathlength with a range from 0.015 to 1 mm.

2. Sample preparation of solid

a. **Mull technique:** In this technique, the finely grinded sample is mixed with Nujol (mulling agent) in a mortar to make a thick paste. A thin film is applied onto the salt plates and mounted in a path of IR beam.

    b. **Solid in solution:** If a solid sample can be dissolved in a non-aqueous solvent provided that the solvent does not absorb radiation in the wavelength range to be studied. A drop of solution is placed on the surface of alkali metal disc and solvent is evaporated to dryness leaving a thin film of the solute.

    c. **Pressed pellet technique:** In this technique, a small amount of finely ground solid sample is mixed with potassium bromide (KBr) and compressed into a thin transparent pellet using a hydraulic press. The pellets are transparent to IR radiation and used for analysis.

C. Chemicals

1. Water free methylene chloride (CH_2Cl_2), carbon tetrachloride (CCl_4), ACS grade, 99.5%.
2. Acetylacetone ($C_5H_8O_2$, reagent, >99%).
3. Benzoic acid ($C_7H_6O_2$, ACS grade, >99.5%).
4. Mineral oil: "Nujol".
5. Potassium bromide (KBr, IR grade, predried and desiccated).
6. Unknown samples provided by instructor.

D. Apparatus

1. Dispersive or Fourier Transform infrared spectrophotometer.
2. Sodium chloride flats.
3. Demountable cell and holder.
4. Standard sealed liquid cell.
5. KBr disc assembly.
6. Agate mortar and pestle.

E. Procedure

> **Precaution**: the optical parts and absorption cell used in this experiment are made of NaCl or KCl and will be damaged by moisture. Take any necessary measures to avoid the contact of vulnerable parts with moisture. All reagents used in this experiment should be water free. In addition the optical part and cells are fragile, and must be handled carefully.

1. Prepare the instrument: Follow the procedures prepared by your instructor for operation of the instrument.

2. Acquire IR spectrum of acetylacetone (liquid) with a standard sealed cell

    a. Clean the sealed cell by introducing some CCl_4 followed by purging with nitrogen gas.
    b. Prepare 3.5% acetylacetone (v%) solution by diluting 3.5 mL acetylacetone in 100 mL volumetric flask with CCl_4.
    c. Introduce acetylacetone solution into the cell and close it.
    d. Mount the cell onto the sample holder in the IR spectrophotometer.
    e. Scan the spectrum of acetylacetone from 4000 cm^{-1} to 500 cm^{-1} and record the spectrum.
    f. Follow the same procedure to measure IR spectrum of CCl_4 (**blank**).
    g. Correct the sample (acetylacetone) IR spectrum with blank.

3. Acquire IR spectrum of acetylacetone (liquid) with a demountable cell

    a. Place a drop of the pure acetylacetone onto a NaCl flat. You should handle NaCl flats only from their edges.
    b. Place a second NaCl flat over the first one so that a thin film of acetylacetone between the two flats is obtained. Make sure that no air bubbles are contained within the thin liquid film.
    c. Mount the two NaCl flats containing the liquid film into the demountable cell holder and fix the cell assembly.
    d. Mount the cell onto sample holder in the instrument.
    e. Scan the spectrum of the liquid in the range from 4000 cm^{-1} to 500 cm^{-1} and record your spectrum.

    f.   Demount the cell and the NaCl flats from the cell assembly and clean the NaCl flats with water free CH_2Cl_2.

    g.   Aerate the flats with dried N_2 and store them in a desiccator.

    h.   Reassemble the cell without applying sample and scan IR spectrum (blank).

4. Acquire IR spectrum of acetylacetone with a KBr disc

    a.   Follow instructions for correct use of the KBr disc hydraulic press.

    b.   Demount the KBr die assembly and place an adequate amount of predried, desiccated and finely powdered KBr between the two small stainless steel flats and reassemble the components.

    c.   Apply a pressure of 10 tons to the die, hold for 20 seconds, then slowly release the pressure and remove the KBr disc from the die assembly.

    d.   Mount the KBr disc on the appropriate holder in the spectrophotometer and scan the IR spectrum in the range from 4000 cm^{-1} to 500 cm^{-1} (this is the **blank**).

    e.   Remove the KBr disc from the instrument. Apply a drop of liquid acetylacetone to moisten the disc surface. Allow about 1 min for the solvent to dry.

    f.   Mount the KBr disc in its appropriate place in the spectrophotometer and scan the spectrum in the range from 4000 cm^{-1} to 500 cm^{-1}.

5. Acquire IR spectrum of benzoic acid (solid) with Nujol mull method

    a.   Grind 2 mg benzoic acid in a mortar till the sample particulates are very fine. Remove a tiny portion of the sample into a small mortar, add 1 drop of Nujol and grind again.

    b.   Transfer the resulting mull or an appropriate portion of it and squeeze between two NaCl flats.

    c.   Mount the flats properly in the cell holder and adjust the cell assembly.

    d.   Record the IR spectrum of the solid sample in the range from 4000 cm^{-1} to 500 cm^{-1}.

    e.   Follow the same procedure to measure IR spectrum for Nujol oil alone (**blank**).

> Watch video to learn how to prepare solid sample with "Nujol" and sealed cell:
> **https://www.youtube.com/watch?v=g_pCDAi5kGI**

6. Acquire IR spectrum of benzoic acid with KBr pellet method

    a.   Finely grind 10 mg of benzoic acid with 500 mg KBr till a very fine powder is obtained.

    b.   Demount the KBr die assembly and load the mixture as directed. Reassemble and apply a 10 tons pressure on the disc and hold for 20 seconds.

    c.   Slowly release the pressure, demount the KBr die assembly, and remove the resulting KBr disc.

    d.   Mount the disc in the appropriate cell holder and record the IR spectrum in the range from 4000 cm^{-1} to 500 cm^{-1}.

    e.   Repeat steps a - d using only KBr to acquire **blank** spectrum.

> Watch video to learn how to prepare IR KBr pellet:
> **https://www.youtube.com/watch?v=lTAHqg_Q_5I**

7. Acquire IR spectrum of unknown sample

Choose one or more sample preparation methods for the unknown sample. Acquire IR spectrum.

8. Clean-up and waste disposal: Turn off the instrument. Dispose any organic waste in properly labeled waste container.

F. Result report

1. Include all IR spectra obtained with different sample preparation methods, including both analytes and blank spectra.

2. Compare all blank IR spectra. Discuss the advantage/disadvantage of each sample preparation method in terms of background absorption of different methods.
3. Compare analyte spectra (actylacetone and benzoic acid) obtained from different sample preparation methods. Discuss major interference for different methods, and how they are reflected on your IR spectra.
4. Include IR spectrum of the unknown sample in your report. Identify the unknown sample based on the IR spectrum. Discuss how you identify the compounds (absorption bands vs. functional groups). Or if your IR spectrum does not provide enough information to identify the unknown compound, what other information is needed?

G. Questions for discussion

1. Compare results obtained with all sample preparation methods tested in this experiment. Which method is more applicable for quantitative analysis?
2. Try to interpret as many peaks present in the frequency region on the IR spectra of acetylacetone and benzoic acid as possible.
3. Discuss advantages of a double-beamed IR spectrophotometer over a single-beamed instrument.

H. Supplementary experiments

Many organic compounds in a typical chemistry lab can be used in this experiment with one or more sample preparation methods. Try different types of organic compounds (aromatic, ketone, aldehyde, alcohol, carboxyl acid etc.) with appropriate sample preparation techniques and compare their IR spectra. Table 5-1 lists some organic compounds which can be used in this experiment.

Table 5-1 *Organic compounds can be used in qualitative IR spectroscopy experiment.*

Ketone aldehyde	Benzophenone Methyl ethyl ketone Benzaldehyde iso-Butylraldehyde	Acetone Cyclohexanone Acetaldehyde Acetophenone
Alcohol	n-Butyl alcohol sec-Butyl alcohol	Benzyl alcohol tert-Butyl alcohol
Nitro, ester	Benzonitrile Nitrobenzene o-Nitrotoluene	Etyl acetate Propionic anhydride Phthalic anhydride
Amide	Acetamide Acetanilide	Dimethyl formamide

I. Reference

1. Sawyer, D. T., W. R. Heineman and J. M. Beebe, 1984. Chemistry Experiments for Instrumental Methods. Wiley.
2. Gebel, E. M, M. A. Kaleuati and B. J. Finlayson-Pitts, 2003. Measurement of Organics Using Three FTIR Techniques: Absorption, Attenuated Total Reflectance, and Diffuse Reflectance. J. Chem. Educ. 80(6): 672.
3. Larkin, P., 2011. Infrared and Raman Spectroscopy: Principles and Spectral Interpretation. Elsevier.
4. Smith, C. B., 2011. Fundamentals of Fourier Transform Infrared Spectroscopy. 2nd Ed. CRC Press.
5. Günzler, H. and H.-U. Gremlich, 2002. IR Spectroscopy: An Introduction. Wiley-VCH.

Experiment 5B: Lab Demonstration—Interpretation of IR Spectrum

A. Objectives

1. To approximate the frequency of vibrational movement of chemical bonds.
2. To get familiar with the regions (frequency vs. fingerprint) of IR spectrum.
3. To correlate IR absorption bands with chemical bonds and vibrational movements.
4. To practice interpreting IR spectra.

B. Procedure

Part I Approximation of group frequencies

1. Introduction

The IR region of absorption is due to change in the vibrational/rotational state in a molecule. The vibrational movement of a chemical bond between two atoms in a molecule can be modeled with a simple harmonic oscillator composed of 2 rigid balls connected by a spring, and the stretching frequency of a bond can be approximated by Hooke's Law.

According to Hooke's law, the frequency of the vibration (v) of the spring is related to the mass and the force constant of the spring, k, by the following formula

$$v = \frac{1}{2\pi}\sqrt{\frac{k}{\mu}} \qquad \text{(5B-1)}$$

where μ is reduced mass, which is given

$$\mu = \frac{m_1 m_2}{m_1 + m_2} \qquad \text{(5B-2)}$$

where m_1 and m_2 are masses (kg) of the 2 rigid balls connected by a spring. The relation between frequency and wavenumber (cm^{-1}) are defined as

$$\bar{v} = \frac{v}{c} \qquad \text{(5B-3)}$$

where c is light speed (3 x 10^{11} cm/s). Formula (5B-1) can be reduced to

$$\bar{v} = \frac{1}{2\pi c}\sqrt{\frac{k}{\mu}} = 5.3 \times 10^{-12}\sqrt{\frac{k}{\mu}} \qquad \text{(5B-4)}$$

The force constant of single, double and triple bonds are approximately 0.5, 1, and 1.5 x 10^3 N/m respectively. The reduced mass μ can be calculated from the two atoms in a bond. Therefore, the wave-number of the vibrational movement of a bond can be calculated.

Example: Calculate the approximate wavenumber of absorption band due to stretching vibration of C-H bond.

Solution: For C-H single bond, the force constant k is about 0.5 x 10^3 N/m.

m_1 = (1 x 10^{-3} kg/mole) / (6 x 10^{23} atom/mole) = 1.67 x 10^{-27} kg
m_2 = (12 x 10^{-3} kg/mole) / (6 x 10^{23} atom/mole) = 2.0 x 10^{-26} kg
μ = (1.67 x 10^{-27} kg x 2.0 x 10^{-26} kg) / (1.67 x 10^{-27} kg + 2.0 x 10^{-26} kg) = 1.54 x 10^{-27} kg

Substitute k and μ into Eqn. 5B-4

$$\bar{v} = \frac{1}{2\pi}\sqrt{\frac{k}{\mu}} = 5.3 \times 10^{-12} \text{ s/cm} \sqrt{\frac{0.5 \times 10^3 \text{N/m}}{1.54 \times 10^{-27} \text{Kg}}} = 3020 \text{ cm}^{-1}$$

The C-H stretching band in organic compounds is in between 2850 and 3300 cm^{-1} in difference structures. The theoretical calculation is pretty close.

2. Exercise

Exercise 5B-I Use method given above to calculate approximate group wavenumbers of absorption due to chemical bonds, and compare with the observed value.

Bond	Frequency range (cm^{-1})	Calculated frequency (cm^{-1})
C-H	2850 – 3300	3020
O-H	3500 – 3650	2990
C=O	1690 – 1760	1563
C-O	1050 – 1300	1105
N-H	3300 – 3500	3060
C-N	1180 – 1360	3000
C≡N	2210 – 2280	5197

Part II: IR spectrum regions

Exercise 5B-II The purpose of this exercise is to get you familiar with the different regions of a typical IR spectrum. Referring to Figure 5-5 and Table 5-2, carefully read through the **Introduction**, answer the following questions:

a. Why the IR spectrum is divided into group frequency and fingerprint regions?
b. What kind of information can be obtained from the fingerprint region? How this information can be used to interpret structure of organic compound?
c. What kind of information can be obtained from the group frequency region? How this information can be used to interpret organic structure?
d. Why the majority of double bonds and triple bonds fall in narrow band on the IR spectrum?
e. Why the single bond involving H atom fall in high wavenumber region (>3000 cm^{-1})?

Introduction

Group frequency region vs. fingerprint region: The interpretation of infrared spectra involves the correlation of absorption bands in the spectrum of an unknown compound with the known absorption frequencies for types of bonds. Table 5-2 lists common types of bonds and their corresponding absorption bands (wavenumber ranges), and properties of the bands such as **intensity** (weak, medium or strong) and **shape** (broad or sharp) in the spectrum. Identification of an organic compound from an IR spectrum can be considered a two-step process.

The first step is to determine presence of functional groups by examining the absorption bands falling in the region called **group frequency region** (1250-3600 cm^{-1}). In this region (Figure 5-5), the approximate frequency (or wavenumber) at which a functional group absorbs IR radiation can be calculated (Part I). These frequencies, called group frequencies, provide valuable information of the presence of specific functional groups.

The second step is to compare the IR spectrum of unknown sample with known compounds for the entire region. The fingerprint region (600–1200 cm^{-1}) is especially useful since small difference in the structure of a compound results in significant changes in the appearance and distribution of absorption bands in this region. Therefore, a close match between two spectra in the fingerprint region plus the group frequency region is almost certain evidence that the two compounds are identical.

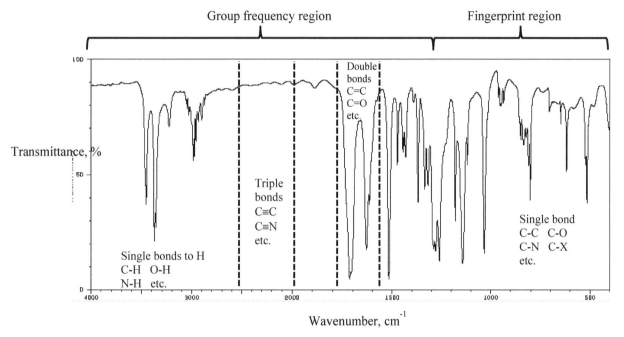

Figure 5-5 Organic functional groups and IR absorption bands.

Functional group regions: According to formula 5B-4, the frequency (wavenumber) of a specific bond is determined by type of the bond (single, double or triple) and the masses of the two atoms in the bond. That's why the wavenumbers of bonds involving two heavier elements (C, O, N) increase in the order of single, double and triple bonds due to increase in forces constant from single to triple bond. In addition, since the atomic masses of C, N and O are not significantly different, the reduced mass (μ) of bond involving any combination of these three atoms (or the same atoms of these atoms) are not significantly different. This explains why the absorption of double bonds fall in a narrow range (1550–1700 cm^{-1}), and the same scenario for the triple bonds (2000–2500 cm^{-1}).

In the case of single bond involving one hydrogen and a heavier atom (C, O, N), even the force constant is low, the reduced mass is low too. And the absorption bands of such bond fall in high wavenumber region (3000–4000 cm^{-1}).

Table 5-2 *Group frequencies (wavenumber), strength and vibration type of organic functional groups.*

Bond	Compound Type	Frequency range, cm^{-1}	Intensity	Vibration type
C-H	Alkanes	2960-2850	Strong	stretch
		1470-1350	Variable	scissoring and bend
C-H	Alkenes	3080-3020	Medium	stretch
		1000-675	Strong	bend
C-H	Aromatic Rings	3100-3000	Medium	stretch

Bond	Compound Type	Frequency range, cm^{-1}	Intensity	Vibration type
C-H	Phenyl Ring Substitution Bands	870-675	Strong	bend
	Phenyl Ring Substitution Overtones	2000-1600	Weak	fingerprint region
C-H	Alkynes	3333-3267	Strong	stretch
		700-610	Broad	bend
C=C	Alkenes	1680-1640	Med-weak	stretch
C≡C	Alkynes	2260-2100	Weak	stretch
C=C	Aromatic Rings	1600, 1500	Weak	stretch
C-O	Alcohols, Ethers, Carboxylic acids, Esters	1260-1000	Strong	stretch
C=O	Aldehydes, Ketones, Carboxylic acids, Esters	1760-1670	Strong	stretch
O-H	Monomeric - Alcohols, Phenols	3640-3160	Strong broad	stretch
	Hydrogen-bonded - Alcohols, Phenols	3600-3200	Broad	stretch
	Carboxylic acids	3000-2500	Broad	stretch
N-H	Amines	3500-3300	Medium	stretch
		1650-1580	Medium	bend
C-N	Amines	1340-1020	Medium	stretch
C≡N	Nitriles	2260-2220	Variable	stretch
NO$_2$	Nitro Compounds	1660-1500	Strong	asymmetrical stretch
		1390-1260	Strong	symmetrical stretch

Part III: Interpretation of IR spectrum (1)

1. Introduction

The qualitative aspects of infrared spectroscopy are one of the most powerful attributes of this analytical technique. The basic principle of qualitative IR spectroscopy is based on the fact that structural features of the molecule produce characteristic and reproducible absorptions in the IR spectrum. Therefore, an IR spectrum of an unknown compound can by compared with IR spectra from known species to find a "match". This is usually done with computer program and a built-in database. In the absence of a suitable reference database, it is possible to characterize, and possibly even identify of an unknown sample based on the same principles.

2. Exercise

From the practice in Part I and II, you learn that the IR absorption bands are closely related to the structural features of the molecule, either the backbone of the structure (C-C, C=C, C≡C etc.), or functional groups (O-H, C=O etc.). In this exercise, you will go one step further to look into the details how to extract information from IR spectrum and interpret into structural features of organic compounds.

Three groups of organic compounds and their IR spectra are given in the following exercises (5B-III to 5B-V). Group 1: Pentane, 1-pentene, 1-pentyne and toluene; Group 2: Pentanone, pentanoic acid, ethyl acetate, and propionalhyde; Group 3: Pentanol, diethyl ether, pentylamine, and nitropentane. For each compound, identify the characteristic absorption bands and associated bonds and type of vibrational movements. This practice aims to help you get familiar with characteristic absorption bands of IR spectra of different types of compounds (alkane, aromatic, ketone, ester etc.).

Exercise 5B-III. Four organic compounds and their IR spectra are given. 1. For each compound, identify the characteristic absorption bands, fill in blank the approximate wavenumber (cm⁻¹) of each characteristic peak, and mark the peaks on the spectra. 2. Compare the structures and spectra of given compounds, familiarize yourself with the correlation between chemical bonds and IR absorption bands.

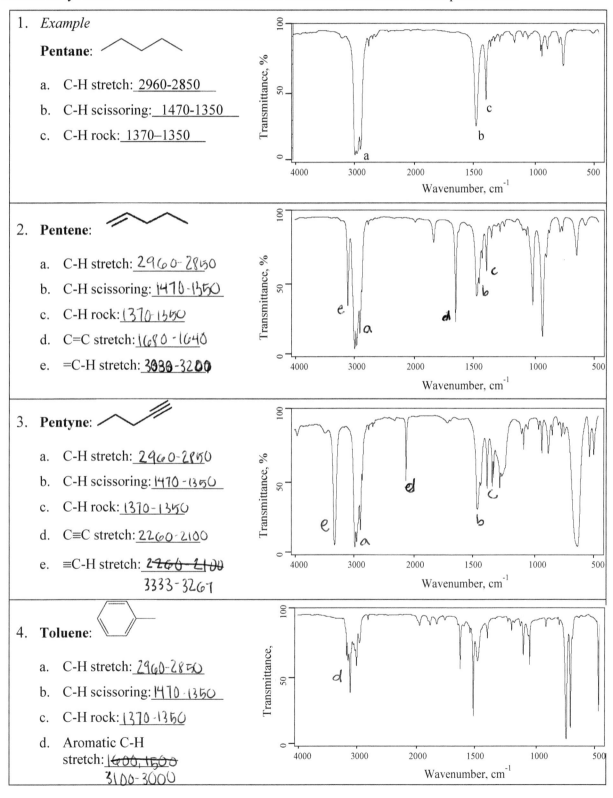

1. *Example*

    Pentane:

    a. C-H stretch: 2960-2850

    b. C-H scissoring: 1470-1350

    c. C-H rock: 1370–1350

2. **Pentene**:

    a. C-H stretch: 2960-2850

    b. C-H scissoring: 1470-1350

    c. C-H rock: 1370-1350

    d. C=C stretch: 1680-1640

    e. =C-H stretch: 3030-3200

3. **Pentyne**:

    a. C-H stretch: 2960-2850

    b. C-H scissoring: 1470-1350

    c. C-H rock: 1370-1350

    d. C≡C stretch: 2260-2100

    e. ≡C-H stretch: 2260-2100
        3333-3267

4. **Toluene**:

    a. C-H stretch: 2960-2850

    b. C-H scissoring: 1470-1350

    c. C-H rock: 1370-1350

    d. Aromatic C-H
        stretch: 1600,1500
        3100-3000

Exercise 5B-IV. Four organic compounds and their IR spectra are given. 1. For each compound, identify the characteristic absorption bands, fill in blank the approximate wavenumber (cm⁻¹) of each characteristic peak, and mark the peaks on the spectra. 2. Compare the structures and spectra of given compounds, familiarize yourself with the correlation between chemical bonds and IR absorption bands.

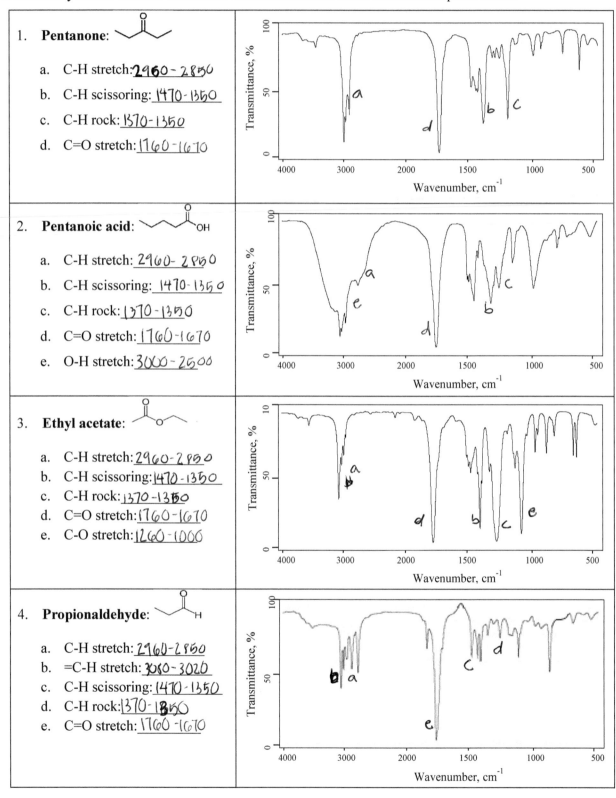

1. **Pentanone**:

   a. C-H stretch: 2960-2850
   b. C-H scissoring: 1470-1350
   c. C-H rock: 1370-1350
   d. C=O stretch: 1760-1670

2. **Pentanoic acid**:

   a. C-H stretch: 2960-2850
   b. C-H scissoring: 1470-1350
   c. C-H rock: 1370-1350
   d. C=O stretch: 1760-1670
   e. O-H stretch: 3000-2500

3. **Ethyl acetate**:

   a. C-H stretch: 2960-2850
   b. C-H scissoring: 1470-1350
   c. C-H rock: 1370-1350
   d. C=O stretch: 1760-1670
   e. C-O stretch: 1260-1000

4. **Propionaldehyde**:

   a. C-H stretch: 2960-2850
   b. =C-H stretch: 3060-3020
   c. C-H scissoring: 1470-1350
   d. C-H rock: 1370-1350
   e. C=O stretch: 1760-1670

Exercise 5B-V. Four organic compounds and their IR spectra are given. 1. For each compound, identify the characteristic absorption bands, fill in blank the approximate wavenumber (cm⁻¹) of each characteristic peak, and mark the peaks on the spectra. 2. Compare the structures and spectra of given compounds, familiarize yourself with the correlation between chemical bonds and IR absorption bands.

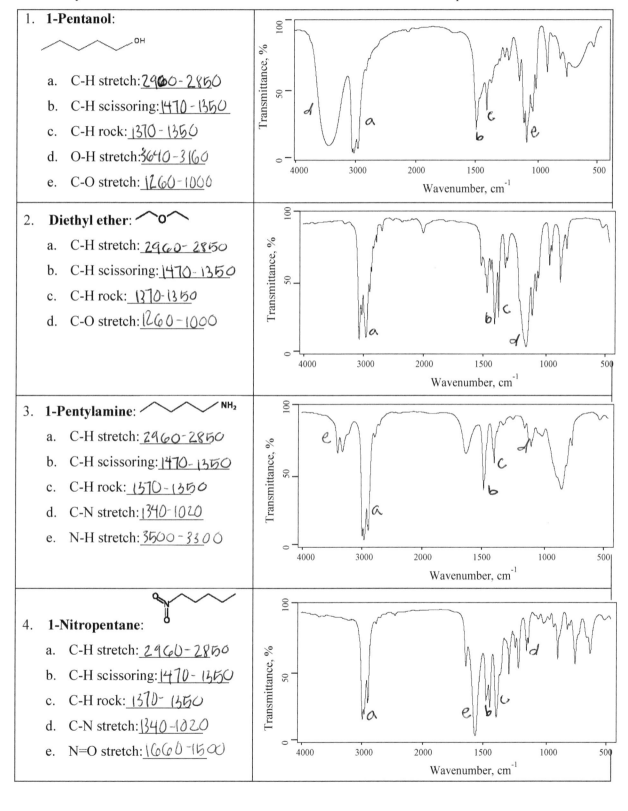

1. **1-Pentanol**:
   a. C-H stretch: 2960-2850
   b. C-H scissoring: 1470-1350
   c. C-H rock: 1370-1350
   d. O-H stretch: 3640-3160
   e. C-O stretch: 1260-1000

2. **Diethyl ether**:
   a. C-H stretch: 2960-2850
   b. C-H scissoring: 1470-1350
   c. C-H rock: 1370-1350
   d. C-O stretch: 1260-1000

3. **1-Pentylamine**:
   a. C-H stretch: 2960-2850
   b. C-H scissoring: 1470-1350
   c. C-H rock: 1570-1350
   d. C-N stretch: 1340-1020
   e. N-H stretch: 3500-3300

4. **1-Nitropentane**:
   a. C-H stretch: 2960-2850
   b. C-H scissoring: 1470-1350
   c. C-H rock: 1370-1350
   d. C-N stretch: 1340-1020
   e. N=O stretch: 1660-1500

Part IV: Interpretation of IR spectra (2)

In this exercise, you are given two groups of compounds and two groups of IR spectra. Use the knowledge you learn from Part II and III, match each compound with the IR spectrum. This is one step further than Part III. Table 5-3 provides a step-wise approach for interpretation of IR spectrum. Try to follow the order in Table 5-3 and use the information in Table 5-2 to solve the IR spectra on the next 2 pages.

Table 5-3 *A step-wise approach to solve simple organic structures based on IR spectrum.*

Procedure	Absorption Band	Functional Group Indicated
Check the C–H stretching bands around 3000	Are any or all to the **right** of 3000?	Alkyl groups
	Are any or all to the **left** of 3000?	Aromatic group in the molecule
Check carbonyl band in the region 1760-1690. If present	Is an O–H band also present?	A carboxylic acid group
	Is a C–O band also present?	An ester
	Is an aldehydic C–H band also present?	An aldehyde
	Is an N–H band also present?	An amide
	Are none of the above present?	A ketone
Is a broad O–H band in the region 3500-3200 present? If present	Is an O–H band present?	An alcohol or phenol
Look for a single or double sharp N–H band in the region 3400-3250. If present	Are there two bands?	A primary amine
	Is there only one band?	A secondary amine
Other structural features to check for:	Are there C–O stretches?	An ether (or an ester if there is a carbonyl band too)
	Is there a C=C stretching band?	An alkene
	Are there aromatic stretching bands?	An aromatic
	Is there a C≡C band?	An alkyne
	Are there -NO_2 bands?	A nitro compound

Reference

1. Skoog, D. A., F. J. Holler and S. R. Crouch, 2007. Principles of Instrumental Analysis. 6th ed. Thomson Brooks/Cole Publishing. Belmont, CA.
2. Sawyer, D. T., W. R. Heineman and J. M. Beebe, 1984. Chemistry Experiments for Instrumental Methods. Wiley.
3. Hendra, P., C. Jones and G. Warnes, 1990. Fourier Transform Raman Spectroscopy: Instrumentation and Chemical Applications. Ellis Horwood, NY.
4. Larkin, P., 2011. Infrared and Raman Spectroscopy: Principles and Spectral Interpretation. Elsevier.
5. Silverstein, M. R., F. X. Webster and D. Kiemle, 2005. Spectrometric Identification of Organic Compounds. 7th ed. Wiley.
6. Jones, N. T., K. J. Graham and C. P. Schaller, 2012. A Jigsaw Classroom Activity for Learning IR Analysis in Organic Chemistry. J. Chem. Educ. 89(10): 1293.
7. John Coates, Interpretation of Infrared Spectra, A Practical Approach, in: Encyclopedia of Analytical Chemistry, R.A. Meyers (Ed.). pp. 10815–10837, John Wiley & Sons Ltd, Chichester, 2000. (Online access: **http://infrared.als.lbl.gov/BLManual/IR_Interpretation.pdf**).
8. Online IR tutorial: **https://www.youtube.com/watch?v=5jX0cnKl0I4**

Exercise 5B-VI. Match each IR spectrum (right column) to a compound (left column). Identify 3-4 characteristic absorption bands which help you to make the identification, mark them on the spectra.

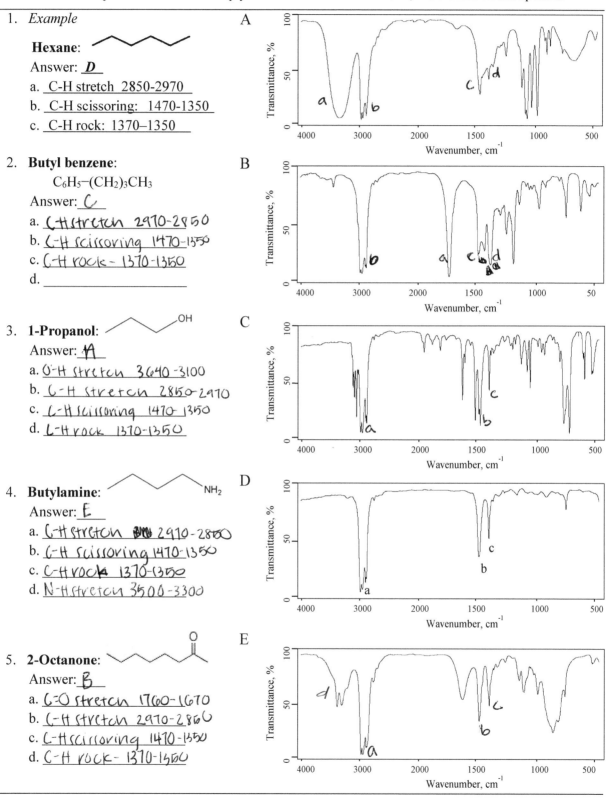

1. *Example*

   Hexane:

   Answer: _**D**_
   a. _C-H stretch 2850-2970_
   b. _C-H scissoring: 1470-1350_
   c. _C-H rock: 1370–1350_

2. **Butyl benzene**:

   $C_6H_5-(CH_2)_3CH_3$

   Answer: _C_
   a. _C-H stretch 2970-2850_
   b. _C-H scissoring 1470-1350_
   c. _C-H rock - 1370-1350_
   d. _____

3. **1-Propanol**:

   Answer: _A_
   a. _O-H stretch 3640-3100_
   b. _C-H stretch 2850-2970_
   c. _C-H scissoring 1470-1350_
   d. _C-H rock 1370-1350_

4. **Butylamine**:

   Answer: _E_
   a. _C-H stretch 2910-2850_
   b. _C-H scissoring 1470-1350_
   c. _C-H rock 1370-1350_
   d. _N-H stretch 3500-3300_

5. **2-Octanone**:

   Answer: _B_
   a. _C=O stretch 1760-1670_
   b. _C-H stretch 2970-2850_
   c. _C-H scissoring 1470-1350_
   d. _C-H rock - 1370-1350_

Exercise 5B-VII. Match each IR spectrum (right column) to a compound (left column). Identify 3-4 characteristic absorption bands which help you to make the identification, mark them on the spectra.

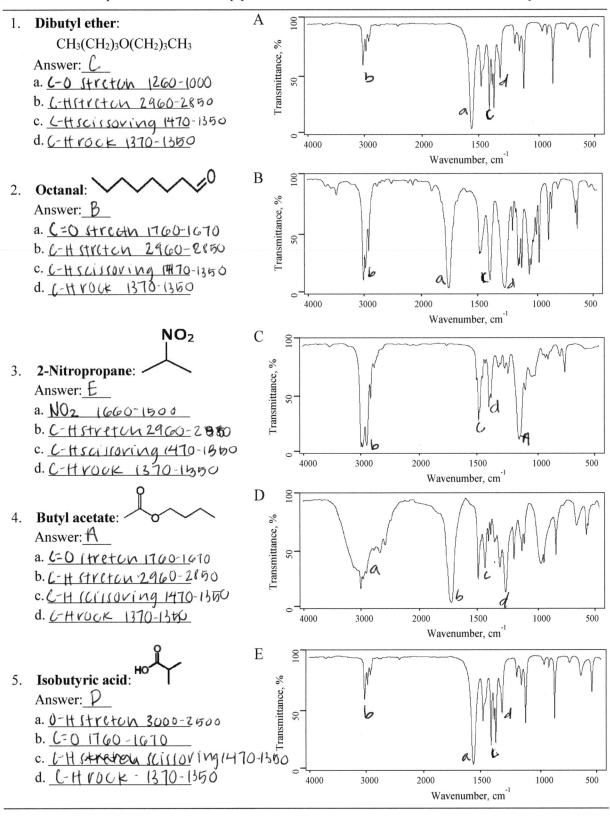

1. **Dibutyl ether**:
   $CH_3(CH_2)_3O(CH_2)_3CH_3$
   Answer: C
   a. C-O stretch 1260-1000
   b. C-H stretch 2960-2850
   c. C-H scissoring 1470-1350
   d. C-H rock 1370-1350

2. **Octanal**:
   Answer: B
   a. C=O stretch 1760-1670
   b. C-H stretch 2960-2850
   c. C-H scissoring 1470-1350
   d. C-H rock 1370-1350

3. **2-Nitropropane**:
   Answer: E
   a. NO₂ 1660-1500
   b. C-H stretch 2960-2850
   c. C-H scissoring 1470-1350
   d. C-H rock 1370-1350

4. **Butyl acetate**:
   Answer: A
   a. C=O stretch 1760-1670
   b. C-H stretch 2960-2850
   c. C-H scissoring 1470-1350
   d. C-H rock 1370-1350

5. **Isobutyric acid**:
   Answer: D
   a. O-H stretch 3000-2500
   b. C=O 1760-1670
   c. C-H stretch scissoring 1470-1350
   d. C-H rock 1370-1350

EXPERIMENT 5C: QUANTITATIVE IR ANALYSIS OF XYLENE MIXTURE

A. Objectives

1. To learn the principle of quantitative infrared spectroscopy.
2. To determine the composition of a mixture of dimethylbenzene isomers (*o*-, *m*- and *p*-xylene).

B. Introduction

The quantitative IR spectroscopy is based on the fact that the IR absorption of analyte follows Beer's Law. However, the typical IR spectrophotometers measure transmittance rather than absorbance, and it's necessary to convert transmittance to absorbance for quantitative purpose.

There are two ways to convert transmittance to absorbance in IR spectrophotometry. With FTIR spectrometer, interferograms of an empty sample cell and a sample cell are obtained first, and then Fourier transform is applied to both interferograms to obtain IR spectra. The transmittance of the sample (T) is obtained from the transmittance of the empty cell (T_0) and sample cell (T_s) by

$$T = T_s / T_0 \quad (5C\text{-}1)$$

The absorbance of the sample is calculated from

$$A = - \log T \quad (5C\text{-}1)$$

Another way to obtain sample absorbance from a single absorption band is the baseline method shown in Figure 5-6. In case the IR spectrum can be provided as absorbance vs. wavenumber, the sample absorbance is obtained by subtracting baseline from the maximum absorbance.

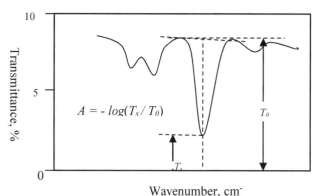

Figure 5-6 Baseline method for determining the absorbance of an IR absorption maximum.

Xylenes refer to the three isomers of dimethylbenzene (Figure 5-7). The IR absorption bands of xylene isomers (Figure 5-8) are distinguishable and absorbance of each isomer can be measured to determine the concentration of each isomer in a mixture without separating them from each other.

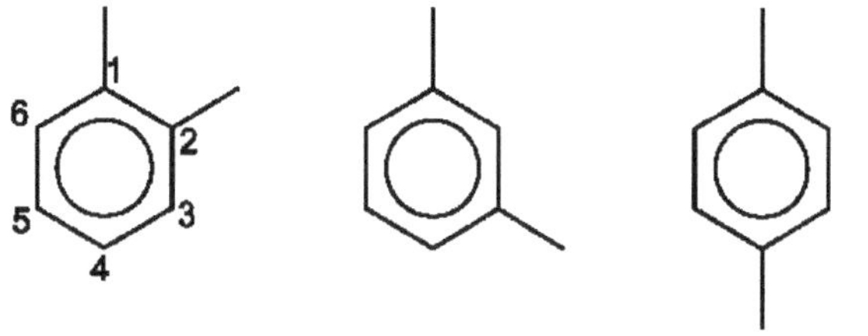

Figure 5-7 The isomers are distinguished by the designations *ortho-* (*o*-), *meta-* (*m*-), and *para-* (*p*-), which specify to which carbon atoms the two methyl groups are attached.

1,2-dimethylbenzene   1,3-dimethylbenzene   1,4-dimethylbenzene
    (*ortho*-xylene)   (*meta*-xylene)   (*para*-xylene)

69

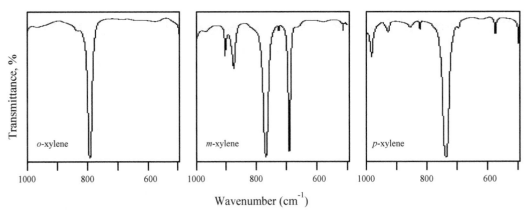

Figure 5-8 Partial IR spectra of xylene isomers between 500 and 1000 cm^{-1}.

C. Chemicals

1. Cyclohexane (C$_6$H$_{12}$, anhydrous, 99.5%).
2. Xylene isomers (*o*-, *m*-, *p*- xylene individual pure standard, >99%).
3. Commercial xylene mixture (ACS grade, >98.5%).

D. Apparatus

1. IR spectrophotometer or FTIR spectrometer.
2. Sandwich IR cells or demountable IR cell.
3. Volumetric flasks, 10, 25 mL.
4. Analytical balance.
5. Pipet, 1, 5 mL.

E. Procedure

1. Preparation of solutions

   a. *Preparation of mixed xylene stock standard*: Pipet 1 mL each xylene isomer into a 25 mL volumetric flask. Bring to mark with cyclohexane. Label this flask "Std1". This yields a mixed standard with 35.2 mg/mL *o*-xylene, and 34.4 mg/mL *m*- and *p*-xylene.

   b. *Preparation of diluted mixed standard*: Pipet 5 mL of Std1 into a 10 mL volumetric flask and bring to mark with cyclohexane. Label this standard "Std2". Pipet 2 mL of Std1 into another 10 mL volumetric flask, fill with solvent and make up to the mark. Label this as "Std3".

   c. *Preparation of sample*: Pipet 1 mL of commercial xylene mixture into a 10 mL volumetric flask. Bring to mark with cyclohexane.

2. Prepare the instrument: follow the procedures prepared by your instructor for operation of the instrument.

   Operation tips:
   1. For quantitative IR spectrometer, it's important that the pathlength of radiation is consistent. Some sample preparation method might not be suitable. Demountable cells or sealed sandwich cells are recommended.
   2. The optical parts and windows are salt, measures needed to avoid moisture.
   3. The optical parts and windows are also fragile, handle with extreme caution.

3. Standard calibration

   a. Depending on types of sample cell used, follow proper procedure to clean the cell. Ask your instructor if you are not very sure about how to handle the process.

   b. Acquire a blank spectrum using the cell filled with cyclohexane.

   c. Acquire the spectra of standard solutions.

4. Measurement of sample

    a. Follow the same procedure in Step 3 to acquire IR spectrum of sample mixture.

    b. Recognize characteristics peaks for all three xylene isomers. Determine the absorbance of each peak.

5. Cleanup and waste disposal: dispose organic waste in properly labeled waste container.

F. Result report

1. Include all IR spectra in your final report. Show how you determine the absorbance of xylene isomers for standards and samples.

2. Calculate absorbance with the baseline method described in Introduction. If FTIR instrument is used, assess absorbance with both methods described in Introduction and compare the results from the two methods.

Isomer	Wavenumber v (cm^{-1})	T_0	T_s			A		
			Std1	Std2	Std3	Std1	Std2	Std3
o-xylene	739							
m-xylene	768 (or 691)							
p-xylene	795							

3. Tabulate the concentration of standard and absorbance of xylene isomers in each standard. Construct calibration curve for all xylene isomers by plot absorbance vs. concentration for each xylene isomer.

	o-xylene		m-xylene		p-xylene	
	C (mg/mL)	A_{739}	C (mg/mL)	$A_{768(or\ 691)}$	C (mg/mL)	A_{795}
Std1	35.2		34.4		34.4	
Std2						
Std3						
Standard calibration	m	b	m	b	m	b

4. Finally, calculate absorbance of each xylene isomer in the unknown sample and calculate concentration of each xylene isomer in the unknown.

Isomer	v (cm^{-1})	T_0	T_s	A	C (mg/mL)
o-xylene	739				
m-xylene	768 (or 691)				
p-xylene	795				

G. Questions for discussion

1. Why quantitative IR absorption spectroscopy is not as common as quantitative UV/Vis absorption spectroscopy?

2. The sample cell for quantitative IR absorption spectrometer is more complicated than the cell used in UV/Vis absorption spectrometer. Discuss the main difference and explain why.

3. Compare the IR spectra of three xylene isomers, discuss how the positioning of the two methyl group affect IR absorption.

H. Supplementary experiment

Introduction: A better approach to quantify the composition of a xylenes mixture is to calculate concentration of each isomer based on the principle introduced in Experiment 3C for multi-component mixture. With this method, molar absorptivities for the three xylene isomers (C_8H_{10}) are computed at the three analytical wavelengths. Utilizing three equations and a simultaneous solution will allow the calculation of each isomeric concentration from the three absorbance values.

Wave number (cm⁻¹)	Formula
768 or 691	$A_{768\ or\ 691} = \varepsilon_{1o}\, b\, C_o + \varepsilon_{1m}\, b\, C_m + \varepsilon_{1p}\, b\, C_p$
739	$A_{739} = \varepsilon_{2o}\, b\, C_o + \varepsilon_{2m}\, b\, C_m + \varepsilon_{2p}\, b\, C_p$
795	$A_{795} = \varepsilon_{3o}\, b\, C_o + \varepsilon_{3m}\, b\, C_m + \varepsilon_{3p}\, b\, C_p$

Procedure: 1) Acquire IR spectra of standard with known concentration for each isomer at three wavenumbers. Calculate absorbance and absorptivity of each isomer at all three wavenumbers using the method illustrated in the main experiment. 2) For unknown sample, acquire IR spectrum, and calculate absorbance at three wavenumbers. 3) Use the equations above to solve concentrations of xylene isomers.

I. Reference

1. Skoog, D. A., F. J. Holler and S. R. Crouch, 2007. Principles of Instrumental Analysis. 6th ed. Thomson Brooks/Cole Publishing. Belmont, CA.
2. Günzler, H. and H-U. Gremlich, 2002. IR Spectroscopy: An Introduction. Wiley-VCH.
3. Griffiths, P., J. A. De Haseth, 2007. Fourier Transform Infrared Spectrometry (Chemical Analysis: A Series of Monographs on Analytical Chemistry and Its Applications). Wiley-Interscience.
4. Hartkopf, A., R. R. Schroeder and C. H. Meyers, 1974. Quantitative analysis of xylene mixtures by refractometry. J. Chem. Educ. 51(6): 405.

NUCLEAR MAGNETIC RESONANCE SPECTROSCOPY

CHAPTER

6

I. BASIC PRINCIPLES

Quantum description of NMR: NMR is based on the interaction between a positively charged spinning nucleus in an atom and an externally applied magnetic field (B_0). The nuclei of the atoms bonded to each other in molecules spin on an axis like a top (Figure 6-1A). In the absence of B_0, the axes about which the nuclei spin are oriented randomly. When B_0 is applied, the nuclei align parallel or antiparallel to the external field. The parallel orientation is slightly lower in energy and thus slightly favored. The energy difference is very small and corresponds to radio frequency energy which is unique for every molecule and will give the information regarding the nature of the compounds and the presence of various functional groups and their environment. A specific nucleus of an isotope has spin if its atomic or mass number is odd number, such as ^{1}H, ^{13}C, ^{19}F, ^{31}P.

Quantum mechanics provides a description of the energy states of a spinning nucleus in an external magnetic field as in Figure 6-1B. I is spin quantum number, m is magnetic quantum number.

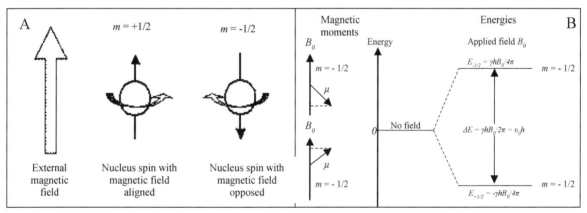

Figure 6-1 Two ways to describe a spinning nucleus in a magnet field: (A) spin top model; (B) quantum way to describe magnetic moments and energy levels for a nucleus with a spin quantum number of ½.

For the nuclei of ^{1}H, ^{13}C, ^{19}F, ^{31}P, quantum number $I = 1/2$. When these nuclei are brought into an external magnetic field, the nuclei are oriented in two directions, which corresponding to two magnetic quantum number, $m = 1/2$ (lower energy state) and $m = -1/2$ (higher energy state). The energy E of the two orientations (quantum states) are given by

$$E_{+1/2} = -\frac{\gamma h B_0}{4\pi} \ \ (m = \tfrac{1}{2}) \quad (6\text{-}1)$$

$$E_{-1/2} = \frac{\gamma h B_0}{4\pi} \ \ (m = -\tfrac{1}{2}) \quad (6\text{-}2)$$

where γ is the **magnetogyric (gyromagnetic) ratio** ($T^{-1}s^{-1}$), which is different for each type of nucleus. h is Plank's constant (6.626 x 10^{-34} Js). B_0 is the intensity of the external magnet field (SI unit, tesla or T). The product of γ and B_0 is called **Larmor frequency**, ω, which is the angular frequency associated with the spin transition of the electron spin precession. The difference between the two states is

$$\Delta E = \frac{\gamma h B_0}{2\pi} = \frac{h\omega}{2\pi} \qquad (6\text{-}3)$$

Nuclear magnetic resonance (NMR) spectroscopy uses the transition between these two energy states to detect and quantify nuclei. The magnitude of the energy splitting between these levels for nuclei in a strong magnetic field is in the range of radio frequency (RF) radiation. Absorption of the RF radiation causes nucleus spin to realign or flip into the higher-energy direction. The frequency of RF radiation absorbed is determined by Larmor frequency under the resonance condition

$$\Delta E = \frac{\gamma h B_0}{2\pi} = v_0 h \qquad (6\text{-}4) \qquad \text{and}$$

$$v_0 = \frac{\gamma B_0}{2\pi} = \frac{\omega}{2\pi} \qquad (6\text{-}5)$$

where v_0 is the frequency of the resonant radiation absorbed.

Chemical shift: The frequency of RF radiation, which is absorbed by a given nucleus, is strongly affected by its chemical environment. Nearby nucleus which generates a small magnetic field can perturb the local magnetic field, causing slight shift in the RF frequency of the nucleus. This shift provides a wealth of spectral information that can be used to elucidate the chemical structure of the molecule. This shift in resonance frequencies caused by nearby nuclei is called **chemical shift**, and measured as a difference relative to a reference compound. For ^1H NMR spectroscopy the most common reference compound is tetramethylsilane (TMS), $Si(CH_3)_4$.

The chemical shift, δ, is given by

$$\delta = \left(\frac{v_{sample} - v_{ref}}{v_{ref}} \right) \times 10^6 \qquad (6\text{-}6)$$

where δ has units of ppm, v_{sample} is resonance frequency of sample, and v_{ref} is resonance frequency of reference compounds (e.g. TMS in ^1H NMR).

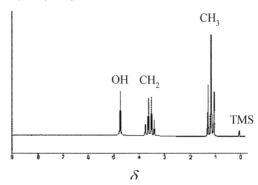

Figure 6-2 NMR spectrum of ethyl alcohol.

Spin-spin splitting: The effective magnetic field for a specific proton is also affected by the orientation of neighboring nuclei. This effect is known as **spin-spin coupling** which can cause splitting of the signal for each type of nucleus into two or more lines (Figure 6-2). The pattern of **spin-spin splitting** caused by neighboring nuclei is governed by the so-called ***n + 1* rule**: if a set of protons has *n* neighboring, non-equivalent protons, it will be split into *n* + 1 sub-peaks. An example is given in Figure 6-2, the peak of protons on $-CH_2-$ group is split to 4 peaks since there are 3 protons attached to the neighboring $-CH_3$ group. Similarly, the peak of protons on $-CH_3$ group is split to 3 sub-peaks.

Coupling constant: The distance between peaks in a spin-spin splitting multiplets is called the **coupling constant**, *J*, which is measured in *Hz*, not *ppm*. To obtain *J* value, the distance between peaks in a multiplet is measured in *ppm*, the *J* value is then calculated as the product of the distance in *ppm* and the field strength in *mHz*.

For example, on a 60 *mHz* machine, the distance of the subpeaks of chloroethane is measured to be 0.12 *ppm*. Therefore, there are 60 *Hz* for every 1 *ppm* on the spectrum. Multiplying 0.12 *ppm* by 60 *Hz*/1 *ppm* gives the *J* value of 7.2 *Hz*.

$$J = 0.12 \ ppm * (60 \ Hz \ / \ 1 \ ppm) = 7.2 \ Hz$$

Qualitative Application: All five characteristic NMR signals, chemical shift, spin-spin splitting, line width, coupling constant and relative intensity, provide structural information of organic compounds. Comparison of a spectrum from literature or authentic specimen with that of an unknown specimen may be used to confirm the identity of the specimen. For simple structure, NMR spectrum may provide plenty information to illustrate the structure. For complicated structure, information NMR is commonly combined with other techniques (IR, MS etc.) to solve the structure.

Quantitative NMR: Proton NMR is intrinsically quantitative. For a specific molecule, the intensity of the signal is proportional to the number of a specific type of protons. For example, in Figure 6-2, the ratio of integral area of CH_2 protons to the integral area of CH_3 protons is 2 to 3. In a mixture, if all types of protons in the same and different molecules are resolved, the intensity of the signal is determined by both the number of the same type of protons in a molecule and the concentration of the molecule which bears the type of proton. Method of quantitative analysis based on NMR for single compound and multicomponent mixture have been reported. However, the primary application of NMR is to resolve structure of molecules (qualitative analysis).

II. BASIC INSTRUMENTATION

There are two general types of NMR instrument: **continuous wave** (CW) and **Fourier Transform** (FT) NMR. Early experiments were conducted with CW instruments, and currently FT instruments dominate the market.

CW NMR spectrometers are similar in principle to optical spectrometers. The sample is held in a **strong magnetic field**, and the frequency of the **source** is slowly scanned. The signal generated by absorption of energy is detected, amplified and recoded. Figure 6-3 shows components of a CW NMR, which includes powerful magnet, radio frequency signal generator, amplifier, detector, etc.

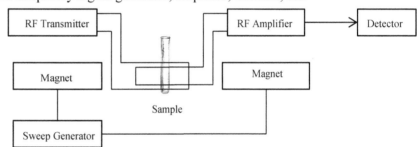

Figure 6-3 Components of a typical NMR.

In FT-NMR, all frequencies in a spectrum are irradiated simultaneously with a **radio frequency pulse**. Following the pulse, the nuclei return to thermal equilibrium. A **time domain emission signal** is recorded by the instrument as the nuclei relax. A **frequency domain spectrum** is obtained by Fourier Transform.

Compared to CW NMR, FT NMR is a less intuitive way to get the same information. Rather than allowing only one wavelength at a time to pass through to the detector as in the CW NMR, FT NMR lets through a beam containing many different wavelengths of light at once, and measures the total beam intensity. This makes it possible to improve the signal to noise ratio through averaging multiple scans.

General Reading

1. Skoog, D. A., F. J. Holler and S. R. Crouch, 2007. Principles of Instrumental Analysis. 6th Ed. Thomson Brooks/Cole Publishing. Belmont, CA.
2. Sawyer, D. T., W. R. Heineman and J. M. Beebe, 1984. Chemistry Experiments for Instrumental Methods. Wiley.
3. Richards, S. A. and J. C. Hollerton, 2010. Essential Practical NMR for Organic Chemistry. Wiley.
4. Online book by J. P. Hornak: **http://www.cis.rit.edu/htbooks/nmr/inside.htm**
5. Video series to introduce basics of NMR by Magritek: **http://www.magritek.com/support-videos**

EXPERIMENT 6A: PROTON NMR SPECTRA, CHEMICAL SHIFTS, AND COUPLING CONSTANTS

A. Objectives

1. To understand basic principles of NMR spectroscopy and basic NMR instrumentation.
2. To illustrate chemical shifts and spin-spin coupling and how they are related to the molecular structural properties on a NMR spectrum.
3. To acquire NMR spectrum of organic compounds with NMR spectrometry.
4. To learn the basic principle of quantitative analysis of NMR.

B. Chemicals

1. Deuterated chloroform ($CDCl_3$, 99.8 atom%D).
2. Absolute ethanol (CH_3CH_2OH, >99.8%).
3. Benzene (C_6H_6, anhydrous, >99.8%).
4. Tetramethylsilane (TMS, ACS grade, >99.5%).
5. Chloroethane (C_2H_5Cl, >98%).
6. Bromoethane (C_2H_5Br, >98%).
7. Iodoethane (C_2H_5I, >99%).
8. Premium gasoline (sample).

C. Apparatus

1. NMR spectrometer, 60 MHz.
2. NMR tubes.
3. Pipets, 100 µL, 1 mL, 5mL.
4. Capped test tube, 5 mL and 20 mL.

D. Procedure

> **Safety Precautions:** Magnetic field in modern NMR is powerful enough to erase credit cards and destroy watches. You should always place your watch, wallet, and any other metal jewelry, etc. on the table near the door before you approach the NMR spectrometer console!

1. Preparation of solutions

   a. *Preparation of 10% (v/v) benzene and ethanol solution*: Add 500 µL benzene, 100 µL TMS and 4.4 mL $CDCl_3$ in a 5 mL capped test tube. Mix and cap the tube. Prepare 10% (v/v) ethanol solution in the same way.

   b. *Preparation of 7% (v/v) ethyl halides*: Add 350 µL chloroethane, 100 µL TMS and 4.55 mL $CDCl_3$ in a 5 mL capped test tube. Prepare bromoethane and iodoethane solutions in the same way.

   c. *Unknown sample*: Add unknown amount of benzene and ethanol in $CDCl_3$. Add TMS to make its concentration approximately 1% (v/v).

2. Preparation of instrument

   Depending on the instrument used in this experiment, instructor needs to prepare a detailed operational guideline. The following are some general procedures for operating common FT NMR instrument, but might not apply to NMR instrument used in your lab. Students must conduct the following procedures under supervision of the instructor.

   Loading and setting parameters: Load a sample with deuterated solvent (e.g. $CDCl_3$) in the spectrometer. Under supervision of the instructor, adjust parameters, or load the parameters preset by the instructor.

   Setting the spinning: Set the spinning at rate of 20-50 revolutions per second. The purpose of spinning is to average out some of the field inhomogeneities in the x-y plane.

Locking the magnetic field: Locking is simply the adjustment of the deuterium lock field (Z_0) such that the deuterated solvent's resonance (the deuterium signal) is centered on a predefined lock frequency. The spectrometer uses this information to compensate for any drifting of the magnetic field (i.e. small loss over time of field strength).

Shimming: The purpose of shimming is to compensate for inhomogeneities in the primary magnetic field by producing a small magnetic field through pairs of wire loops called shim coils. Shimming is a relative complicated and time-consuming process. In addition, shimming must be carried out each time a new sample is introduced into the spectrometer.

Acquisition of NMR spectrum: The NMR signal acquired from FT NMR is call **Free Induction Decay (FID)**, which convert to normal NMR spectrum through Fourier Transform (FT). A few additional parameters are needed to be specified before you acquire the first FID.

3. Qualitative analysis of benzene and ethanol

    a. Add 10% (v/v) ethanol solution into NMR tube, load the sample onto NMR.
    b. Acquire NMR spectra. Integrate the peaks, and record area of the peak around 5.2 ppm in the data table below.
    c. Follow the same procedure to obtain NMR spectrum for 10% benzene. Integrate the peak area.

	C	δ (ppm)	Integral Area (A_{STD})
Ethanol	10%	5.2	
Benzene	10%	7.0-8.0	

4. Quantitative determination of mixture of benzene and ethanol

    a. Acquire NMR spectrum of unknown sample. Integrate peaks which are due to benzene protons and proton in the OH group of ethanol.
    b. Calculate content of benzene and ethanol in unknown sample by

$$C_a = \frac{A_a}{A_{STD}} \times C_{STD} \qquad (6A\text{-}1)$$

where C_a and C_{STD} are concentrations of analytes and standard (10% in this experiment), respectively; A_a and A_{STD} are integral areas of corresponding peaks of benzene (~7.0-8.0 ppm) or ethanol (~5.2 ppm) of the unknown sample and standard respectively.

	δ (ppm)	Integral Area (A_a)	C (%)
Ethanol	5.2		
Benzene	7.0-8.0		

5. Effect of electronegativity on the chemical shift

    a. Acquire proton NMR spectra of 7% (v/v) chloro-, bromo- and iodoethane.
    b. Tabulate chemical shift (δ) and coupling constant (J) of the peaks due to protons on the methyl group (-CH_3) and halogenated methyl group (-CXH_2) for three compounds.
    c. Plot δ vs. the Paulin electronegativities (χ, the Greek letter chi).

	χ	-CH_3		-CXH_2	
		δ (ppm)	J (Hz)	δ (ppm)	J (Hz)
CH_3CH_2Cl	3				
CH_3CH_2Br	2.8				
CH_3CH_2I	2.5				

6. Proton NMR spectra of premium gasoline

    a. Add 30 µL gasoline and 0.5 mL of CDCl₃ in NMR tube. Add 2 drops of TMS. Load sample to NMR. Record NMR spectrum.

    b. Determine the chemical shifts for each peak and identify the type of protons associated with each peak. Figure 6-4 is an example of NMR spectrum of a gasoline sample.

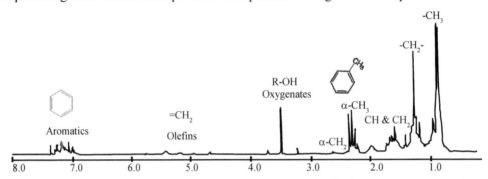

Figure 6-4 NMR spectrum of a gasoline sample.

E. Result report

1. Include the NMR spectra of 10% benzene and ethanol standard, and spectrum of unknown sample. Tabulate the types of protons, chemical shift, spin-spin splitting, integral areas of all peaks for both ethanol and benzene.

2. Calculate concentration of benzene and ethanol in unknown sample using formula 6A-1.

3. Include the NMR spectra of 7% chloro-, bromo- and iodoethane. Visually examine how the electronegativities (χ) of halogen atoms affect chemical shift of peaks due to protons on methyl (-CH₃) and halogenated methyl (-CH₂X) groups.

4. Plot chemical shift (δ) vs. Paulin electronegativity (χ).

5. Include the NMR spectrum of gasoline sample. Identify the type of protons associated with each peak.

F. Questions for discussion

1. Why NMR quantitative analysis can be done without a standard calibration?

2. Discuss how electronegativity of atom affects chemical shift of protons attached to the same carbon and the adjacent carbon based on δ - χ plot.

3. Does the substituent effect have influence on the coupling constant?

4. Predict the chemical shifts of fluoroethane (χ_F = 4.0) based on the δ - χ plot obtained in this experiment.

5. Discuss how NMR spectrum helps to identify main components of a complex mixture such as gasoline. What kind of qualitative and quantitative information can be extracted from NMR spectrum of a complex mixture of organic compounds.

G. Reference

1. Sawyer, D. T., W. R. Heineman and J. M. Beebe, 1984. Chemistry Experiments for Instrumental Methods. Wiley.

2. Richards, A. S. and J. C. Hollerton, 2010. Essential Practical NMR for Organic Chemistry. Wiley.

3. King, R. W. and K. R. Williams, 1989. The Fourier-transform in chemistry - NMR: A glossary of NMR terms, J. Chem. Educ. 67: A100-5.

4. King, R. W. and K. R. Williams, 1989 The Fourier-transform in chemistry Part 1. Nuclear magnetic resonance: Introduction. J. Chem. Educ. 66: A213-9.

5. King, R. W. and K. R. Williams, 1989. The Fourier-transform in chemistry Part 2. Nuclear magnetic resonance: The single pulse experiment. J. Chem. Educ. 66: A243-8.

EXPERIMENT 6B: QUANTITATIVE ANALYSIS OF CHLORINATED ETHANOL MIXTURE BY PROTON NMR

A. Objectives

1. To learn the basic principles of quantitative proton NMR spectroscopy.
2. To demonstrate the application of proton NMR in quantitative analysis of organic mixture.

B. Introduction

A very significant advantage of NMR determinations is that they do not require availability of pure analyte for calibration purposes. The generation of a calibration curve is, therefore, not absolutely necessary for NMR quantitative measurement. The only requirements are: i) distinguishable signals from analyte and (internal) standard can be integrated separately; ii) the numbers of protons giving rise to these signals are known.

The composition of mixtures can be quantitatively determined by proton NMR spectroscopy with the following formula if distinguishable signals from each component can be integrated separately

$$C_a = C_i \times \frac{A_a}{A_i} \times \frac{N_i}{N_a} \qquad (6B\text{-}1)$$

where A_a and A_i are integral areas of the peaks chosen for analyte and internal standard, N_a and N_i are the number of protons giving rise to the relevant analyte and standard signals respectively.

In this particular experiment, the composition of a mixture of 1,1,1-trichloroethane and 1,1,2-trichloroethane is assayed by ^1H NMR spectroscopy with trichloroethylene as internal standard. The chemical shifts of interest, in ppm on the δ scale, is listed bellow

	Abr.	Formula	Structure	FW	Density (mg/mL)	δ(ppm)
Trichloroethylene	TCE	$CHCl=CCl_2$		131.39	1.46	6.5
1,1,1-Trichloroethane	1,1,1-TCE	$CH_3\text{-}CCl3$		133.4	1.32	2.8
1,1,2-Trichloroethane	1,1,2-TCE	$CH_2Cl\text{-}CHCl_2$		133.4	1.435	3.9 or 5.8

C. Chemicals

1. Deuterated chloroform ($CDCl_3$, 99.8 atom%D).
2. Tetramethylsilane (TMS, ACS grade, >99.5%).
3. Trichloroethylene (C_2HCl_3, ACS grade, >99%).
4. 1,1,1-trichloroethane ($C_2H_3Cl_3$, ACS grade, >99%).
5. 1,1,2-trichloroethane ($C_2H_3Cl_3$, analytical grade).

D. Apparatus

1. NMR spectrometer, 60 MHz.
2. NMR tubes.
3. Pipets, 100 μL, 1 mL, 10 mL.
4. Capped test tubes, 5, 10 mL.

E. Procedure

1. Preparation of standards and sample

a. *Preparation of standards*: Prepare two sets of standard solutions of 1,1,1-trichloroethane (1,1,1-TCE, 10, 20, 30%, v/v) and 1,1,2-trichloroethane (1,1,2-TCE, 10, 20, 30%, v/v) by adding carbon tetrachloride (CCl_4), TMS (reference, 1%, v/v) and trichloroethene (TCE, 5%, v/v, internal standard) in 10 mL capped tubes as in following table (unit, mL).

Tube #	CCl_4	TMS	TCE	1,1,1-TCE	1,1,2-TCE
1	8.4	0.1	0.5	1	0
2	7.4	0.1	0.5	2	0
3	6.4	0.1	0.5	3	0
4	8.4	0.1	0.5	0	1
5	7.4	0.1	0.5	0	2
6	6.4	0.1	0.5	0	3

b. *Preparation of sample*: Prepare sample in a 10 mL tube with 1% TMS (v/v), 5% TCE (v/v), unknown volume of 1,1,1-TCE and 1,1,2-TCE in CCl_4.

2. Preparation of instrument

   Depending on the instrument used in this experiment, instructor needs to prepare a detailed operational guideline. Some general instructions on operating NMR are found in Experiment 6A.

3. Acquirement of NMR spectra

   a. *Standard calibration*: Introduce approximately 0.5 mL of a standard solution into an NMR tube and record the ^1H NMR spectrum between 8.0 and 0.0 on the δ scale. Then integrate the peaks at 6.5, 2.8, 3.9 (or 5.8) ppm. Record the integral areas of proton due to TCE (A_i) and TCE (A_s) in the data table below. Continue in the same manner with the other standards.

Compound		TCE	1,1,1-TCE			1,1,2-TCE	
δ (ppm)		6.5	2.8			3.9 (or 5.8)	
N		1	3			2 (or 1)	
Integral Area		A_i	A_{s1}	A_{s1}/A_i		A_{s2}	A_{s2}/A_i
C (v%)	10%						
	20%						
	30%						

   b. *Sample measurement*: Introduce 0.5 mL of sample into a NMR tube and record the ^1H NMR spectrum. Record integral areas of NMR peak at 6.5, 2.8, 3.9 (or 5.8) ppm.

Compound		TCE (IS)	1,1,1-TCE			1,1,2-TCE	
δ (ppm)		6.5	2.8			3.9 (or 5.8)	
		A_i	A_{a1}	A_{a1}/A_i		A_{a2}	A_{a2}/A_i
Sample	1						
	2						

4. Waste disposal: the chlorinated ethanol are toxic, dispose all waste in an appropriately labeled container.

F. Result report

1. Construct external standard calibration with data in **3.a** of Procedure by plotting integral area of each compound (A_s) vs. concentration. Calculate concentrations of 1,1,1-TCE and 1,1,2-TCE in unknown sample with the external standard calibration.

Compound		1,1,1-TCE	1,1,2-TCE
δ (ppm)		2.8	3.9 (or 5.8)
External Standard Calibration	m		
	b		
Sample 1	Area (A_a)		
	C (v%)		
Sample 2	Area (A_a)		
	C (v%)		

2. Construct internal standard calibration with data in **3.a** of Procedure by plotting ratios of integral area of each compound to internal standards (A_s/A_i) vs. concentration. Calculate concentrations of 1,1,1-TCE and 1,1,2-TCE in unknown sample with the internal standard calibration.

Compound		1,1,1-TCE	1,1,2-TCE
δ (ppm)		2.8	3.9 (or 5.8)
Internal Standard Calibration	m		
	b		
Sample 1	Area ratio (A_a/A_i)		
	C (v%)		
Sample 2	Area ratio (A_a/A_i)		
	C (v%)		

3. Refer to Introduction and Eqn. 6B-1, calculate concentrations of three compounds in unknown sample using Eqn. 6B-1(no external/internal standard calibration needed).

Compound		TCE (IS)		1,1,1-TCE		1,1,2-TCE	
Proton # (N)		1		3		2 (or 1)	
δ (ppm)		6.5		2.8		3.9 (or 5.8)	
		A_i	C_i (v%)	A_{a1}	C_{a1} (v%)	A_{a2}	C_{a2} (v%)
Sample	1		5%				
	2		5%				

G. Questions for discussion

1. Compare results of unknown sample from all three standard calibration methods. Based on your experience in this lab, discuss advantage/disadvantage of each standard calibration method.
2. Explain why the second internal standard calibration method (**F.3**) can only be used in NMR.
3. Why is it not necessary to use the same NMR tube for all solutions measured?

H. Reference

1. Richards, A. S. and J. C. Hollerton, 2010. Essential Practical NMR for Organic Chemistry. Wiley.
2. King, R. W. and K. R. Williams, 1989. The Fourier-transform in chemistry - NMR: A glossary of NMR terms. J. Chem. Educ. 67: A100-5.
3. Wallace, T., 1984. Quantitative Analysis of a Mixture by NMR Spectroscopy. J. Chem. Educ. 61(12): 1074.

EXPERIMENT 6C: DETERMINATION OF EQUILIBRIUM CONSTANT OF KETO-ENOL TAUTOMERISM REACTION

A. Objectives

1. To evaluate the equilibrium composition of keto-enol mixture with proton NMR spectroscopy.
2. To demonstrate assignment of NMR spectral features to specific protons based on chemical shift and spin-spin splitting patterns.
3. To determine the equilibrium composition of a keto-enol mixture quantitatively.
4. To examine the effect of solvent, concentration, substitution and on the keto-enol tautomerism reaction.

B. Introduction

Keto-enol tautomerism: In organic chemistry, **keto-enol tautomerism** refers to a chemical equilibrium between a **keto** form (compound containing a carbonyl group, C=O) and an **enol** (compound containing a pair of doubly bonded carbon atoms adjacent to a hydroxyl, C=C-OH). The enol and keto forms are said to be tautomers of each other. The keto form predominates at equilibrium for most ketones. Nonetheless, the enol form is important for some reactions. Furthermore, the deprotonated intermediate in the interconversion of the two forms, referred to as an enolate anion, is important in carbonyl chemistry, in large part because it is a strong nucleophile.

The equilibrium constant of **keto-enol tautomerism**, K_{eq}, is defined as

$$K_{eq} = \frac{[enol]_{eq}}{[keto]_{eq}} \qquad (6C\text{-}1)$$

where [enol] and [keto] are molar concentration of the enol and keto tautomers at equilibrium.

NMR study of keto-enol tautomerism: Keto-enol tautomerism can be characterized with ^{1}H NMR. First, the keto and enol tautomers have distinct ^{1}H NMR spectra; and second, the relative abundance of keto and enol tautomers can be quantified based on the size of the characteristic peaks. Therefore, the equilibrium constant of keto-enol tautomerism, which is the ratio of molar concentration of enol to keto tautomers, can be obtained from a single ^{1}H NMR spectrum without quantifying keto and enol tautomers (Figure 6-5).

Figure 6-5 The tautomerism reaction and partial ^{1}H NMR spectrum of 2,4-pentandione in CDCl₃. The peaks at 2.0 and 2.2 ppm are due to protons of the methyl group in enol and keto tautomers respectively. Since both structures have the same number of protons contributing to these two peaks, the ratio of integral area of peak 1 (2.0 ppm) to peak 2 (2.2 ppm) equals to molar ratio of enol to keto tautomers, which equals to the equilibrium constant of the keto-enol tautomerism reaction.

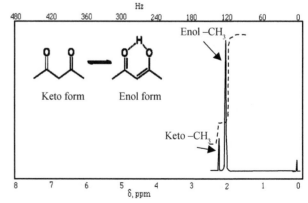

C. Chemicals

1. Deuterated chloroform ($CDCl_3$, 99.8 atom%D).
2. Tetramethylsilane (TMS, ACS grade, >99.5%).
3. Acetylacetone (AcAc, $C_5H_8O_2$, >99%).
4. Carbon tetrachloride (CCl_4, anhydrous, >99.5).
5. Cyclohexane (C_6H_{12}, ACS grade, >99%).
6. Benzene (C_6H_6, ACS grade, >99%).
7. Methanol (CH_3OH, anhydrous, >99.8%).
8. Chloroform ($CHCl_3$, anhydrous, >99%).
9. Acetonitrile (C_2H_3N, anhydrous, >99.8%).
10. 3-Phenylacetylacetone ($C_{11}H_{12}O_2$, 98%).
11. Dibenzoylmethane ($C_{15}H_{12}O_2$, >98%).
12. Benzoylacetone ($C_{10}H_{10}O_2$, >98%).
13. 3-Methylacetylacetone ($C_6H_{10}O_2$).
14. Hexafluoroacetylacetone ($C_5H_2F_6O_2$, 98%).

D. Apparatus

1. NMR Spectrometer.
2. NMR tubes.
3. Capped test tubes, 5 mL.
4. Pipet, 1, 5 mL.

E. Procedure

Part I Determination of keto-enol equilibrium constant

> **Safety Precautions:**
> 1. Protect your own properties (credit card, watch etc.) from the strong magnetic field of the NMR.
> 2. Most chemicals used in this experiment are toxic. Prepare solutions under fume hood. Wear goggles, gloves and lab coat.

1. Preparation of sample

   Fill the NMR tube to a height of ~4 cm with $CDCl_3$ (3-finger level) and add 2 drops AcAc, 1 drop of TMS. Cap the tube and invert it several times to ensure mixing.

2. Preparation of instrument

   Depending on the instrument used in this experiment, instructor needs to create a detailed operational guideline. Some general instructions on operating NMR can be found in Experiment 6A.

3. Determination of keto-enol equilibrium constant

   a. Under supervision of the instructor, load the sample, set instrument parameters. Acquire NMR spectrum. If FTNMR instrument is used, convert FID to normal NMR spectrum. Scan two more NMR spectra for the same sample.

   b. Assign peaks to the specific protons of the keto and enol tautomers. Integrate all peaks. Enter the integral areas of peaks due to protons attached to methyl groups of keto and enol forms into the data table below.

Sample	A_{enol} (δ=2)	A_{keto} (δ=2.2)	K_{eq}
1			
2			
3			

   c. Calculate equilibrium constant of keto-enol tautomerism reaction as described in Introduction.

Part II Solvent, concentration, substitution effects on keto-enol equilibrium

1. Solvent effects

    a. Prepare the following solutions 24 hours before experiment.

    Prepare solutions of 0.2 mole fraction (N_A) of AcAc in cyclohexane, CCl$_4$, benzene, methanol, and acetonitrile by pipetting appropriate amount of each solvent (data table below) and AcAc into a 5 mL stoppered test tube. Also, prepare a sample of pure AcAc and a saturated AcAc sample in deionized water. The dielectric constants of the solvents at 20°C are given for data processing.

#	Solvent	V_{AcAc} (µL)	$V_{solvent}$ (µL)	Dielectric constant (20°C)	A_{enol} (δ=2)	A_{keto} (δ=2.2)	K_{eq}
1	CCl$_4$	500	1898	2.023			
2	Cyclohexane	500	2114	2.2379			
3	Benzene	500	1745	2.284			
4	Methanol	500	792	32.66			
5	Acetonitrile	500	1022	37.5			
6	Water	500	3100	80.36			
7	Pure AcAc	/	/	/			

    b. Allow the sample to stand for 24 h to come to equilibrium.
    c. Fill the NMR sample tubes 3/8-full with the samples and add to each tube a drop or two of TMS, which serves as internal standard.
    d. Acquire the ^{1}H NMR spectra of all samples.
    e. *Data treatment*: Calculate equilibrium constant of keto-enol tautomerism reaction in each solution following procedure in Part I. Compare in tabular form the equilibrium constant to solvent polarity (i.e. dielectric constant) for each solvent.

2. Concentration effects

    a. Prepare the following solutions 24 hours before experiment.

    Prepare AcAc solutions of 0.4, 0.6 and 0.8 of molar fraction (N_A) in cyclohexane and in acetonitrile by mixing appropriate volume of AcAc with solvents in 5 mL capped test tube. Try to measure the volumes as close to the number as possible. Include the result of 0.2 Na solutions in Step 1.

N_A	V_{AcAc} (µL)	$V_{Cyclohexane}$ (µL)	A_{enol} (δ=2)	A_{keto} (δ=2.2)	K_{eq}
0.2 N_A	500	2157			
0.4 N_A	1000	1618			
0.6 N_A	1500	1079			
0.8 N_A	2000	539			

N_A	V_{AcAc} (µL)	$V_{Acetonitrile}$ (µL)	A_{enol} (δ=2)	A_{keto} (δ=2.2)	K_{eq}
0.2 N_A	500	1043			
0.4 N_A	1000	782			
0.6 N_A	1500	522			
0.8 N_A	2000	261			

b. Allow the sample to stand for 24 h to come to equilibrium.
c. Fill the NMR sample tubes 3/8-full with the samples and add to each tube a drop or two of TMS, which serves as internal standard.
d. Acquire the NMR spectra of all samples.
e. *Data treatment*: Calculate equilibrium constant of keto-enol tautomerism reaction in each solution following procedure in Part I. For each of the two solvents, plot equilibrium constants vs. mole fraction of AcAc.

3. Substitution effects

a. Prepare the following solutions 24 hours before experiment.

Prepare 0.2 N_A concentration of 3-phenylacetylaceton, dibenzoylmethane, benzoylacetone, 3-methylacetylacetone, 1,1,1-trichloroacetylacetone, and hexafluoroacetylacetone in chloroform (solvent) by pipetting 500 mL these compounds and appropriate volume of CCl_4 into capped test tubes.

Substituted AcAc	V_{sub} (μL)	$V_{solvent}$ (μL)	A_{enol} (δ=2)	A_{keto} (δ=2.2)	K_{eq}
3-Phenylacetylacetone	500	1331			
Dibenzoylmethane	500	1434			
Benzoylacetone	500	1352			
3-Methylacetylacetone	500	1177			
Hexafluoroacetylacetone	500	1853			

b. Allow the sample to stand for 24 h to come to equilibrium.
c. Fill the NMR sample tubes 3/8-full with the samples and add to each tube a drop or two of TMS, which serves as internal standard.
d. Acquire the ^{1}H NMR spectrum for each sample.
e. Data treatment: Calculate equilibrium constant of keto-enol tautomerism reaction for each substituted AcAc. Examine how the substitute groups affect the equilibrium constant.

F. Result report

Part I Determination of keto-enol equilibrium constant

1. Include the original ^{1}H NMR spectrum and integration result in your report.
2. Tabulate structural features, chemical shift, multiplicity, and peak areas. Match each peak with protons in either keto or enol structure.
3. Pick the two peaks used to calculate K_{eq} of the keto-enol tautomerism reaction.
4. Calculate K_{eq} for each NMR scan.

Part II Solvent, concentration, substitution effects

1. Based on the result of experiment Part II-1, discuss how the electronegativity of solvent affects the keto-enol equilibrium in terms of polarity of keto and enol forms. Which form is favored by hydrogen bonding and why?
2. Based on the result of experiment Part II-2, discuss how the concentration of AcAc affects the keto-enol equilibrium.
3. Based on the result of experiment Part II-3, discuss how the substitution group can affect the keto-enol equilibrium.

G. Questions for discussion

1. Discuss briefly your assignments of chemical shifts and spin–spin splitting patterns of AcAc.
2. Why are sweep width and offset frequency important?

3. What pulse sequence did you use and why?
4. What is the purpose of acquiring more than one scan in NMR? How does acquiring 16 or 64 scans instead of 1 scan improve the spectrum?

H. Reference

1. Skoog, D. A., F. J. Holler and S. R. Crouch, 2007. Principles of Instrumental Analysis. 6th ed. Thomson Brooks/Cole Publishing. Belmont, CA.
2. Richards, A. S. and J. C. Hollerton, 2010. Essential Practical NMR for Orgasnic Chemistry. Wiley.
3. Sawyer, D. T., W. R. Heineman and J. M. Beebe, 1984. Chemistry Experiments for Instrumental Methods. Wiley.
4. Garland, C., J. Nibler and D. Shoemaker, 2009. Experiments in Physical Chemistry. 8th Ed. McGraw Hill.
5. King, R. W. and K. R. Williams, 1989. The Fourier-transform in chemistry Part 1. Nuclear magnetic resonance: Introduction. J. Chem. Educ. 66: A213-9.
6. King, R. W. and K. R. Williams, 1989. The Fourier-transform in chemistry Part 2. Nuclear magnetic resonance: The single pulse experiment, J. Chem. Educ. 66: A243-8.
7. King, R. W. and K. R. Williams, 1989. The Fourier-transform in chemistry - NMR: A glossary of NMR terms, J. Chem. Educ.67: A100-5.

CHAPTER 7

ATOMIC SPECTROSCOPY

Atomic spectroscopy is the determination of elemental composition by electromagnetic or mass spectrum. Atomic spectroscopy is closely related to molecular spectroscopy. It can be divided based on mechanisms of **atomization** or by the type of spectroscopy used.

The main division of atomic spectroscopy is between optical and mass spectrometry. **Atomic mass spectrometry (AMS)** generally gives significantly better analytical performance, but is also significantly more complex. This complexity translates into higher costs in purchase, operation, training and maintenance etc. In contrast, optical atomic spectroscopy is generally less expensive and has performance adequate for many tasks; hence, it is still more common than AMS. **Atomic absorption (AAS)** and **emission (AES) spectrometry** are the most common optical spectroscopic techniques.

In atomic spectroscopy, a sample must be vaporized and atomized. For atomic mass spectrometry, a sample must also be ionized. Vaporization, atomization, and ionization are usually accomplished with a single source. Alternatively, one source may be used to vaporize a sample while another is used to atomize and ionize. An example is **laser ablation inductively-coupled plasma (LA-ICP)** atomic MS, where a laser is used to vaporize a solid sample and an ICP is used to atomize and ionize the vapor.

Atomic sources can be adapted in many ways. **Flames** are the most common due to their low cost and their simplicity. ICP, especially when used with mass spectrometers, are recognized for their outstanding analytical performance and their versatility. With the exception of flames and graphite furnaces, which are most commonly used for AAS, most sources are used for AES. Table 7-1 and 7-2 summarizes some atomization/ionization techniques and their applicability to AAS, AES and AMS (Table 7-1) and to different types of samples (Table 7-2). More information on the basic principles and instrumentation of AAS, AES and ICP/MS can be found in each experiment of this chapter.

Table 7-1 *Atomization/ionization techniques applicable to AAS, AES and AMS.*

	Flame	Spark	Graphite furnace	Arc	Glow discharge	ICP	Direct-current plasma	Laser ablation
AAS	✓		✓		✓			
AES		✓		✓	✓	✓	✓	✓
AMS		✓			✓	✓	✓	✓

Table 7-2 *Atomization/ionization techniques applicable to different types of samples.*

	Flame	Spark	Graphite furnace	Arc	Glow discharge	ICP	Direct-current plasma	Laser ablation
Liquid	✓	✓	✓			✓	✓	
Sold		✓	✓	✓	✓			✓
Gas	✓				✓	✓	✓	

General Reading

1. Skoog, D. A., F. J. Holler and S. R. Crouch, 2007. Principles of Instrumental Analysis. 6th ed. Thomson Brooks/Cole Publishing. Belmont, CA.
2. Lajunen, L. H. J., P Peramaki, 2005. Spectrochemical Analysis by Atomic Absorption and Emission. Royal Society of Chemistry.

EXPERIMENT 7A: DETERMINATION OF SODIUM AND POTASSIUM IN WATER WITH AAS

A. Objectives

1. To learn the basic principles and instrumentation of AAS.
2. To conduct measurement of sodium and potassium in drinking water with AAS.

B. Introduction

Basic principles of AAS: Atomic-absorption spectroscopy (AAS) uses the absorption of light to measure the concentration of gas-phase atoms. Since samples are usually liquids or solids, the analyte atoms or ions must be vaporized in a flame or graphite furnace. The atoms absorb ultraviolet or visible light and make transitions to higher electronic energy levels. The analyte concentration is determined from the amount of absorption. Applying the Beer's Law directly in AAS is difficult due to variations in the atomization efficiency from the sample matrix, and nonuniformity of concentration and path length of analyte atoms (in graphite furnace AAS). Concentration measurements are usually determined from a working curve after calibrating the instrument with standards of known concentrations.

Basic instrumentation of AAS: A typical atomic absorption spectrometer has light source, atomizer, monochromator, detector (transducer) and readout device (Figure 7-1).

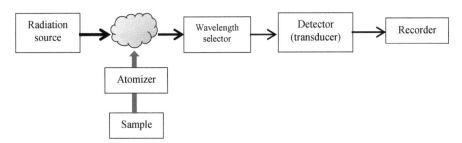

Figure 7-1 Components of a typical AAS instrument.

1. **Radiation Source**: There are two types of light source in AAS, the classic line source (LS) and continuum source (CS). In LS AAS, source radiation is emitted by the same element analyzed with high resolution of the source light spectrum; therefore, high resolution monochromator is not required. The disadvantage is that usually a separate lamp is required for each element to be determined. In CS AAS, a continuum spectrum over the entire spectral range is provided by lamps such as deuterium lamps. Thus, high resolution monochromator is required in CS AAS. CS lamp usually only used for background correction purposes.

2. **Atomizer**: The most common atomizers in AAS are flame and graphite furnace. Flame AAS can only analyze solutions, while graphite furnace AAS can accept solutions, slurries, or solid samples. Flame AAS uses a slot type burner to increase the path length, and therefore to increase the total absorbance. Sample solutions are usually aspirated with the gas flow into a nebulizing/mixing chamber to form small droplets before entering the flame.

3. **Light separation and detection**: AAS uses monochromators and detectors for UV and visible light. The main purpose of the monochromator is to isolate the absorption line from background light due to interferences. Simple dedicated AA instruments often replace the monochromator with a bandpass interference filter. Photomultiplier tubes are the most common detectors for AAS.

C. Chemicals

1. Sodium chloride (NaCl, ACS grade, >99%).
2. Potassium chloride (KCl, ACS grade, >99%).
3. Hydrochloric acid (HCl, ACS grade, 37%, concd).
4. Lithium carbonate (Li_2CO_3, ACS grade, >99%).

D. Apparatus

1. Basic flame/graphite furnace AAS.
2. Flasks, 100, 1000mL.
3. Analytical balance (0.0001 g).
4. Pipets, 1, 5, 10 mL.

E. Procedure

1. Preparation of standard solutions and samples

   a. *Preparation of 100 ppm Na^+ and K^+ stock solution*: Weigh 0.2542 g of sodium chloride, transfer to 1 L volumetric flask, bring to mark with deionized water. Weight 0.1907 g potassium chloride, transfer to 1 L volumetric flask, and bring to mark with deionized water.

   b. *Preparation of Na^+ standard solutions*: Pipet 0.5, 1, 2.5, 5, 10 mL of 100 ppm Na^+ solution into five 100 mL volumetric flasks. Bring to mark with deionized water. This yields sodium standard solutions of 0.5, 1.0, 2.5, 5.0, 10 ppm.

   c. *Preparation of spiked sample for Na^+ analysis*: Add 5 mL of 100 ppm sodium stock solution into a 100 mL volumetric flask. Bring to mark with sample (e.g. drinking water).

   d. *Preparation of 100 ppm lithium internal standard*: Weigh 0.2473 g of Li_2CO_3 into 1 L volumetric flask, add ca. 300 mL of deionized water. Slowly add 15 mL of concentrated hydrochloric acid. After CO_2 has been released, add deionized water to mark.

   e. *Preparation of K^+ standard solutions with Li^+ as internal standard*: Pipet 0, 0.5, 1, 2.5, 5, 10 mL of 100 ppm K^+ standard solution into six 100 mL volumetric flasks. Add exactly 5 mL 100 ppm Li^+ internal standard in each flask. Bring to mark with deionized water. This yields K^+ standard solutions of 0.5, 1.0, 2.5, 5.0, 10 ppm with 5 ppm Li^+.

   f. *Preparation of sample with internal standard for K^+ analysis*: Add 5 mL of 100 ppm Li^+ stock solution into a 100 mL volumetric flask. Bring to mark with sample.

   > **Safety Precautions**:
   > 1. Both atomic absorption and emission instruments generate high temperature and large amount of heat from flame or graphite furnace or other atomizers. Proper safety attire (goggles, lab coats, long pants, closed-toed shoes, etc.) must be worn as always when working with these instruments.
   > 2. If you operate the instrument for the first time, read the procedures thoroughly, and consult your instructor if you have question. Stop operation when you are not sure. It's highly recommended that you should operate the instrument under supervision if you are first time user.

2. Preparation of instrument

   Based on system used, a standard operating procedure (SOP) should be developed and used as guideline. The following are some general procedures in conducting experiment with common AAS instrument.

   a. Turn on the main power of instrument and computer (or other recording device)
   b. Set up the sample introduction system.
   c. Install proper lamp and/or filter for sodium analysis.
   d. Set and optimize instrumental parameters.
   e. Check the instrument performance by introducing blank and mixed standard. Run multiple injections to check repeatability of signals of interest.

3. Quantitative analysis of sodium with external standard calibration

   a. Prepare the instrument following the procedures prepared by the instructor. Install proper lamp and/or filter for sodium analysis if necessary.

b. Run blank and all Na$^+$ calibration standards. Record all results on data table below.
c. Construct external standard calibration curve with a spreadsheet.

	Standard					Standard Calibration	
C (ppm)	0.5	1.0	2.5	5.0	10	m	b
A							

d. Run the original and spiked unknown sample. Record signal (absorbance) in data table below.
e. Calculate concentration of sodium in original and spiked sample.
f. Calculate recovery of sodium.

		Original	Spiked	Recovery (%)
Sample 1	A			
	C (ppm)			
Sample 2	A			
	C (ppm)			

4. Quantitative analysis of potassium with internal standard calibration

a. Prepare instrument for potassium analysis.
b. Run blank, all K$^+$ calibration standards and unknown sample for potassium. Record all results in data table below.
c. Prepare instrument for lithium analysis.
d. Run blank, all K$^+$ calibration standards and unknown sample for lithium. Record all results in data table below.

Standard	1	2	3	4	5	Calibration		Sample
C_K (ppm)	0.5	1	2.5	5	10	m	b	
A_K								
A_{Li}								
A_K/A_{Li}								

e. Calculate ratio of absorbances (A_K/A_{Li}) for all standards and unknown sample.
f. Construct calibration curve by potting A_K/A_{Li} ratio vs. K$^+$ concentration. Run linear regression on spreadsheet to obtain internal standard calibration parameters (m and b).
g. Calculate K concentration in unknown sample with the internal standard calibration.

5. Cleanup and waste disposal: there is no hazardous waste generated in this experiment, solutions can be vacated to the drain.

F. Result report

1. Construct external standard calibration for sodium analysis.
2. Calculate the concentration of sodium in the original and spiked (take into account of the dilution when spiking the sample) samples. Calculate recovery of sodium.
3. Construct internal standard calibration for potassium analysis.
4. Calculate the concentration of potassium in the unknown sample.

G. Questions for discussion

1. Compare atomic and molecular absorption spectrum. Why the atomic absorption line is so sharp?
2. Compare the two standard calibration methods. Discuss advantages/disadvantage of each method.
3. Is the sodium recovery close to 100%? Explain what information provided by the recovery.

H. Supplementary experiments

Table 7-3 lists elements can be used in this (AAS) and next (AES) experiments, and wavelengths for AAS and AES analysis.

Table 7-3 *Major and trace elements and wavelength for AAS and AES analysis.*

Major Elements	Symbol	Atomic Mass	AAS Wavelength, nm	AES Wavelength, nm
Sodium	Na	22.99	330.2	588.9
Potassium	K	39.098	404.4	766.4 (404.4)
Lithium	Li	6.94	323.3	670.8
Calcium	Ca	40.078	422.7	317.933 (315.887)
Magnesium	Mg	24.305	285.2	279.079 (285.213)
Aluminum	Al	26.981	309.3	308.215 (309.271)
Iron	Fe	55.845	248.3	259.94
Manganese	Mn	54.938	279.5	257.61
Strontium	Sr	87.62	460.7	421.552
Trace Elements	Symbol	Atomic Mass	AAS Wavelength, nm	AES Wavelength, nm
Antimony	Sb	121.76	217.6	206.833
Arsenic	As	74.921	193.7	193.696
Barium	Ba	137.327	553.6	455.403 (493.409)
Beryllium	Be	9.012	234.9	313.042
Cadmium	Cd	112.411	228.8	226.502 (228.80)
Chromium	Cr	51.966	357.9	267.716 (205.552)
Cobalt	Co	58.933	240.7 (242.5)	228.616
Copper	Cu	63.546	324.8	324.754
Lead	Pb	207.2	217.0 (283.3)	220.353
Molybdenum	Mo	95.94	313.3	202.030 (203.844)
Nickel	Ni	58.693	232	231.604 (221.647)
Selenium	Se	78.96	196	196.09
Tin	Sn	118.71	235.5 (286.3)	189.989
Vanadium	V	50.9415	318.4	292.402
Zinc	Zn	65.409	213.9	213.856 (202.551)

I. Reference

1. Skoog, D. A., F. J. Holler and S. R. Crouch, 2007. Principles of Instrumental Analysis. 6th ed. Thomson Brooks/Cole Publishing. Belmont, CA.
2. Sawyer, D. T., W. R. Heineman and J. M. Beebe, 1984. Chemistry Experiments for Instrumental Methods. Wiley.
3. Lajunen, L. H. J. and P. Peramaki, 2005. Spectrochemical Analysis by Atomic Absorption and Emission. Royal Society of Chemistry.
4. Buffin, P. B., 1999. Removal of Heavy Metals from Water: An Environmentally Significant Atomic Absorption Spectrometry Experiment. J. Chem. Educ. 76(12): 1678.
5. Online introduction: **http://en.wikipedia.org/wiki/Atomic_absorption_spectroscopy**

EXPERIMENT 7B: SIMULTANEOUSLY ANALYSIS OF SODIUM, POTASSIUM AND CALCIUM IN WATER SAMPLE WITH AES

A. Objectives

1. To learn the basic principle and instrumentation of atomic emission spectroscopy (AES).
2. To conduct measurement of sodium, potassium and calcium in drinking water simultaneously with AES.

B. Introduction

AAS vs. AES: In atomic emission spectroscopy (AES), atoms are evaporated and excited to high energy level by high temperature generated by a flame (2000–3100°K) or an inductively coupled plasma (ICP, 5000–6000°K) or other means. When the excited atom returns to the ground state, it emits radiation which is detected. Hence, the light source in AES is the excited atoms self, there is no need for a separate light source.

In contrast to AAS in which multi-elemental measurement is unusual, atomic emission spectrometry is inherently a multi-elemental procedure. In a high-temperature flame or plasma, the emission occurs from all elements at the same time. It is therefore possible to perform simultaneous multi-elemental determinations simply by means of a multichannel detection system.

In addition, AES generally is more sensitive for most elements than AAS. AAS can be performed under relatively low temperature, while the emission efficiency increases with temperature in AES, and higher temperature is preferred in AES.

Flame AES vs. ICP-AES: Flame AES and ICP AES are the most common AES techniques, and the theories are similar (Figure 7-2). Compared to flames, plasmas produce much higher temperature, and hence much higher atomization ratios. ICP AES has number of advantages over flame AES primarily due to the higher atomization temperature, and has replaced the classic flame AES as preferred method. However, flame AES could be advantageous for Group IA or IIA elemental analysis since greater ionization occurring at higher temperatures could be problematic for these elements.

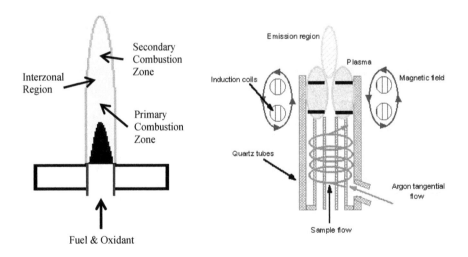

Figure 7-2 A laminar flow burner (flame, left) and ICP plasma (right).

Basic instrumentation of AES: A typical single beam atomic emission spectrometer has all components in a single beam atomic absorption spectrometer except light source. The following is a schematic diagram of a single beam AES (Figure 7-3).

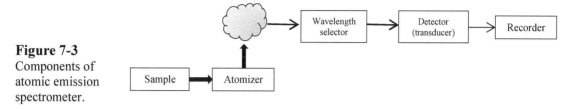

Figure 7-3
Components of atomic emission spectrometer.

1. **Atomizer**: In addition to flame and ICP mentioned earlier, some less common ways of atomization such as electronic ark and spark are also available.

2. **Wavelength selector**: Generally, AES requires wavelength selector with higher resolution than in the AAS; especially when multi-elemental analysis is conducted. This is because the atomic emission spectrum is much more complicated and frequently made up of large number of lines. Prism and grating type of monochromators are common wavelength selectors in AES. Although the spectrum provides more information for qualitative analysis, the chance of spectral interferences in quantitative analysis increases.

3. **Detector (transducer)**: There are a few types of design to meet the need of AES, generally based on multi-elemental analysis. The most common type of wavelength separation and detection in AES is simultaneous multichannel detection, which provides an advantage of simultaneous measurement of multiple elements in one run. Two-dimensional **charge-injection device** (CID) and **charge-coupled device** (CCD) are the most common multichannel detectors.

C. Chemicals

1. Sodium chloride (NaCl, ACS grade, >99%).
2. Potassium chloride (KCl, ACS grade, >99%).
3. Lithium carbonate (Li_2CO_3, ACS grade, >99%).
4. Calcium chloride ($CaCl_2$, ACS grade, >96%).
5. Nitric acid (HNO_3, trace metal grade, 67-70%, concd).

D. Apparatus

1. Basic AES system with flame or ICP atomizer.
2. Volumetric flasks, 100, 1000 mL.
3. Pipets, 1, 5, 10 mL.

E. Procedure

1. Preparation of standard solutions

   a. *Preparation of 2% HNO_3*: Add ca. 300 mL deionized water into 1 L volumetric flask. Add 28 mL concentrated HNO_3 slowly with swirling. Bring to mark with deionized water.

   b. *Preparation of 100 ppm Na^+, K^+ and Ca^{2+} mixed stock solution*: Weigh 0.2540 g NaCl, 0.1910 g of KCl and 0.2772 g of $CaCl_2$, transfer to 1 L volumetric flask with ca. 300 mL deionized water. Slowly add 28 mL concentrated HON_3. Bring to mark with deionized water.

   c. *Preparation of 100 ppm lithium internal standard*: Weigh 0.2470 g Li_2CO_3 into 1 L volumetric flask, add ca. 300 mL of deionized water. Slowly add 28 mL concentrated HON_3. After CO_2 has been released, add deionized water to mark.

   d. *Preparation of mixed standard solutions*: Pipet 100, 200, 400, 800, and 1600 µL of 100 ppm mixed stock solution into five 100 mL volumetric flasks. Add 400 µL 100 ppm lithium stock solution to each flask. Bring to mark with 2% HNO_3. This yields mixed standard solutions of 0.1, 0.2, 0.4, 0.8, 1.6 ppm of Na^+, K^+ and Ca^{2+} with 0.4 ppm Li^+ (internal standard) in each standard.

e. *Preparation of sample*: Pipet 10 mL tap water to a 100 mL volumetric flask, add 400 μL 100 ppm lithium stock solution, followed by 2.8 mL concentrated HNO_3. Bring to mark with deionized water.

2. Preparation of instrument

Based on system used, a standard operating procedure (SOP) should be developed and used as guideline. The following are some general procedures in conducting experiment with both flame and ICP AES instrument.

a. Turn on the main power of instrument and computer (or other recording device).
b. Set up the sample delivery device.
c. Start the emission source (flame or ICP).
d. Set and optimize instrumental parameters for sample introduction device, emission source and detector.
e. Calibrate detector (wavelength alignment etc.) with standard solution.
f. Set up the emission wavelengths used in this experiment as follow

Elements	Na^+	K^+	Ca^{2+}	Li^+ (IS)
λ (nm)	588.9	766.4 or 404	393 or 397	670.8

g. Check the instrument performance by introducing blank and mixed standard. Run multiple injections to check repeatability of signals of interest.

> **Safety Precautions**: The AES source generates high temperature and large amount of heat. Proper safety attire (goggles, lab coats, long pants, closed-toed shoes, etc.) must be worn as always when working with AES instrument.

3. Quantitative analysis with external standard calibration

a. Run blank (deionized water) and the mixed standards from lowest concentration (0.1 ppm) to highest (1.6 ppm). Run the unknown sample.
b. In your report, construct external standard calibration curves for Na^+, K^+ and Ca^{2+}.
c. Calculate concentration of Na^+, K^+ and Ca^{2+} in the unknown sample.

Data table 3.1 *External standard calibration and sample data processing.*

	C (ppm)	Atomic Emission Intensity			
		Na^+	K^+	Ca^{2+}	Li^+ (IS)
Standard	0.1				
	0.2				
	0.4				
	0.8				
	1.6				
Standard Calibration	*m*				
	b				
Sample	Signal				
	C (ppm)				

4. Quantitative analysis with internal standard calibration

a. Use data in Data table **3.1**, construct internal standard calibration curves for Na^+, K^+ and Ca^{2+} with Li^+ as internal standard (Data table **3.2**).

b. Calculate concentrations of Na^+, K^+ and Ca^{2+} in the unknown sample with internal standard calibration.

Data table 3.2 *Internal standard calibration and sample data processing.*

	C (ppm)	Intensity Ratio		
		I_{Na}/I_{Li}	I_K/I_{Li}	I_{Ca}/I_{Li}
Standard	0.1			
	0.2			
	0.4			
	0.8			
	1.6			
IS Calibration	m			
	b			
Sample	I_s/I_i			
	C (ppm)			

5. Cleanup and waste disposal: the diluted HNO_3 acid solution waste can be neutralized with soda and vacated to the drain.

F. Result report

1. Construct both external and internal standard calibration curves for sodium, potassium and calcium.
2. Calculate the concentrations of sodium, potassium and calcium in unknown sample(s) with both external and internal standard methods.
3. Compare results of unknown sample from different calibration methods.

G. Questions for discussion

1. Discuss advantages/disadvantages of AES vs. AAS.
2. Discuss advantages/disadvantages of external and internal standard calibrations.
3. A chemical interference can arise when calcium is being measured and phosphate is present. The calcium and phosphate will combine to form calcium phosphate ($Ca_3(PO_4)_2$). Calcium phosphate does not completely atomize in an air-acetylene flame. Therefore, an excess of lanthanum chloride ($LaCl_3$) is added. Discuss how $LaCl_3$ reduce the chemical interference by phosphate.

H. Supplementary experiments

Table 7-3 lists major and trace elements which can be included in this experiment.

I. Reference

1. Skoog, D. A., F. J. Holler and S. R. Crouch, 2007. Principles of Instrumental Analysis. 6th ed. Thomson Brooks/Cole Publishing. Belmont, CA.
2. Sawyer, D. T., W. R. Heineman and J. M. Beebe, 1984. Chemistry Experiments for Instrumental Methods. Wiley.
3. Harris, D. C., 2010. Quantitative Chemical Analysis. 8th Ed. W. H. Freeman.
4. Hiefje, G. M., 2000. Atomic emission spectroscopy—it lasts and lasts and lasts. J. Chem. Educ. 77: 577–583.
5. Online introduction on ICP/AES: **http://xa.yimg.com/kq/groups/3004572/678782447/name/ICP.pdf**

EXPERIMENT 7C: HEAVY METALS ANALYSIS IN WATER SAMPLE WITH ICP/MS

A. Objectives

1. To understand basic principles and basic instrumentation of ICP/MS.
2. To measure metals in water sample using ICP/MS with external and internal standard calibration.
3. To discuss the importance of quality assurance/quality control in ICP/MS analysis.

B. Introduction

Basic principles: An ICP/MS combines a high-temperature **inductively coupled plasma** (ICP) ion source with a **mass spectrometer** (MS). The sample is introduced to plasma where the analyte elements are converted to ions. This ionized sample is then sent through a series of powerful magnets called a mass spectrometer, which separates sample ions on the basis of their **mass/charge ratio** (M/Z). These ions are then measured by a detector to establish sample composition.

ICP/MS is a relatively new technique for the determination of trace elements in variety of samples. It offers better sensitivity than graphite furnace AAS with the multi-element speed of ICPOES. In comparison to ICP/OES, the mass spectra are much simpler than the optical emission spectra. Most heavy elements exhibit hundreds of emission lines, but they have only 1-10 natural isotopes in the mass spectrum. The standard and sample preparation techniques are very similar to those in AAS and ICP/OES. In addition, ICP/MS has a remarkable advantage over other atomic analytical techniques that it can determine the individual isotope.

> Visit: **http://minerals.cr.usgs.gov/icpms/index.html** for more information

Basic instrumentation: An ICP-MS consists of a **sample introduction system**, **ICP torch** and **radio frequency** (RF) coil, an **interface**, **mass spectrometer**, **ion detector** (transducer), and a computer with software to control the instrument and record the signals. A vacuum system is required for the interface and mass spectrometer (Figure 7-4).

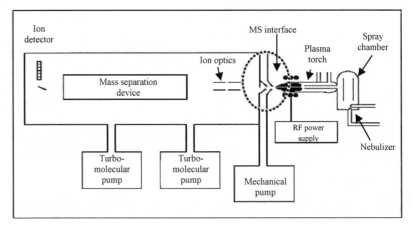

Figure 7-4 Components of a typical ICP/MS instrument.

1. **Sample introduction system**: The most common sample introduction device in ICP/MS is composed of a **nebulizer** and **spray chamber**. This is a device which converts liquids into an aerosol, and the aerosol is introduced to the plasma to generate the ions. Less commonly, the **laser ablation** is particularly useful for solid samples. In this method, a laser is focused on the sample and creates a plume of ablated material which can be swept into the plasma.

2. **ICP torch and RF coil**: Generates the high temperature (~8000°C) argon **plasma**, which serves as the ion source of the ICP-MS through a process called **ionization**. The plasma is made by

partially ionizing argon gas (Ar → Ar$^+$ + e$^-$). The energy required for this reaction is obtained by pulsing an electrical current in wires that surround the argon gas.

3. **Interface**: Links the ICP ion source (atmospheric pressure) to the high vacuum mass spectrometer. The interface region in the ICP-MS transmits the ions traveling in the argon sample stream at atmospheric pressure (1-2 torr) into the low pressure region of the mass spectrometer (<1 x 10^{-5} torr). This is done through the intermediate vacuum region created by the two interface cones, the **sampler** and **skimmer cones**.

4. **Vacuum system**: Provides high vacuum for ion optics, mass spectrometer, and detector. The vacuum is created and maintained by a series of pumps. The first stage is usually based on a roughing pump, most commonly a standard rotary vane pump. This removes most of the gas. Later stages have their vacuum generated by more powerful vacuum systems, most often turbomolecular pumps.

5. **Ion optics**: Guides the desired ions into the quadrupole while assuring that neutral species and photons are discarded from the ion beam.

6. **Mass spectrometer**: Acts as a mass filter to sort ions by their mass-to-charge ratio (m/z). The most commonly used type of mass spectrometer is the **quadrupole mass filter**.

7. **Detector**: Counts individual ions exiting the mass spectrometer. The channel electron multiplier (CEM) has been used on earlier ICP-MS instruments. The discrete dynode type detectors, which generally have wider linear dynamic ranges than CEMs, has replaced CEM in recent years. This is important in ICP-MS as the concentrations analyzed may vary from sub-ppt to high ppm.

8. **Data handling and system controller**: Controls all aspects of instrument control and data handling to obtain final concentration results.

C. Chemicals

1. Mixed standard, 10 ppm stock solution. Prepare mixed stock solutions from pure chemicals or purchase from commercial sources. Elements (isotopes) used in this experiment: ^{66}Zn, ^{75}As, ^{135}Ba.

2. Mixed internal standard: 2000 ppb stock solution prepared from 10 ppm solution. For simplicity, single internal standard (yttrium) is recommended in this experiment.

3. Nitric acid (HNO$_3$, trace metal grade, 67-70%, concd).

D. Apparatus

1. Basic ICP/MS unit with nebulizer, ICP plasma, interface, MS (quadruple) detector, a peristaltic pump for introducing sample to the nebular, a computer and software. An autosampler is optional.

2. Sample tube with caps, five 50 mL, a few 10 mL for samples.

3. Pipets: 100 μL, 1mL, 5 mL.

E. Procedure

1. Preparation of calibration/QC standards and sample

    a. *Preparation of 2% HNO₃ stock solution*: In a 1000 mL flask with ca. 500 mL deionized water, slowly add 28 mL of concentrated HNO₃. Bring to mark with deionized water.

    b. *Preparation of 2 ppm internal standard*: Transfer 20 ml 10 ppm yttrium solution to 100 ml volumetric flask. Bring to mark with 2% HNO₃.

    c. *Preparation of blank, calibration standards, quality control (QC) standard*: In five 50 mL flasks, add 10 ppm mixed standard, 2 ppm internal standard and dilute to mark with 2% HNO₃. The following table (next page) lists the volume of mixed standard and internal standard stock solution needed for each solution.

    d. *Sample preparation*: In a 10 mL volumetric flask, add 100 μL internal standard stock (2 ppm) and 280 μL concentrated HNO₃. Bring the final volume to 10 mL with the **unknown sample**.

	C (ppb)	Total V (mL)	Mixed Std V (μL)	IS Stock (μl)
Blank	0	50	0	500
Std 1	10	50	50	500
Std 2	20	50	100	500
Std 3	100	50	500	500
QC Std	50	50	250	500

2. Set up ICP/MS instrument

Depending on the instrument used, the instructor needs to prepare a standard operation proce-dures (SOP) according to manufacturer's instructions. The following lists some general proce-dures in ICP/MS analysis based on Perkin Elmer Elan ICP/MS.

a. Turn on the power for the instrument.
b. Turn on the computer. Open the program.
c. Open the argon gas. Adjust the pressure to required level.
d. Turn on vacuum. Wait for the pressure to reach required level.
e. Start plasma. Wait for the instrument to stabilize.
f. Set up the autosampler (if used).
g. Tune and optimize the instrumental parameters.
h. Evaluate instrument performance.
i. Set up the instrumental method to specify instrument parameters, standard calibration method, quality control process, data collection and processing etc.
j. Set up sample list.
k. Run calibration/quality control standard solutions and unknown samples.

3. External standard calibration

Modern ICP/MS instruments come with software can handle different standard calibration methods. Instructor can set up standard calibration methods on computer, and show students how each of them works. For practice purpose, students will manually construct calibration curves for selected elements, and calculate the concentrations of elements in unknown samples. The results from the manual calibration can be compared with the results from the computer generated results. The following procedures might need to be modified for the instrument used.

a. Run blank, standards, quality control and samples.
b. Tabulate the intensity of selected elements (^{66}Zn, ^{75}As, ^{135}Ba) and internal standard (Y).
c. Correct the intensity of calibration standards, QC standards and samples with blank.
d. Construct external standard calibration for the selected elements. Use Data processing table 3.1.

Data table 3.1 *Data treatment of external standard calibration.*

Element	Intensity of blank	Intensity of standard						External standard calibration	
		10 ppb		20 ppb		100 ppb		calibration	
		Raw	Blk Crtd	Raw	Blk Crtd	Raw	Blk Crtd	m	b
^{66}Zn									
^{75}As									
^{135}Ba									

e. Calculate concentrations of elements in QC standard and unknown sample with external standard calibration. Calculate recovery of the quality control (QC) standard. Use data processing table 3.2.

Data table 3.2 *Data processing of QC standard and sample based on external standard calibration.*

Element	Intensity of blank	QC standard 50 ppb		Calculated value (ppb)	Recovery (%)	Sample		Sample C (ppb)
		Raw	Blk Crtd			Raw	Blk Crtd	
^{66}Zn								
^{75}As								
^{135}Ba								

4. Internal standard calibration

Again, the instructor can set up the software program for internal standard calibration. For practice purpose, students will manually construct internal standard calibration curves for selected elements, and calculate the concentrations of elements in unknown samples. The results from the manual calibration can be compared with the results from the computer generated results, and the results from the external standard calibration in Step **3**. The following are general procedures for application of internal standard calibration method.

a. Since the internal standard (yttrium) already included in all blank, calibration standards, QC standard, and unknown sample. Student will use the same results in Step **3**, but include internal standard this time.

b. Tabulate the intensity of each element in standards ($I_{Blk\ Crtd}$, blank corrected intensity from Data table **3.1**), intensity of Y (IS) of each standard (I_{IS}, slightly different for each standard).

c. Calculate the ratios of intensities (blank corrected) of calibration standards for selected elements to internal standard (I/I_{IS}) using data in Data table 3.1.

d. Plot I/I_{IS} vs. concentrations, and conduct correlation analysis to obtain calibration parameters.

Data table 4.1 *Data processing of internal standard calibration.*

Element		^{66}Zn	^{75}As	^{135}Ba
10 ppm	$I_{Blk\ Crtd}$			
	I_{IS}			
	$I_{Blk\ Crtd}/I_{IS}$			
20 ppm	$I_{Blk\ Crtd}$			
	I_{IS}			
	$I_{Blk\ Crtd}/I_{IS}$			
100 ppm	$I_{Blk\ Crtd}$			
	I_{IS}			
	$I_{Blk\ Crtd}/I_{IS}$			
Calibration	m			
	b			

e. Calculate the I/I_{IS} ratios of selected elements for QC standards and sample using data in Data table 4.2 (next page).

Data table 4.2 *Data processing of QC standard and sample based on internal standard calibration.*

Element	QC standard I/I_{IS}	Calculated value (ppb)	Recovery (%)	Sample I/I_{IS}	Sample C (ppb)
^{66}Zn					
^{75}As					
^{135}Ba					

    f. Calculate the concentrations of selected elements in QC standard and unknown sample using the internal standard calibration.

5. Cleanup and waste disposal: there is no hazardous waste generated in this experiment. The diluted nitric acid waste can be neutralized with base (soda) and vacated into drain.

F. Result report

1. Construct external standard calibration for selected elements. Calculate concentrations of selected elements in samples and the QC standard with external standard calibration. Calculate recoveries of selected elements.
2. Construct internal standard calibration for selected elements. Calculate concentrations of selected elements in samples and the QC standard with internal standard calibration. Calculate recoveries of selected elements.

G. Questions for discussion

1. Most qualitative analysis needs blank correction. Discuss specifically why it's necessary to correct with blank in ICP/MS.
2. Compare the results of external and internal standard calibration in terms of linearity of calibration curves, QC standard recovery. Compare the results of unknown sample between the external and internal standard calibrations.
3. Based on the result from this experiment, discuss what advantages internal standard calibration has over external standard calibration in ICP/MS?

H. Reference

1. Skoog, D. A., F. J. Holler and S. R. Crouch, 2007. Principles of Instrumental Analysis. 6th ed. Thomson Brooks/Cole Publishing. Belmont, CA.
2. Harris, D. C., 2010. Quantitative Chemical Analysis, 8th Ed., Freeman, New York.
3. Thoms, R., 2013. Practical Guide to ICP-MS: A Tutorial for Beginners. 3rd Ed. CRC Press.
4. Nelms, S., 2005. Inductively Coupled Plasma Mass Spectrometry Handbook. Blackwell.
5. EPA METHOD 200.8, Determination of trace elements in waters and wastes by inductively coupled plasma-mass spectrometry.
6. Online introduction: **http://en.wikipedia.org/wiki/Inductively_coupled_plasma_mass_spectrometry**
7. Online introduction: **http://minerals.cr.usgs.gov/icpms/intro.html**

GAS CHROMATOGRAPHY

CHAPTER

8

I. BASIC PRINCIPLES

Chromatography in general: Chromatography involves a sample being carried in a **mobile phase**. The mobile phase is then forced through an immobile, immiscible **stationary phase**, the components are separated from each other as they travel through the stationary phase. Techniques such as **gas chromatography** (GC) and **high performance liquid chromatography** (HPLC) use **columns** - narrow tubes packed with stationary phase, through which the mobile phase is forced. The sample is transported through the column by continuous addition of mobile phase. This process is called **elution**.

Gas chromatography (GC): GC is one of the most important tools in analytical chemistry, since it can offer an extremely wide range of applications, combined with very high measurement sensitivity and selectivity.

In GC, the mobile phase is a **carrier gas**, usually an inert gas such as helium or an unreactive gas such as nitrogen. The stationary phase is a microscopic layer of liquid or polymer on an inert solid support, inside a piece of glass or metal tubing called a column. The analysis is initiated by introduction of the sample into the gas stream at the beginning of the column. The various constituents of the sample then migrate through the column at a rate that is determined by their partition coefficients between the two phases. Provided that the partition characteristics of the various components in the sample are sufficiently different, a **separation** is obtained.

As the individual components emerge from the column in the gas phase, they pass through a **detector**, which generates an electrical signal proportional in magnitude to the concentration of the substance. The output of the detector is displayed as a "**chromatogram**" - a trace showing each sample constituent as a "**peak**" on a horizontal **baseline**. A range of detection systems is available, the choice for a particular application depending on considerations such as the type of sample being analyzed and the required detection sensitivity and selectivity.

Qualitative Analysis by GC: GC can be used to identify the chemical composition of sample materials. The basis for this purpose lies in the fact that, under fixed column temperature and carrier gas flow rate, the time taken for a substance to pass through a particular column (**retention time**, t_R) is fixed and repeatable. The "t_R" of a substance is a parameter can be used as evidence of identity. However, a substance's retention time may not be unique and care must be exercised in assigning an identity based solely on retention time measurements. The combination of a GC, to achieve a separation of a sample component, with a **mass spectrometer** detection system which gives chemical structure information has become a popular and powerful means to overcome this problem.

Quantitative Analysis by GC: Quantitative measurements made by GC are based on the fact that the electrical output generated by the detector (the peak) is proportional to the concentration of sample analyte in the carrier gas stream. Today's GC instruments are normally equipped with a computer based data processing system, which generates area of each peak either automatically or manually.

II. BASIC INSTRUMENTATION

A basic GC system has **carrier gas**, an **injector** (manual or automatic), a **column** housed in an **oven** which provides temperature control of the column, a **detector** and a **recorder** (Figure 8-1). In today's GC, a computer and software are commonly used to record the GC signals and control the GC components.

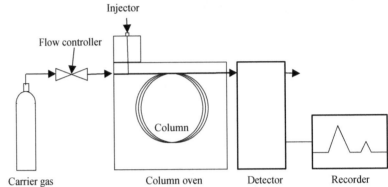

Figure 8-1 Components of a typical gas chromatography system.

1. **Column**: Two types of **capillary columns** are commonly used as stationary phase in modern GC. Coated - simple coating of stationary phase on the inside of a fused silica tube, and bonded - chemically bound via a silane bond. Selection of GC column for a specific analysis is usually done by an experienced GC expert, and is beyond the scope of this manual.
2. **Carrier gas**: Nitrogen, helium and hydrogen are the most common carrier gases used in GC. Contrary to common perception, hydrogen is a safe carrier gas with high efficiency.
3. **Detectors**: A wide range of detectors have been developed for use in gas chromatography, some of the most common detectors are listed below.

    a. **Flame ionization detector** (FID): In FID, a clean hydrogen flame is generated, and the organic substance eluted from the column is burnt to generate a signal to be detected. Hence, with a few exceptions, FID responds to all organic substances which can be burnt. This makes FID the most widely used gas chromatography detector with high sensitivity, wide linear response range, low cost, and ease of use.
    b. **Electron capture detector** (ECD): In ECD, a radiation source generates an electron current between a pair of electrodes. When the components are eluted and enter the ECD, the substances exhibiting a high affinity for electrons decrease the electron current, and this signal is recorded. Many substances do not have such an affinity for electrons, and are not detected by ECD. Thus, the ECD provides a selective response to electron capturing species, such as halogenated organic compounds, polycyclic aromatic hydrocarbons, polychlorinated biphenyls, tin and lead organic compounds.
    c. **Mass spectrometer detector** (MSD): The MSD has become the most important detector used in GC since MSD provides positive identification of the sample constituents to be made. A more detailed introduction on MSD can be found in Experiment 8C.

General Reading

1. Skoog, D. A., F. J. Holler and S. R. Crouch, 2007. Principles of Instrumental Analysis. 6th ed. Thomson Brooks/Cole Publishing. Belmont, CA.
2. Sawyer, D. T., W. R. Heineman and J. M. Beebe, 1984. Chemistry Experiments for Instrumental Methods. Wiley.
3. Harold, M. M., M. M. James, 2009. Basic Gas Chromatography. Wiley-Interscience, 2nd Ed.
4. Seader, J. D. and E. J. Henley and D. K. Roper, 2010. Separation Process Principles. 3rd Ed. Willey.
5. Colin, P., 2012. Gas Chromatography. Elsevier. 1st Ed.
6. Online introduction: **http://en.wikipedia.org/wiki/Gas_chromatography.**

EXPERIMENT 8A: RESPONSE AND RESOLUTION OF GAS CHROMATOGRAPHY

A. Objectives

1. To learn the basic principles of chromatography including chromatographic separation, peak efficiency, resolution etc.
2. To learn the basic instrumentation of gas chromatography and FID/ECD detector.
3. To gain experience in temperature programming and method development for GC.
4. To evaluate GC retention and separation of simple compounds.

B. Chemicals

1. Dichloromethane (CH_2Cl_2, ACS grade, 99.5%).
2. Chloroform ($CHCl_3$, anhydrous, >99%).
3. Carbon tetrachloride (CCl_4, anhydrous, >99.5%).

C. Apparatus

1. GC with FID and/or ECD detector.
2. Microsyringe, 10 μL.
3. Pipets, 100 and 1000 μL.
4. GC vials.

D. Procedure

1. Instrument preparation

   The instructor should prepare an operating procedure including basic steps of starting the instrument, GC parameters setup, sample injection method, etc. If an autosampler is used, include the process to set up the autosampler. The following instrument preparation procedure is generalized based on Agilent GC system with CHEMSTATION software, instructor need to modify to adapt for the system used.

   a. Start-up of GC/FID or ECD: check the following

      - Carrier gas: adjust outlet pressure as required by manufacturer;
      - FID gases: check pressure of gases, adjust pressure as specified by manufacturer;
      - The septum on the column inlet: change septa if necessary;
      - Autosampler and syringe: fill the washing vial and change syringe if necessary;
      - Turn on the GC and FID/ECD power if it's not on;
      - Turn on the computer and start up instrument program. Make sure that the communica-tion between all components and computer program is set up.

   b. Set up the METHOD: depending on the specific GC system and the column used, instructor needs to develop/optimize instrumental conditions to satisfy the separation and detection of the target analytes. The following are GC and FID conditions recommended for this experiment, which may be modified based on the specific system used.

      - GC condition

         ✓ GC column: a variety of capillary column (30 m x 0.25 mm) should be sufficient to separate the target analytes (e.g. Agilent DB5 capillary column, 0.25mm x 30 m, or similar);
         ✓ Carrier gas: helium;
         ✓ Flow rate: 1.0 mL/min;
         ✓ Temperature program: set as specified in each experiment;
         ✓ Run time: 5 minute;

✓ Injector: 180°C.

- FID condition

    ✓ Temperature: 300°C;
    ✓ Make up gas: nitrogen, 25 mL/min;
    ✓ FID H$_2$ flow: 30 mL/min;
    ✓ FID air flow: 350 mL/min.

2. Determination of theoretical plate number and plate height of column

    a. Prepare CHCl$_3$/CCl$_4$ samples by adding 20 µL CHCl$_3$/CCl$_4$ and 1 mL CH$_2$Cl$_2$ in GC auto-sampler vials. (**Note**: when ECD is the primary detector, use methanol as solvent to minimize the solvent signal).

    b. Set and hold oven temperature at 50°C. Inject 0.1 µL CHCl$_3$ sample. Run CCl$_4$ sample under the same condition. Record the retention time for both CHCl$_3$ and CCl$_4$ in data table below.

    c. Expand the peaks corresponding to CHCl$_3$ and CCl$_4$, print it out. Measure peak height, base width, and half height width as shown in Figure 8-2.

Compounds	Oven temp (°C)	Flow rate (mL/min)	t_R (min)	$W_{1/2}$ (min)	W_h (min)	N	H
CHCl$_3$							
CCl$_4$							

    d. Calculate theoretical plate number and height with the formula below

$$\text{plate number: } N = 5.55 \times \left(\frac{t_R}{W_{1/2}}\right)^2 \qquad (8A\text{-}1)$$

$$\text{plate height: } H = \frac{L}{N} \qquad (8A\text{-}2)$$

where L is column length.

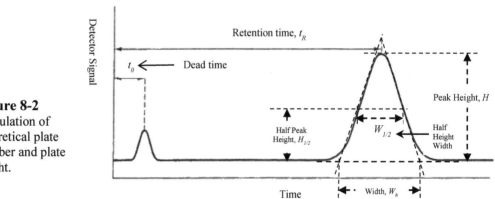

Figure 8-2
Calculation of theoretical plate number and plate height.

3. Effect of changes in temperature program

    a. Prepare a mixed sample with both CHCl$_3$ and CCl$_4$ by adding 20 µL CHCl$_3$ and CCl$_4$ in 1 mL CH$_2$Cl$_2$ in a GC autosampler vial.

    b. Set and hold oven temperature at 50°C. Inject 0.1 µL mixture prepared above. Recognize the two peaks corresponding to CHCl$_3$ and CCl$_4$, and record the retention times in data table (next page).

c. Increase the temperature to 60°C with other conditions remain unchanged, repeat Step **b**. Repeat this procedure (increase oven temperature by 10°C) until the $CHCl_3$ and CCl_4 peaks start to merge.

d. Enter a temperature program in which the oven temperature starting at 50°C and increases to 90°C at a rate of 5°C/min. Inject 0.1 μL sample of the mixed solution and record the retention times of $CHCl_3$ and CCl_4.

Oven Temp (°C)	Flow rate (mL/min)	t_0 (min)	t_R (min) CHCl₃	t_R (min) CCl₄	Δt_R (min)
50°C					
60°C					
70°C					
80°C					
90°C					
Program					

4. Effect of changes in flow rate

a. Set the column flow rate of the carrier gas to 1.5 mL/min (the initial flow rate is 1.0 mL/min). Set the oven temperature for an isothermal run at 50°C, make a 0.1 μL injection of the mixed solution, and record the retention times of $CHCl_3$ and CCl_4 in data table below.

b. Set carrier gas flow rate to 2.0 mL/min with other conditions remain unchanged. Repeat procedure in Step **4.a**.

c. Expand the $CHCl_3$ and CCl_4 peaks by zooming in the specific peak and print it out for measuring base width of the peak. The expanded chromatograms will be used to calculate resolution in Step **7**.

Flow rate (mL/min)	Oven temp. (°C)	t_0 (min)	t_R (min) CHCl₃	t_R (min) CCl₄	Δt_R (min)
1.0					
1.5					
2.0					

5. Capacity factor of $CHCl_3$ and CCl_4

The **capacity factor**, *k*, (also called "capacity ratio", "retention factor") is the time the sample component resides in the stationary phase relative to the time it resides in the mobile phase. It's a measure how much longer a sample component is retarded by the stationary phase than it would take to travel through the column without being retarded by the stationary phase. Mathematically, it is the ratio of the adjusted retention time and the dead time (Figure 8-3).

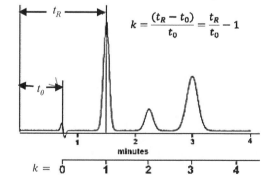

$$k = \frac{(t_R - t_0)}{t_0} = \frac{t_R}{t_0} - 1$$

Figure 8-3 Calculation of capacity factor.

Exercise: Calculate capacity factors of $CHCl_3$ and CCl_4 at different temperatures using GC results in Step 3 (data processing table in next page). (Note: only chromatograms run with isothermal program should be used for this calculation).

Oven Temp (°C)	Capacity factor (k)		Selectivity factor (α)
	$CHCl_3$	CCl_4	
50°C			
60°C			
70°C			
80°C			
90°C			

6. Selectivity factor (α)

In order to separate two components on a given chromatographic system, it is necessary that those two components exhibit different retention behavior. The term which represents this difference is called selectivity. The selectivity (α) is defined for peak pairs and is given by the ratio of the capacity factors of the more retained component (k_2) and the less retained component (k_1).

$$\alpha = \frac{k_2}{k_1} = \frac{t_{R2}-t_0}{t_{R1}-t_0} \qquad (8A-3)$$

The selectivity is always equal to or greater than one. If the selectivity equals one, the two components cannot be separated and their peaks overlap. A higher selectivity always implies a better separation. However, whether a baseline separation is achieved also depends on the peak width.

Exercise: Calculate selectivity for $CHCl_3$ and CCl_4 using the capacity factors derived from Step 5 and the data processing therein.

7. Resolution of two components

Another parameter to characterize the separation of two adjacent peaks is the resolution. It's a measure of how well species have been separated by taking into account of peak widths. Baseline resolution is achieved when $R = 1.5$. It may be expressed according to the equation

$$R_{AB} = \frac{2(t_{RB}-t_{RA})}{W_{hA}+W_{hB}} \qquad (8A-4)$$

where R_{AB} is the resolution, t_{RB} and t_{RA} are the retention time of two adjacent components B and A (B eluted after A), and W_{hA} and W_{hB} are the respective widths of each peak at its base as shown in Figure 8-2.

Exercise: Calculate resolutions of $CHCl_3$ and CCl_4 at different flow rates using results from Step 4.

Flow rate (mL/min)	Base Width (W_h, min)		Resolution (R)
	$CHCl_3$	CCl_4	
1.0			
1.5			
2.0			

8. Cleanup and waste disposal: clean up the area you used and dispose any organic waste as advised by the instructor.

E. Result report

1. Include one chromatogram to show separation of $CHCl_3$ and CCl_4.
2. Calculate the parameters as introduced in the experiment.

   a. Theoretical plate number (N) and heights (H) using data from Step 2.
   b. The capacity factors (k) in Step 5.
   c. The selectivity factor (α) in Step 6.
   d. The resolution (R) in Step 7.

> **Note**: The assessment of dead time (t_0) for GC is not introduced in this experiment. If the instructor does not have this information, assume a dead time (or dead volume) between 1.0 and 1.5 minute, depending on the length of column used.

F. Questions for discussion

1. Discuss how oven temperature affects the elution and resolution of compounds used. Would you expect the dead time to increase or decrease with an increase in oven temperature?
2. Discuss how flow rate affects the elution and resolution of compounds used. Would you expect the dead time to increase or decrease with an increase in flow rate?
3. Discuss the reasons for using temperature programming in gas chromatography rather than simple isothermal separations. Relate this discussion to the specific experiment in this experiment.
4. Why is it important to make the injection quickly and to be consistent in your technique?

G. Supplementary experiments: Kovat's Retention Indices

Introduction: The retention index of a certain chemical compound is its retention time normalized to the retention times of adjacently eluting *n*-alkanes. While retention times vary with the individual chromatographic system, the derived retention indices are relatively independent of these parameters and allow comparing values measured by different analytical laboratories under varying conditions. Tables of retention indices can help identify components by comparing experimentally found retention indices with known values.

Experiment: Using the isothermal method with column temperature of 50°C and flow rate of 0.8 mL/min, record the chromatogram for 0.1 µl injection of a neat mixture of the pentane, hexane, heptane, octane, (nonane and higher straight-chain hydrocarbons if available).

Data treatment: Make a plot between the adjusted retention times for the C5 to C8 hydrocarbons versus the logarithm of the number of paraffinic carbon atoms x 100 (e.g. for C_5, this equals 500 and so on). Perform a linear regression and determine the slope and the intercept of the best-fit line. Use this plot and the adjusted retention times of $CHCl_3$ and CCl_4, calculate the Kovat's retention index for each compound.

H. Reference

1. Skoog, D. A., F. J. Holler and S. R. Crouch, 2007. Principles of Instrumental Analysis. 6th ed. Thomson Brooks/Cole Publishing. Belmont, CA.
2. Harris, D. C., 2010. Quantitative Chemical Analysis, 8th Ed., Freeman, New York.
3. Harold, M. M., and M. M. James, 2009. Basic Gas Chromatography. 2nd Ed. Wiley-Interscience.
4. Poole, C., 2012. Gas Chromatography. Elsevier.
5. Parcher, J. F., 1972. Retention Volume Theories for Gas Chromatography. J. Chem. Educ. 49(7): 472-475.
6. Benson, G. A., 1982. The separation and identification of straight chain hydrocarbons: An experiment using gas-liquid chromatography. J. Chem. Educ. 59 (4): 344.

EXPERIMENT 8B: GC/FID ANALYSIS OF ISOMERIC BUTYL ALCOHOL MIXTURE

A. Objectives

1. To set up GC method for separation of structurally similar organic compounds.
2. To learn the concept and application of internal standard calibration method in GC.
3. To determine the concentration of each component in a mixture with external and internal standard calibration.

B. Introduction

Quantification by GC-FID is typically performed using **external standard calibration**; this approach is selective and is accurate for low level analyses. Its primary disadvantage is that it is greatly affected by the variability of the chromatographic system and the presence of chromatographic interferences in a sample or sample extract.

Internal standard calibration in GC: A more advanced calibration method is the **internal standard calibration.** Internal standard calibration has several advantages over external standard method: 1) it accounts for routine variation in the response of the chromatographic system; 2) it accounts for the variations in the exact volume of sample or sample extract introduced into the chromatographic system.

The application of internal standard in GC is based on the fact that the relative responses of two similar compounds remain constant, although the absolute responses of analytes in GC change from day to day and instrument to instrument. Therefore, the variations can be corrected with an internal calibration standard as reference of the analytes.

In this method, a constant concentration of a non-interfering compound (internal standard) is added to each sample before it is analyzed. The response of analyte relative to the reference, defined as **relative response factor** (RRF), can be determined with standard containing known concentrations of analytes and internal standard. The RRF then can be used to quantify an unknown concentration of one analyte in the presence of a known concentration of the internal standard.

To determine the RRF of an analyte (A) relative to the reference (R, internal standard), a standard containing known concentration of A and R are analyzed. The peak areas and concentrations of the analyte (a_A, C_A) and internal standard (a_R, C_R) are used to calculate the response factors (RFs), f_A and f_R for the analyte and internal standard respectively, as in Eqn. 8B-1.

$$f_A = \frac{a_A}{C_A} \quad \text{and} \quad f_R = \frac{a_R}{C_R} \qquad (8B\text{-}1)$$

The RFs calculated for the analyte and internal standard are then used to establish the RRF of the analyte relative to the internal standard.

$$RRF_{A/R} = \frac{f_A}{f_R} = \frac{a_A C_R}{a_R C_A} \qquad (8B\text{-}2)$$

The RRF can be used to calculate the concentration of analyte A (C_S) in unknown sample in the presence of a known concentration of internal standard (C_R) with Eqn. 8B-2.

$$C_S = \frac{C_R \times \frac{a_S}{a_R}}{RRF_{A/R}} \qquad (8B\text{-}3)$$

where a_S and a_R are signals (integral area) of analyte A and reference R respectively.

Selection of internal standard: selecting suitable internal standard is the key for the success in the internal standard method. The ideal internal standard need to meet the following criteria:

1. It should provide a signal that is similar to the analyte signal in most ways but sufficiently different so that the two signals are distinguishable by the instrument.
2. It must be known to be absent from the sample matrix so that the only source of the standard is the added amount.
3. It should not suppress or enhance the analyte signal, and the change of analyte concentration does not affect the internal standard signal.

Butanol isomers: Butanol or butyl alcohol isomers are alcohols with a 4 carbon structure and the molecular formula of C_4H_9OH. They belong to the higher alcohols and branched-chain alcohols. It is primarily used as a solvent, an intermediate in chemical synthesis, and as a fuel. Like many alcohols, butanol is considered toxic with toxicity in laboratory animal experiments. Butanol is considered as a potential biofuel (butanol fuel) which can be used in cars designed for gasoline (petrol) without any change to the engine (unlike 85% ethanol), and it contains more energy for a given volume than ethanol and almost as much as gasoline. Table 8-1 lists the nomenclature, boiling points and density of four butanol isomers.

Table 8-1 *Structure and property of butanol isomers.*

	Structure	FW	Boiling point (°C)	Density (g/mL)
n-butanol		74.12	118	0.81
sec-butanol		74.12	99	0.808
iso-butanol		74.12	108	0.802
tert-butanol		74.12	82	0.775

C. Chemicals

1. Methanol (CH_3OH, ACS grade, >99.8%).
2. *n*-Butanol (*n*-$C_4H_{10}O$, ACS grade, 99.4%).
3. *sec*-Butanol (2-$C_4H_{10}O$, ACS grade, >99%).
4. *iso*-Butanol (2-Methyl-1-propanol, ACS grade, >99%).
5. *tert*-Butanol (*tert*-$C_4H_{10}O$, ACS grade, >99%).

D. Apparatus

1. Basic GC with FID detector.
2. Pipet, 1 mL.
3. Volumetric flasks, 100 mL.
4. Micro syringe, 1 μL.

E. Procedure

1. Preparation of standard

   a. *Preparation of 1% (v/v) mixed stock standard*: In 100 mL volumetric flask, pipet 1 mL *n*-butanol, *sec*-butanol, *iso*-butanol and *tert*-butanol, dilute with methanol to mark.
   b. *Preparation of calibration standard*: Pipet 0.1, 0.2, 0.5 and 1 mL 1% (v/v) mixed stock standard into 100 mL volumetric flasks. Dilute with methanol to mark. This yields standard of 0.001%, 0.002%, 0.005% and 0.01% (v/v) of mixed standards.

c. *Preparation of unknown samples*: Two unknown samples are prepared. Unknown #1 has unknown concentrations for all four butanol isomers (for external calibration method), Unknown #2 has known concentrations of *tert*-butanol (used as internal standard) and unknown concentrations of all other three butanol isomers.

2. Preparation of instrument

Follow the similar procedure as in Experiment 8A to set up instrument parameters. Conduct the following procedure to optimize the GC conditions for separation of butanol isomers

a. Inject 0.1 µL of mixed standard (1%, v/v) to check the separation of butanol isomers. Modify the temperature program to improve the separation of butanol isomer if necessary. The following is a temperature program based on a 30 m x 0.53 mm ID fused silica capillary column bonded with DB-Wax (Agilent), which is capable to separate the butanol isomers (EPA Method 8015B). Use this program as starting point if you use different instrument.

- Initial temperature: 45°C, hold for 4 minutes.
- Program: 45°C to 220°C at 12°C/min.
- Final temperature: 220°C, hold for 3 minutes.

b. Once the instrumental conditions are finalized, inject individual isomer of butanol to determine the identity of each peak in the mixed standard by comparing retention time.

3. External standard calibration method

a. Run calibration standards, integrate each peak corresponding to the 4 butanol isomers. Record the peak areas for each peak.
b. Construct external standard calibration curve for each isomer by plotting peak areas vs. concentration and run linear regression for each isomer.

Compound	t_R (min)	Integral Area				Standard calibration	
		0.001%	0.002%	0.005%	0.01%	m	b
n-butanol							
sec-butanol							
iso-butanol							
tert-butanol							

c. Run Unknown #1, identify each isomers, integrate the peaks identified. Record the results.
d. Calculate concentrations of isomers in Unknown #1 with external standard calibration curves.

Compound	t_R (min)	Integral Area	Concentration (%)
n-butanol			
sec-butanol			
iso-butanol			
tert-butanol			

4. Internal standard calibration method

a. Inject 0.1 µL of Unknown #2 and run GC with the same condition as in 3. Identify and integrate all peaks of butanol isomers. Record results.
b. Calculate response factor for each isomers using results from Step 3. You can use any standard. An alternate way to obtain response factor (RF) is to use the slope of the external standard calibration curves (why?).

   c. Calculate relative response factor (RRF) for *n*-butanol, *sec*-butanol and *iso*-butanol with *tert*-butanol as internal standard.

   d. Calculate concentrations of *n*-butanol, *sec*-butanol and *iso*-butanol in Unknown #2 with Eqn. 8B-3.

Compound	t_R (min)	RF	RRF	Integral Area	Concentration (%)
n-butanol					
sec-butanol					
iso-butanol					
tert-butanol			1	$a_R =$	$C_R =$

   e. Calculate concentrations of all four butanol isomers in Unknown #2 with the external standard calibration obtained in Step 3.

Compound	t_R (min)	Integral Area	Concentration (%)
n-butanol			
sec-butanol			
iso-butanol			
tert-butanol			

   f. Compare results from the internal (Step **4.d**) and external (Step **4.e**) standard calibration for Unknown #2.

5. Cleanup and waste disposal: dispose organic waste in properly labeled waste container.

F. Result report

1. Include chromatograms of one mixed standard to show the separation of butanol isomers. Mark the butanol isomers.
2. Construct external calibration curves with a spreadsheet.
3. Calculate the concentration of butanol isomers in Unknown #1 with the external standard calibration.
4. Calculate the response factors (RF) of butanol isomers based on results in Step 3. Calculate relative response factors (RRF) of three other isomers with *tert*-butanol as internal standard.
5. Calculate concentrations of *n*-butanol, *sec*-butanol and *iso*-butanol in Unknown #2 based on the relative response factors.
6. Calculate concentrations of all isomers in Unknown #2 with external standard calibration obtained in Step 3. Compare results from the two methods.

G. Questions for discussion

1. What the advantage and disadvantages of external and internal standard calibration method used in this experiment?
2. Discuss the factors affecting the separation of butanol isomers.

H. Reference

1. Skoog, D. A., F. J. Holler and S. R. Crouch, 2007. Principles of Instrumental Analysis. 6th ed. Thomson Brooks/Cole Publishing. Belmont, CA.
2. Harris, D. C., 2010. Quantitative Chemical Analysis, 8th Ed., Freeman, New York.
3. Seader, J. D., E. J. Henley and D. K. Roper, 2010. Separation Process Principles. 3rd Ed. Willey.
4. Riee, W. G., 1987. Determination of impurities in whiskey using internal standard techniques: A GC experiment for quantitative analysis. J. Chem. Educ. 64(12):1055.
5. EPA Method 8015B. 1996. Nonhalogenated Organics Using GC/FID.
6. Online book section: **http://onlinelibrary.wiley.com/doi/10.1002/9783527611300.app6/pdf** (Basic quantitative capillary GC).

EXPERIMENT 8C: THE KINETICS AND MECHANISM OF THE BROMINATION OF DISUBSTITUTED ARENES BY GC/MS

A. Objectives

1. To study the basic principles and instrumentation of GC/MS.
2. To learn how to identify unknown organic compounds from a reaction with GC/MS.
3. To study kinetics of the bromination of disubstituted arenes.

B. Introduction

B*asic principle of GC/MS*: GC/MS is a method that combines the features of gas chromatography (GC) and mass spectrometry (MS). The combination of the separation capability of GC and the qualitative power of MS provides chemists an extremely powerful tool which finds probably the widest applications.

The coupling between GC and MS is technically less challenging than that in LC/MS (Chapter 9). Since the analyte is eluted from the GC column as vapor, it can be easily introduced to a device called **ion source** in the MS. The ions generated by ion source are then introduced to an **ion analyzer**, and detected by an ion detector. A **mass spectrum** is recorded as a plot of abundance of different ions vs. **mass to charge ratio(M/Z)** of the ion.

B*asic instrumentation*: In GC/MS, MS plays a role as a detector similar to FID/ECD. A typical MSD consists of an ion source, an ion analyzer and an ion detector. Figure 8-4 illustrates a quadruple MSD which is the most commonly used MSD in modern GC/MS.

1. **Ion source**: The most commonly used ion source in GC/MS is **electron impact** (EI, Figure 8-4). In an EI source, sample molecules are bombarded by electrons generated by a heated filament between a cathode and an anode. The electrons accelerated towards a positive target by a 70 volt potential. When an electron strikes on its way a neutral sample molecule, it knocks out one of its electrons. Additional energy absorbed by the molecule induces vibrational and rotational movement, and results in **fragmentation** of the molecule.

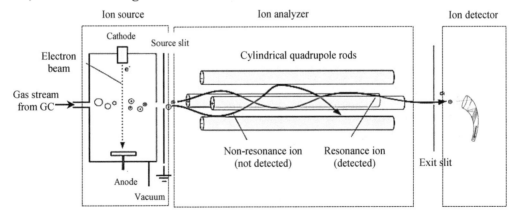

Figure 8-4 A quadrupole mass spectrometer detector connected to GC. The MS detector has an ionization device, the quadrupole ion analyzer and an ion detector.

2. **Ion analyzer**: The ionized species from ion source is introduced into an **ion analyzer**. The ions are separated in ion analyzer based on their mass to charge ratio (M/Z). The most commonly used ion analyzer in GC/MS is **quadrupole** ion analyzer (Figure 8-4). A less popular ion analyzer is **time-**

of-flight (TOF) ion analyzer, which sees increasing application in recent years. The mechanism how these ion analyzers separate and detect ions is out of the scope of this manual.

3. **Ion detector**: The most commonly used ion detector is the **electron multiplier** - a continuous dynode device which amplifies the electrical signal by many orders of magnitude.

C. Chemicals

1. Bromine (Br₂, ACS grade, >99.5%).
2. Sodium hydroxide (NaOH, ACS grade, >97%).
3. Chlorobenzene (C₆H₅Cl, ACS grade, >99.5%).
4. 1,2-Dichlorobenzene (C₆H₄Cl₂, GC grade, >99%).
5. Bromobenzene (C₆H₅Br, GC grade, >99.5%).
6. 1,2-Dibromobenzene (C₆H₄Br, GC grade, >97%).
7. Aluminum chloride (AlCl₃, anhydrous, >98%).

D. Apparatus

1. A basic GC/MS (with EI ion source and quadruple ion analyzer).
2. Pipets, 1, 5 mL.
3. Volumetric flasks, 100 mL.
4. Micro syringe, 1 µL.

E. Procedure

> **Safety Precautions**:
> 1. Bromine is volatile and highly toxic. All operation with bromine must be conducted under a working fume hood.
> 2. Owing to the evolution of small amounts of HBr over the course of the reaction and the toxicity of halogenated arenes, all procedures are to be conducted in the fume hood and ALL students are required to wear protective clothing, safety glasses and gloves.

1. Preparation of solutions

   a. *Preparation of 1% (v/v) chloro- and bromobenzene mixed stock solution*: In 100 mL volumetric flask, add 1 mL each of mono- and disubstituted chloro- and bromobenzene. Bring to mark with dichloromethane.

   b. *Preparation of chloro- and bromobenzene working standards*: In four 100 mL volumetric flasks, add 1, 2, 3, 4 mL of mixed stock standard solution. Bring to mark with dichloro-methane.

   c. *Preparation of 2.2 M bromine*: Transfer 5.67 mL of bromine into 100 mL flask, bring to mark with dichloromethane. This yields bromine solution of 2.2 M.

   d. *Preparation of 22 mM 1,2-dichlrobenzene*: Add 0.223 mL of 1,2-dichlorobenze into 100 mL volumetric flask, bring to mark with dichloromethane.

   e. *Preparation of 2 M NaOH solution*: Weight 8 g NaOH to 100 mL volumetric flask, bring to mark with deionized water. Dissolve and mix thoroughly.

2. GC/MS analysis: The following GC and MS conditions are based on EPA Method 8260B for volatile organic compounds.

   a. GC condition

   - GC column: a capillary column (30 m x 0.25mm or similar) is recommended.
   - Carrier gas: helium.
   - Flow Rate: 1.0 mL/min.
   - Program: 50°C, hold for 5 minutes, 50°C to 150°C at 5°C/min, Final temperature: 150°C, hold until all expected compounds have eluted.
   - Injector: splitless at 180°C

   b. MS condition

   - Scan range: 30 to 350 amu.
   - Scan time: 1 sec/scan.
   - Ionization mode: electron impact.
   - Electron energy: 70 volt.
   - Solvent delay: 2 min.
   - Background mass: 45 m/z.
   - Reaction tube, 30 mL.

3. Standard calibration

   a. Run the mixed standard solutions with 0.1 µL of injection.
   b. Identify all compounds in the mixed standard with help of mass spectra.
   c. Integrate each peak on total ion chromatogram (TIC) of chloro- and bromobenzene in the mixed standards. Record results.
   d. Construct calibration for each compound in standards with linear regression on a spreadsheet.

Compound	t_R (min)	Integral Area				Calibration	
		0.01%	0.02%	0.03%	0.04%	m	b
Chlorobenzene							
1,2-Dichlorobenzene							
Bromobenzene							
1,2-Dibromobenzene							

4. Bromination of disubstituted arene

   a. Combine 120 mg of anhydrous aluminum chloride (pre-weighed in a vial) with 4 mL of 2.2 M bromine solution in dichloromethane in a dry 30 mL test tube. The solution is stirred with the aid of a flea magnetic stir bar.
   b. Add 4 mL of 22 mM 1,2-dichlorobenzene in dichloromethane.
   c. During the course of the reaction, take aliquots (100 µL) at regular time intervals (every 30 seconds for the first 5 minutes; every 1 minute for the next 5 minutes; every 10 minutes for the next 30 minutes; every 30 minutes for the next 2 hours; take a final aliquot near the end of the lab period).
   d. Add the aliquots to 0.25 mL of 2 M aqueous NaOH in a small test tube and gently shake the test tube until the color of bromine disappears. This stops the reaction.
   e. Inject 1 µL portion of the bottom layer (dichloromethane) into the inlet of the GC/MS.

5. Kinetics of bromination of dichlorobenzene

   a. Run all the samples with conditions specified in Step **2**.
   b. Identify the four compounds in the samples and all possible reaction products with help of mass spectra.
   c. Integrate the four peaks on total ion chromatogram (TIC) corresponding to the four compounds in the mixed standards. Calculate concentrations in the samples. Record your results.

Compound	Chlorobenzene		1,2-Dichlorobenzene		Bromobenzene		1,2-Dibromobenzene	
Time (min)	Area	C (%)	Area	C (%)	Area	C (%)	Area	C (%)
0								
0.5								
1								
1.5								
2								
3.5								
4								
4.5								
5								

6								
7								
9								
10								
20								
30								
60								
90								
120								
150								

6. Cleanup and waste disposal: the organic waste generated in this experiment is toxic. Follow the appropriate procedure to dispose waste, or consult the instructor. **Don't vacate the waste to the sink!**

F. Result report

1. Include a TIC to show the separation of the four compounds in mixed standard.
2. Conduct linear regression for each compound in the mixed standard to construct external standard calibration on a spreadsheet.
3. Tabulate the reaction time of each sample and the integral areas of identified compounds. Calculate concentrations of the four compounds in the mixed standard if present in the sample.
4. Plot concentration of reactant (1,2-dichlorobenzene) and reaction products identified vs. time.

G. Questions for discussion

1. Why aluminium chloride must be added to the reaction mixture?
2. What is the purpose of the vacuum system in the mass spectrometry detector? Would the detector function without it?
3. What is Selected Ion Monitoring (SIM)? Would this process have helped in identifying the various components analyzed in this experiment? Why or why not?
4. Why should water not be used as a solvent when using electron impact (EI) as the ionization source?

H. Supplementary Experiment: Identification and Quantification of BTEX in Gasoline by GC/MS

Introduction

BTEX refers to **b**enzene, **t**oluene, **e**thyl benzene and the three **x**ylene isomers, a group of structurally similar volatile organic compounds. BTEX are regulated toxic compounds while benzene is also an EPA target carcinogen. They are typically found near petroleum production and storage sites. The investigation of these compounds, especially in drinking water at low levels, is critical to protect public health.

Chemicals

1. Mixed standard solution 1 mg/mL of benzene, toluene, ethylbenzene, o-xylene, m-xylene, and p-xylene each in methanol can be purchased from commercial supplier (e.g Sigma-Aldrich)
2. Methanol (CH_3OH, HPLC grade, >99.8%).

Apparatus

1. Basic GC/MS.
2. Pipet, 1, 5 mL.
3. Volumetric flask, 100 mL.

Procedure

1. Preparation of BTEX standard

   a. *Preparation of 1mg/L stock standard*: Add 0.1 mL of 1 mg/mL BTEX mixed standard in 100 mL volumetric flask, bring to mark with methanol.

   b. *Preparation of calibration standard solutions*: Add 0.5, 1, 2, 5 mL of 1 mg/L stock standard in four 100 mL volumetric flasks, bring to mark with methanol. This yields calibration standard solutions with 5, 10, 20, 50 µg/L of each compounds.

   c. *Preparation of gasoline sample*: Add 1 mL of lead free commercial gasoline into a 100 mL volumetric flask, bring to mark with methanol.

2. *Preparation of instrument*: Follow similar procedure in the main experiment to prepare instrument. Start with the similar GC and MS conditions described in main experiment to optimize the instrumental parameters. Use gasoline sample to achieve best separation of components in sample.

3. *Run standard*: Once instrumental condition is finalized, run calibration standards to establish external standard calibration for BTEX compounds.

4. *Run sample*: Run gasoline sample. Identify BTEX compounds in sample by comparing retention time of each compound in the standard. Confirm your identification with mass spectra derived from MSD. Quantify the BTEX compounds if present in the sample.

Data treatment

Construct external standard calibration for BTEX compounds. Quantify these compounds in gasoline sample if present. The gasoline is dominated by straight-chained hydrocarbon followed by branched hydrocarbons. Examine the mass spectra of individual compounds, try to identify as many as aromatic compounds as possible.

I. Reference

1. Skoog, D. A., F. J. Holler and S. R. Crouch, 2007. Principles of Instrumental Analysis. 6th ed. Thomson Brooks/Cole Publishing. Belmont, CA.

2. Seader, J. D., E. J. Henley and D. K. Roper, 2010. Separation Process Principles. 3rd Ed. Willey.

3. Harris, D. C., 2010. Quantitative Chemical Analysis, 8th Ed., Freeman, New York.

4. McMaster, M. 2008. GC/MS: A Practical User's Guide. 2nd Ed. Wiley-Interscience.

5. Annis, D. A., D. M. Collard and L. A. Bottomley, 1995. Bromination of Disubstituted Arenes: Kinetics and Mechanism: GC/MS Experiments for the Instrumental Analysis and Organic Chemistry Labs. J. Chem. Educ., 72(5): 460, DOI: 10.1021/ed072p460.

6. Pfennig, W. B. and A. K. Schaefer, 2011. The Use of Gas Chromatography and Mass Spectrometry To Introduce General Chemistry Students to Percent Mass and Atomic Mass Calculations. J. Chem. Educ. 88(7): 970–974.

7. EPA METHOD 8260B. Volatile organic compounds by gas chromatography/Mass spectrometry (GC/MS). Online access: **http://www.epa.gov/osw/hazard/testmethods/sw846/pdfs/8260b.pdf**

HIGH PERFORMANCE LIQUID CHROMATOGRAPHY

I. BASIC PRINCIPLES

In **high performance liquid chromatography** (HPLC), the mobile phase is a liquid (mixture of solvents), and the stationary phase are adsorptive particles or particles coated with other materials. The stationary phase is packed into a column which can hold high pressure. A high performance pump(s) is used to deliver mobile phase through the column. The sample is introduced between the pump and the column. The analyte components are separated in the column and then detected by a detector. The most commonly used HPLC is **partition chromatography**, in particular, **reverse phase HPLC (RP-HPLC)**, on which we will focus in this chapter.

In partition chromatography, the solute is distributed between the liquid mobile phase and a second, immiscible liquid that is coated on or bonded to solid particles as the stationary phase. Compounds that partition more strongly into the stationary liquid phase are retained longer in the column. This type of chromatography is termed **normal phase** if the stationary phase is more polar than the mobile phase; and it's called **reverse phase** if the mobile phase is more polar than the stationary phase.

Bonded phase columns have the stationary phase chemically bonded to the solid support and are the most popular column for partition chromatography. For example, *n*-octadecane can be bonded directly to silica by attachment to surface hydroxyl groups to form what is termed a **C18 column**. The extent of partitioning of a solute into the stationary phase can be controlled by varying the solvent polarity. A less popular option is the stationary phase involving a liquid coated on solid support particles.

HPLC vs. GC: Compared to GC, HPLC has several advantages. First, HPLC is not limited to volatile compounds, making the application of HPLC much wider than GC. Second, with liquid as mobile phase, a greater control and wider selection of mobile and stationary phase is possible. Unlike in GC, most detectors adapted to HPLC are non-destructive, this makes it possible to incorporate more detectors into one system to acquire more information on the analytes.

Qualitative analysis by HPLC: Each component in a mixture can be qualitatively identified by comparing retention time t_R with that of known substance. This is similar with GC. Today's HPLC system is commonly equipped with **diode array detector** which acquire UV/Vis spectrum online, providing valuable information on the identity of analytes. More advanced instrument coupled with **mass spectrometry detector (MSD)** has qualitative power through acquiring mass spectra of analyte.

Quantitative analysis by HPLC: The traditional HPLC is primarily a quantitative technique. The basic principle of quantitative HPLC analysis is based on the fact that the area (or height) of a peak is proportional to the concentration of that component in the original mixture. Thus a calibration curve can be prepared by plotting either peak height or peak area as a function of concentration for a series of standards.

II. BASIC INSTRUMENTATION

An basic HPLC instrument (Figure 9-1) typically includes a **sampler** by which the sample mixture is injected into the HPLC, one or more mechanical **pumps** for pushing liquid through a tubing system, a separation **column**, a digital analyte **detector** (e.g. a UV/Vis or fluorescence detector) for qualitative or quantitative analysis of the separation, and a digital microprocessor for controlling the HPLC components (and user software).

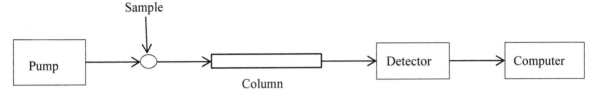

Figure 9-1 Components of a HPLC system.

1. **Injector**: Samples are injected into the HPLC via an injection port, which consists of an **injection valve** and the **sample loop** (Figure 9-2). The sample is drawn into a syringe and injected into the loop via the injection valve. A rotation of the valve rotor closes the valve and opens the loop in order to inject the sample into the stream of the mobile phase.

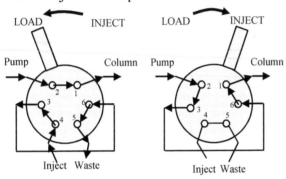

Figure 9-2 The flow paths of a HPLC injection valve. At LOAD position, sample is injected into sample loop while the mobile phase passes by the sample loop and is directed to column. At INJECT position, the mobile phase is connected to the sample loop and wash the sample to the column. Change from LOAD to INJECT position can be done manually or automatically, and marks the start of a HPLC run.

2. **Pump**: The most common HPLC pump is **reciprocating piston pump** which consists of a small motor driven piston which moves rapidly back and forth in a hydraulic chamber that may vary from 35-400 μL in volume. On the back stroke, the separation column valve is closed, and the piston pulls in solvent from the mobile phase reservoir. On the forward stroke, the pump pushes solvent out to the column from the reservoir.

3. **Column**: Holds the stationary phase, is the heart of a LC system. The theory of chromatography column has not changed over time; however there has been continuous improvement in column development. The recent columns are often prepared in stainless steel housing. The packing material generally used is silica or polymer gels. For some analytes such as biomolecules and ionic compounds, contact with metal is not desired, thus polyether ether ketone (PEEK) column housing is used instead.

4. **Detector**: UV-visible absorbance is the most commonly used mode of detection in HPLC. Such detectors enable the effluent from the column to flow through an 8 to 10 μL spectrophotometric cell for detection of compounds at a particular wavelength. **Electrochemical** and **fluorescence detectors** often are used to achieve lower detection limits for certain compounds which are not readily detected by UV/Vis detector. Another less commonly used detector is based on measurement of the **differential refractive index**. A more advanced alternate of UV/Vis detector is **diode array detector** (DAD), which is capable of recording UV/Vis spectrum online, is available for almost all new HPLC systems today. In addition, **mass spectrometry detector** (MSD) for HPLC is also available, and more details on MSD can be found in Experiment 9C.

General Reading

1. Lloyd, R. S., J. J. Kirkland and J. W. Dolan, 2009. Introduction to Modern Liquid Chromatography. 3rd ed. Wiley.
2. Seader, J. D., E. J. Henley and D. K. Roper, 2010. Separation Process Principles. 3rd Ed. Willey.
3. Harris, D. C., 2010. Quantitative Chemical Analysis, 8th Ed., Freeman, New York.

EXPERIMENT 9A: DETERMINATION OF CAFFEINE IN BEVERAGE WITH HPLC

A. Objectives

1. To gain an understanding of the differences between GC and LC.
2. To learn the principle and operation of high performance liquid chromatography (HPLC).
3. To determine concentration of caffeine in beverage with reverse phase HPLC.

B. Chemicals

1. Methanol (CH_3OH, HPLC grade, >99.9%).
2. Caffeine ($C_8H_{10}N_4O_2$, anhydrous, >99.0%).

C. Apparatus

1. HPLC system with UV/Vis detector.
2. Pippets: 100 μL, 1mL, 5 mL.
3. Volumetric flasks: 100, 1000 mL.
4. Test tubes, 10-15 mL.
5. HPLC injection syringe.

D. Procedure

1. Preparation of caffeine standards and samples

    a. *Preparation of 100 ppm of caffeine stock solution*: Accurately weigh 100 mg of caffeine. Transfer to a 1000 mL volumetric flask. Dilute to the mark with 50/50 methanol/water (v/v).

    b. *Preparation of caffeine calibration standards*: Into four 100 mL flask, transfer 10, 25, 50, 75 mL of 100 ppm caffeine stock solution. Bring to mark with 50/50 methanol/water (v/v). This gives caffeine calibration standard solution of 10, 25, 50, and 75 ppm.

    c. *Preparation of sample*: Tea and coffee samples can be prepared from any brand of commercial tea and coffee. Carbonated beverage is degassed overnight. All samples are filtered through 0.45 μm filter, and diluted with methanol at 1:1 (v/v) ratio.

2. Operation of the instrument

    > **Operation tips**
    >
    > 1. Always prime the pump if the system has not been run for a while. Running the pump without solvent will damage the seal in the pump head, and cause expensive repair. Degassing the solvent can prevent accumulation of air bubble in the pump. Watch the pressure (or check the waste outlet) to make sure there is solvent delivered through the system.
    > 2. The lamps used in UV/Vis detector has limited life time. That's why the lamps usually are not automatically turned on when the detector is turned on. Turn off the lamps when you are not running samples.

    a. Instrument condition

    - Column: reverse phase C8 or C18 column which is capable to separate caffeine from the interferences.
    - Eluent: methanol/water = 50/50 (recommended, instructor need to test on their system to examine the separation of caffeine).
    - Gradient: isocratic.
    - Flow rate: 0.8 – 1 mL/min (recommended. Adjust flow rate to obtain a chromatogram with retention time of caffeine between 5-10 minutes).
    - UV detector wavelength: 272 nm.

- Injection volume: 10-25 μL. Make sure the injection volumes are consistent for all standards and samples. If the signal is too high, reduce injection volume or dilute the standards and/or samples.

b. Analysis procedure

- Depending on the system used, the instructor need to develop a detailed operating procedures.
- Modern HPLC systems are commonly equipped with computer and software to control the components and record the signal. In this case, a METHOD which defines the HPLC conditions/parameters/data recorder and processing is required for operation.
- If an autosampler is used, the injection conditions are defined (program controlled) or set up (standalone autosampler) before running sample.

3. Standard calibration

a. Run calibration standards. Record the integral area of caffeine peak for each standard in the data table below.

b. Plot the signal (peak area) vs. concentration in a spreadsheet. Construct external standard calibration for caffeine by linear regression analysis.

Standard	C (ppm)	t_R (min)	Peak area
1			
2			
3			
4			
5			

4. Run sample

a. Run samples (tea, coke, coffee etc.) with the same chromatographic conditions. If the peaks of samples are too high (greater than the highest standard), dilute the samples with eluent. The calculation of final concentration of samples needs to take the dilution into account.

b. Calculate concentration of caffeine in different beverages.

Samples	Dilution factor	t_R (min)	Peak area	Diluted C (ppm)	Original C (ppm)
Undiluted Tea	1				
Diluted Tea					
Undiluted Coffee	1				
Diluted Coffee					
Undiluted Coke	1				
Diluted Coke					

5. Shut down the instrument

a. Turn off lamps of UV/Vis detector (and fluorescence detector if used).

b. Flash the system with 50/50 methanol/water (v/v) for 15-20 minutes. Turn off the pump.

c. Turn off the other components of the instrument. Exit the software.

E. Result report

1. Include UV/Vis spectra of caffeine if you use a UV/Vis detector which is capable of recording UV/Vis absorption spectra (e.g. DAD).
2. Tabulate the integral areas of caffeine in calibration standards and samples.
3. Construct the calibration curve of caffeine by linear regression on a spreadsheet.
4. Use the calibration parameters (formula) to calculate concentration of caffeine in unknown samples.

F. Questions for discussion

1. Explain why reverse phase column is appropriate for caffeine analysis. Could an ion-exchange column be used for determination of caffeine?
2. If you conduct caffeine analysis with UV/Vis spectrometry in Experiment 3B, compare results from the two methods, UV/Vis spectrometry and HPLC. In particular, what are the advantages HPLC has over UV/Vis spectrometry?
3. Explain why it's necessary to dilute the samples if the concentration of caffeine is out of the calibration range.

G. Reference:

1. Sawyer, D. T., W. R. Heineman and J. M. Beebe, 1984. Chemistry Experiments for Instrumental Methods, Wiley.
2. Lloyd, R. S., J. J. Kirkland and J. W. Dolan, 2009. Introduction to Modern Liquid Chromatography. 3rd ed. Wiley.
3. Harris, D. C., 2010. Quantitative Chemical Analysis, 8th Ed., Freeman, New York.
4. Dong, W. M., 2006. Modern HPLC for Practicing Scientists. Wiley-Interscience.
5. McDevitt, V. L., A. Rodriguez and K. R. Williams, 1998. Analysis of Soft Drinks: UV Spectrophotometry, Liquid Chromatography, and Capillary Electrophoresis. J. Chem. Educ. 75, 625-629.
6. Leacock, E. R., J. J. Stankus and J. M. Davis, 2011. Simultaneous Determination of Caffeine and Vitamin B6 in Energy Drinks by High-Performance Liquid Chromatography (HPLC). J. Chem. Educ. 88(2): 232–234.

EXPERIMENT 9B: ANALYSIS OF PARABEN MIXTURE BY HPLC

A. Objectives

1. To learn the principle and operation of high performance liquid chromatography HPLC.
2. To become familiar with the procedure for separation and determination of structurally similar compounds such as parabens with reverse phase HPLC.

B. Introduction

Parabens are esters of **para-hydroxybenzoic** acid, from which the name is derived. Common para-bens include methylparaben, ethylparaben, propylparaben and butylparaben. The general chemical structure of a paraben is shown in Table 9-1, where R symbolizes an alkyl group such as methyl, ethyl, propyl or butyl group.

Table 9-1 *Structural information of common parabens.*

	Abr.	Side group (R)	Formula	FW
Methylparaben	MEP	-CH$_3$	C$_8$H$_8$O$_3$	152.15
Ethylparaben	ETP	-CH$_2$-CH$_3$	C$_9$H$_{10}$O$_3$	166.17
Propylparaben	PRP	-CH$_2$-CH$_2$-CH$_3$	C$_{10}$H$_{12}$O$_3$	180.20
Butylparaben	BTP	-CH$_2$-CH$_2$-CH$_2$-CH$_3$	C$_{11}$H$_{14}$O$_3$	194.23

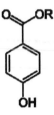

Parabens are widely used as antimicrobial preservatives in cosmetic products. Parabens have a potential of endocrine effect from weak estrogenic activity, and it is known that some estrogens can drive the growth of tumors. As a result, their use of parabens in cosmetic products is limited in the EU countries to a concentration up to 0.4% when used individually and 0.8% as a mixture. In the US, under the FDA and Cosmetic Act (FD&C Act), parabens are typically used at levels ranging from 0.01 to 0.3%. Because of these concerns and regulations, it is necessary to control the level of parabens in cosmetic products, and therefore methods to quantify paraben levels are needed.

All the parabens have similar UV/Vis spectrum with a maximum absorption around 254 nm. The different parabens can be separated on a common reverse phase column. Thus, HPLC is a suitable technique for determination of parabens.

C. Chemicals

1. Methanol (CH$_3$OH, HPLC grade, >99.9%).
2. Acetonitrile (CH$_3$CN, HPLC grade, >99.9%).
3. Methylparaben (analytical standard, 99%).
4. Ethylparaben (analytical standard, 99%).
5. Propylparaben (analytical standard, >99%).
6. Butylparaben (analytical standard, >99%).

D. Apparatus

1. HPLC system with UV/Vis detector (254 nm).
2. Volumetric flasks, 100 mL.
3. Pipet, 1 mL, 5 mL.
4. Analytical balance (0.001 g).

E. Procedure

1. Preparation of standard

   a. *Preparation of 0.4 mg/mL stock standard*: Accurately weight 400 mg of each paraben into 1 L volumetric flask. Dilute with 50/50 methanol/water (v/v) to mark.

b. *Preparation of calibration standards*: Pipet 0.1, 0.2, 0.5, 1 and 2 mL of 0.4 mg/mL stock standard into 100 mL volumetric flasks. Dilute with 50/50 methanol/water (v/v) to mark. This gives mixed standard solutions of 0.4, 0.8, 2, 4 and 8 mg/L of each paraben.

2. Sample preparation

   a. Weight 2.0 g of skin cream into a 50 mL screw-capped plastic tube.
   b. Add 20.0 mL 50% (v/v) aqueous methanol.
   c. The mixture was stirred with a vortex mixer, ultrasonicated for 30 min and then centrifuged for 30 min (5000 rpm).
   d. The solution was filtered through a 0.45 μm membrane filter directly into the HPLC vial.

3. Preparation of instrument

   a. Column: reverse phase C18 column which is capable to separate parabens.
   b. Eluent: actonitrile/water = 40/60 (recommended, test on the system used to examine the separation of parabens).
   c. Gradient: isocratic.
   d. Flow rate: 0.5–1.5 mL/min (adjust flow rate to elute all parabens compounds in approximately 15 minutes).
   e. UV detector wavelength: 254 nm.
   f. Injection volume: 10-15 μL. Make sure the injection volumes are consistent for all standards and samples.

4. Optimization of separation

   a. *Separation of parabens*: Under given chromatographic conditions, the parabens should be eluted in the order from the lighter to heavier (methyl- to butylparaben). Inject individual paraben to confirm the identity of each compound if necessary.
   b. *Effect of eluent composition*: Run a standard solution. If all 4 parabens are separated, increase proportion of acetonetrile by 5%, and run mixed standard in isocratic mode. Repeat this procedure until at least 2 parabens start to merge. If the 4 parabens are not completely separated, reduce the proportion of acetonitrile by 5% and run mixed standard in isocratic mode. Repeat this procedure until all four parabens are completely separated.
   c. *Gradient mode*: Run mixed standard in gradient mode. The following is an example of gradient to start with

Time (min)	%A(CH₃CN)	%B(H₂O)	Curve
0	20	80	linear
2	20	80	linear
10	60	40	linear
13	60	40	linear
15	20	80	linear

5. Standard calibration

   a. Choose the condition (isocratic or gradient) best for separation of parabens, run all calibration standards.
   b. Identify and integrate peaks of parabens. Record results of integral areas in data table (next page).
   c. Construct standard calibration (external) for each paraben by running linear regression analysis between concentration and integral area on a spreadsheet.

C (mg/L)	Integral Area				Calibration Curve							
					MEP		ETP		PRP		BTP	
	MEP	ETP	PRP	BTP	m	b	m	b	m	b	m	b
4												
8												
20												
40												
80												

6. Measurement of unknown samples

   a. Under the same condition used for calibration standard in Step **5**, run the unknown sample.
   b. Identify the four parabens based on retention times (UV/Vis spectra can be used to identify parabens if diode array detector is equipped).
   c. Integrate the paraben peaks. Record the results onto data table below.
   d. Calculate concentration of parabens in unknown sample with calibration in Step **5**.

Sample	Integral Area				C (mg/L)			
	MEP	ETP	PRP	BTP	MEP	ETP	PRP	BTP
1								
2								
3								

7. Shut down the instrument and waste disposal

   a. Dispose the organic waste (standard, sample and eluent) in properly labeled waste reservoir.
   b. Turn off lamps of UV/Vis detector (and fluorescence detector if used).
   c. Flash the system with 50/50 methanol/water (v/v) for 15-20 minutes. Turn off the pump.
   d. Turn off the other components of the instrument. Exit the software.

F. Result report

1. Include UV/Vis spectra of parabens from the standards if you use a UV/Vis detector which is capable of recording spectra (e.g. DAD).
2. Tabulate the retention times and integral areas of calibration standards. Construct the calibration curves for all four parabens on a spreadsheet by running linear regression analysis.
3. Use the calibration parameters to calculate concentrations of parabens in unknown samples.

G. Questions for discussion

1. (Optional) Conduct the following exercise if the practice in Experiment 8A is not conducted. In addition to capacity and selective factor, resolution (R) can be assessed for each pair of neighboring peaks. The method for calculation of parameters in this exercise is introduced in Experiment 8A.

   Calculate and report the capacity factor (k) for methyl, ethyl and propyl parabens, and calculate the selectivity factor (α) between each neighboring pair of parabens for the "best" isocratic separation and the optimized gradient separation. Dead time (t_0) can be obtained from the solvent peak (the first peak on the chromatogram).

CH₃CN/ H₂O	Retention Time (min)				Capacity Factor (*k*)				Selectivity Factor (*α*)		
	MEP	ETP	PRP	BTP	MEP	ETP	PRP	BTP	MEP/ ETP	ETP/ PRP	PRP/ BTP
35/65											
40/60											
45/55											
50/50											
55/45											

2. Discuss how the composition of eluent affects the separation of parabens in HPLC. Which solvent, acetonitrile or water, is considered "strong" solvent? When the compounds are not separated, should you increase or decrease the proportion of "strong" solvent?
3. Discuss why it's necessary to run gradient in some analysis. What advantages/disadvantages does gradient elution offer?

H. Supplementary experiments

1. The procedure in this experiment can be used to analyze other preservatives commonly used in skin care products. Table 9-2 lists some of such preservatives and their molecular and spectral information.
2. The procedure in this experiment can also be used for LC/MS system, in which MSD used to identify the parabens and other preservatives present in the sample.

Table 9-2 *Preservatives and their structural and spectral information.*

Preservatives	Structure	Formula	FW	Wavelength (nm)
2-Bromo-2-nitropropane-1,3-diol (BNPD, Bronopol)		$C_3H_6BrNO_4$	199.98	250
Diazolidinyl urea		$C_8H_{14}N_4O_7$	278.22	210
DMDM hydantoin		$C_7H_{12}N_2O_4$	188.18	210
Imidazolidinyl urea		$C_{11}H_{16}N_8O_8$	388.29	210
Iodopropynylbutylcarbamate (IPBC)		$C_8H_{12}INO_2$	281.09	250
Kathon (MCI/MI)		C_4H_4ClNOS	149.60	274

I. Reference

1. European Scientific Committee on Consumer Product (SCCP), SCCP/0873/05.
2. Federal Food, Drug, and Cosmetic Act (FD&C Act), Chapter VI: Cosmetic Sec. 601 [21 USC § 361] Adulterated cosmetics.

EXPERIMENT 9C: HPLC/MS/MS ANALYSIS OF PERFLUOROOCTANOIC ACID

A. Objectives

1. To learn the basic principle and operation of HPLC/MS/MS.
2. To gain an understanding of advantages and disadvantages of GC/MS and LC/MS.
3. To determine perfluorooctanoic acid in unknown sample with LC/MS/MS.

B. Introduction

Basic principle of *HPLC/MS*: Liquid chromatography-mass spectrometry (**LC-MS**) combines the power of separation capabilities of HPLC with the power of mass analysis capabilities of MS, making it an extremely powerful technique with broad applications and very high sensitivity and specificity. Generally, its application is oriented towards the specific detection and potential identification of chemicals in a complex mixture which can be adapted to HPLC.

Like GC/MS, LC/MS system includes a device for introducing samples (LC), an **interface** for connecting LC and MS, an **ion source** that ionizes analytes, an **electrostatic lens** that efficiently introduces the generated ions, a **mass analyzer** unit that separates ions based on their mass-to-charge (m/z) ratio, and a **detector** unit that detects the separated ions. LC/MS differs from GC/MS in that the mobile phase is liquid, usually a mixture of water and organic solvents. Because of this difference, the interface in LC/MS is different from that of GC/MS and the ionization process is also different.

LC/MS and GC/MS are highly complementary. The primary advantage LC/MS has over GC/MS is that it is capable of analyzing a much wider range of components. Compounds that are thermally labile, exhibit high polarity or have a high molecular mass may all be analyzed using LC/MS, even proteins may be routinely analyzed.

Basic instrumentation: Mass spectrometers work by ionizing molecules and then sorting and identifying the ions according to their mass-to-charge (m/z) ratios. Two key components in this process are the ion source, which generates the ions, and the mass analyzer, which sorts the ions.

1. Ion Source

Several different types of ion sources are used for LC/MS. The most common ion sources are **electrospray ionization (ESI)** and **atmospheric pressure chemical ionization (APCI)**.

ESI source: In ESI (Figure 9-3), the analyte solution flow passes through the electrospray needle that has a high potential (with respect to the counter electrode). This charges the droplets from needle with a same surface charge as on the needle. The droplets are repelled from the needle towards the sampling cone on the counter electrode. As the droplets traverse the space between the needle tip and the cone, solvent evaporation occurs. The droplet shrinks until it reaches the point that the surface tension can no longer sustain the charge at which point a "Coulombic explosion" occurs and the droplet is ripped apart. This produces smaller droplets that can repeat until naked charged analyte molecules form.

APCI source: In APCI, the mobile phase containing eluting analyte is heated to relatively high temperatures (above 400°C), sprayed with high flow rates of nitrogen and the entire aerosol cloud is subjected to a corona discharge that creates ions (Figure 9-3). Unlike ESI where the ionization occurs in the liquid phase, the APCI ionization occurs in the gas phase. A potential advantage of APCI is that it's possible to use a nonpolar solvent as a mobile phase, because the solvent and molecules of interest are converted to a gaseous state before reaching the corona discharge pin. Typically, APCI is a less "soft" ionization technique than ESI, i.e. it generates more fragment ions relative to the parent ion. In

126

addition, APCI allows for the high flow rates typical of standard bore HPLC to be used directly, often without diverting the larger fraction of volume to waste.

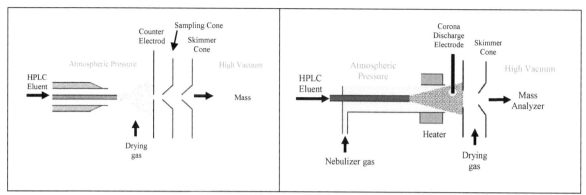

Figure 9-3. Electrospray ionization (ESI, left) source and atmospheric pressure chemical ionization (APCI, right) source.

2. Mass Analyzers

Quadrupole, **time-of-flight (TOF)**, **ion trap** are the most common mass analyzers used in LC/MS. Each has advantages and disadvantages depending on the requirements of a particular analysis.

Quadrupole mas spectrometer: Introduced in Experiment 8C (GC/MS).

TOF: In a TOF mass analyzer, an uniform electromagnetic force is applied to all ions at the same time, causing them to accelerate down a flight tube. Lighter ions travel faster and arrive at the detector first, so the mass-to-charge ratios of the ions are determined by their arrival times.

Ion trap mass analyzer: An ion trap mass analyzer consists of a circular ring electrode plus two end caps that together form a chamber. Ions entering the chamber are "trapped" there by electromagnetic fields. Another field can be applied to selectively eject ions from the trap. Ion traps have the advantage of being able to perform multiple stages of mass spectrometry without additional mass analyzers.

Tandem mass spectrometry: Also known as **MS/MS** or **MS^2**, involves multiple steps of mass spectrometry selection, with some form of fragmentation occurring in between the stages. The first stage of MS serves as separation device for the second stage of MS.

Tandem in space MS/MS is the mode of MS/MS performed by triple-stage quadrupoles or quadrupole-TOF instruments. In tandem in space MS/MS, ions of the specific m/z are first "filtered" by the first quadrupole (**precursor ion**), the ions are then excited to undergo fragmentation within the collision cell which is itself a quadrupole. The fragments (**production ion**) generated then continuously enter the third quadrupole which is rapidly scanned and recorded by ion detector.

*P**erfluorooctanoic acid (PFOA)*: PFOA is a synthetic chemical that does not occur naturally in the environment. PFOA is used to make fluoropolymers, which are substances with valuable properties for applications such as fire resistance and oil, stain, and grease repellence. Toxicological studies have shown that exposure to PFOA can result in developmental/reproductive toxicity, liver damage, and possibly cancer. PFOA is highly persistent in the environment and has been found at very low levels in both the environment and in the blood of the general U.S. population. Recent studies by the EPA have indicated the need for additional testing and monitoring. Detection at levels < 100 ppt in drinking water is required by the European Union. The structure of PFOA is shown below.

$$CF_3 - (CF_2)_6 - COOH$$

This molecule is a carboxylic acid, which is expected to show good sensitivity in negative ion mode using electrospray ionization (ESI).

PFOA have unique chemical and physical properties which adversely affect analysis.

   a. No chromophores: prevents using conventional methodology such as UV/Vis and LC/UV.
   b. Extremely low volatility: eliminating the possibility of using GC for analysis.
   c. Difficult to derivatize for volatile form for GC and GC/MS.
   d. Strong anions: forms strong anions which may adhere to various container surfaces, suspended particulates and biomass, causing it not available for analysis.

C. Chemicals

   1. Perfluorooctanoic acid ($C_8HF_{15}O_2$, 96%).
   2. Methanol (CH_3OH, HPLC grade, >99.9%).
   3. Ammonium acetate ($NH_4C_2H_3O_2$, high purity, demonstrated to be free of analytes and interferences).

D. Apparatus

   1. The LC/MS/MS must be capable of negative ion electrospray ionization (ESI) near the suggested LC flow rate of 0.3 mL/min.
   2. Volumetric flasks, 25, 100 mL.
   3. Pipets, 1, 5 mL.

E. Procedure

   1. Standard preparation

   a. *Preparation of 1000 mg/L stock solution*: Accurately weigh 100 mg of neat standard (PFOA) into a 100 mL volumetric flask. Bring to mark with methanol. Mix thoroughly.
   b. *Preparation of 20 mg/L intermediate standard*: Pipet 500 µL of the stock solution into a 25.0 mL volumetric flask and dilute to volume with methanol.
   c. *Preparation of PFOA standards*: Serially dilute the intermediate standard with methanol to 5.0, 1.0, 0.20, 0.050, 0.010, 0.002 and 0.001 mg/L.
   d. *Preparation of sample*: Prepare sample with unknown concentration of PFOA dissolved in methanol or obtain the unknown from the instructor.

   2. Instrument condition

   a. HPLC condition

   - Column: A reverse phase C18 column (2.1 x 150 mm) packed with 5 µm C18 solid phase particles (Waters #: 186001301 or equivalent) is recommended.
   - Mobile phase: A = 10 mM ammonium acetate in water; B = 10 mM ammonium acetate in 80:20 methanol/water (To prepare 1 L solvent A, add 0.77 g ammonium acetate to 1 L volumetric flask and dilute with reagent water. To make 1 L solvent B, add 0.77 g of ammonium acetate to 1 L volumetric flask, add 200 mL reagent water and bring to mark with methanol).
   - Flow rate: 0.3-0.5 mL/min.
   - Injection volume: 10-20 µL.
   - Isocratic: 85% B.

   b. MS Conditions

   - Mode: negative ESI.
   - Source Temperature: 150 °C.
   - Desolvation temperature: 450 °C.
   - Dwell time (s): 0.05.
   - Capillary voltage: -3.0 kV.
   - Precursor ion: 412.9; and product ion: 369.0.
   - Tune the instrument as needed. See below.

> **Note**: the MS condition and the tuning procedure are based on Waters Micromass triple quadrupole mass spectrometer. Modify the procedure and conduct MS tuning according to the manufacturer specification for system used.

3. ESI-MS/MS tuning

   a. Calibrate the mass scale of the MS with the calibration compounds and procedures prescribed by the manufacturer.
   b. Optimize the [M-H]$^-$ for PFOA by infusing approximately 0.5-1.0 μg/mL PFOA directly into the MS at the chosen LC mobile phase flow rate (0.3-0.5 mL/min). The MS parameters (voltages, temperatures, gas flows, etc.) are varied until optimal responses are determined.
   c. Optimize the product ion (369.0) for PFOA by infusing approximately 0.5-1.0 μg/mL of PFOA directly into the MS at the chosen LC mobile phase flow rate. The MS/MS parameters (collision gas pressure, collision energy, etc.) are varied until optimal responses are determined.

4. Standard calibration

   a. Modern LC/MS/MS are equipped with computer and software which controls all components of the instrument, record, store and process data. Depending on the system used, instructor need to develop an operating procedure for the instrument used.
   b. Run calibration standards and integrate the PFOA peak. Record the result.
   c. Using linear regression analysis, calculate the slope, intercept, and correlation coefficient of standard curve for PFOA. This is done by plotting peak areas vs. concentration.

Standard	C (mg/L)	t_R (min)	Peak area
1			
2			
3			
4			
5			
6			
7			

5. Determination of PFOA in sample

   a. Run unknown sample under the same instrumental conditions.
   b. Calculate PFOA concentration in unknown sample using the calibration curve.

Samples	t_R (min)	Peak area	C (mg/L)
1			
2			

6. Cleanup and waste disposal: PFOA is considered organic contaminant, put all PFOA solution in properly labeled waste container.

F. Result report

1. Include one chromatogram and PFOA mass spectrum in your report to show the identification of PFOA.
2. Construct calibration curve of PFOA using linear regression analysis with a spreadsheet.
3. Calculate concentration of PFOA in unknown sample.

G. Questions for Discussion

1. GC/MS and LC/MS typically use different mechanisms for ionization. Compare the ionization mechanisms between GC/MS and LC/MS. Explain why they are different.
2. Discuss advantages/disadvantages of LC/MS over GC/MS. In particularly, why GC or GC/MS is not suitable for PFOA analysis.

H. Reference

1. Skoog, D. A., F. J. Holler and S. R. Crouch, 2007. Principles of Instrumental Analysis. 6th ed. Thomson Brooks/Cole Publishing. Belmont, CA.
2. Lloyd, R. S., J. J. Kirkland and J. W. Dolan, 2009. Introduction to Modern Liquid Chromatography. 3rd ed. Wiley.
3. McMaster, M., 2006. LC/MS: A Practical User's Guide. Wiley-Interscience.
4. Shoemaker, J. A., P. E. Grimmett and B. K. Boutin, 2009. Determination of selected perfluorinated alkyl acids drinking water by solid phase extraction and liquid chromatography/tandem mass spectrometry (LC/MS/MS). EPA Method 537.
    (Online access: **http://www.epa.gov/microbes/documents/Method%20537_FINAL_rev1.1.pdf**)

CHAPTER

10

OTHER SEPARATION TECHNIQUES

Separation techniques play a key role in today's instrumental analysis. GC and HPLC represent the most widely used techniques. Supercritical fluid chromatography (SFC) was developed from the traditional chromatographic technique, and offers some advantages over GC and HPLC, but still not as common as GC and HPLC. Electrophoresis is another separation technique, in some sense, similar to chromatogramphic techniques. The following table summarizes the common separation techniques including GC and HPLC. This chapter offers three experiments based on separation techniques, IC, SEC and CZE.

Table 10-1 *Common separation techniques.*

Nature of Mobile Phase	Nature of Stationary Phase	Mechanism of Separation	Technique	Name of Chromatographic Method
Gas Chromatography	Liquid	Partition	Column	**Gas Liquid Chromatography (GLC)**
	Solid	Adsorption	Column	Gas Sold Chromatography (GSC)
Liquid Chromatography	Liquid	Partition	Column	Classical Liquid-Liquid Chromatography (LLC)
			Planar	Thin-Layer Chromatography (TLC)
	Bonded Liquid	Modified Partition	Column	**High Performance Liquid Chromatography (HPLC)**
			Planar	High Performance Thin-Layer Chromatography (HPTLC)
	Solid	Adsorption	Column	Classical Liquid-Solid Chromatography (LSC)
			Column	High Performance Liquid Chromatography (HPLC)
			Planar	Thin-Layer Chromatography (TLC)
			Planar	Paper Chromatography (PC)
		Ion Exchange	Column	**Ion Exchange Chromatography (IEC)**
		Exclusion	Column	**Size Exclusion Chromatography (SEC)**
			Column	Gel Permeation Chromatography (GPC)
Supercritical Fluid Chromatography	Liquid/ Solid	Partition/ Adsorption	Column	Supercritical Fluid Chromatography (SFC)
Electrophoresis	Gel	Electropnoretic Mobility	Planar	Slab Electrophoresis
			Capillary	Capillary Gel Electrophoresis (CGE)
	Capillary	Electropnoretic Mobility	Capillary	**Capillary Zone Electrophoresis (CZE)**

General Reading

1. Skoog, D. A., F. J. Holler and S. R. Crouch, 2007. Principles of Instrumental Analysis. 6th Ed. Thomson Brooks/Cole Publishing. Belmont, CA.
2. Seader, J. D., E. J. Henley and D. K. Roper, 2010. Separation Process Principles. 3rd Ed. Willey.
3. Miller, J. M., 2009. Chromatography: Concepts and Contrasts. 2nd Ed. Wiley-Interscience.

EXPERIMENT 10A: DETERMINATION OF ANIONS IN DRINKING WATER BY ION CHROMATOGRAPHY

A. Objectives

1. To become familiar with applications, parameters, and instrumentation of ion chromatography.
2. To separate anions in water sample with ion-exchange column.
3. To determine the concentration of anions present in drinking water.

B. Introduction

Basic principle: **Ion chromatography** (**IC**) is a form of liquid chromatography that uses ion-exchange resins to separate ions based on their interaction with the resin. It's most common application is for analysis of anions for which there are no other rapid analytical methods available. It is also commonly used for cations and biochemical species such as amino acids and proteins.

The stationary phase of IC is ion-exchange resins bonded to inert polymeric particles. For cation separation, the cation-exchange resin is usually a sulfonic ($-SO_3^- H^+$, a strong acid) or carboxylic acid ($-COO^- H^+$, a weak acid). For anion separation, the anion-exchange resin is usually a tertiary amine group ($-N(CH_3)_3^+OH^-$, strong base), or primary mine ($-NH^{3+}OH^-$, weak base). For cation-exchange with a sulfonic acid group the reaction is:

$$xRSO_3^- H^+(s) + M^{x+}(aq) \rightleftharpoons RSO_3^- M^{x+}(s) + xH^+(aq) \qquad (10A\text{-}1)$$

where M^{x+} is a cation with x positive charge, (*s*) indicates stationary phase, and (*aq*) indicates the mobile phase. The equilibrium constant for this reaction is:

$$K_{eq} = \frac{[RSO_3^- M^{x+}]_s[H^+]^x_{aq}}{[RSO_3^- H^+]^x_s[M^{x+}]_{aq}} \qquad (10A\text{-}2)$$

Different cations have different values of K_{eq} and are therefore retained on the column for different lengths of time. The time at which a given cation elutes from the column can be controlled by adjusting pH of the mobile phase. Most ion chromatography instruments use two mobile phase reservoirs containing buffers of different pH, and a programmable pump that can change the pH of the mobile phase during the separation.

IC is primarily a quantitative method, which is based on the fact that the size of IC signal (height or area of chromatogram peak) is proportional to the concentration of analyte (ion). The instrument is standardized with a series of standards with known concentrations. Figure 10-1 shows separation of common anions on an anion-exchange column.

Figure 10-1. A Chromatogram of anion standards separated on an ion exchange resin. Peak identities (1-7): fluoride, chloride, nitrite, bromide, nitrate, phosphate, and sulfate.

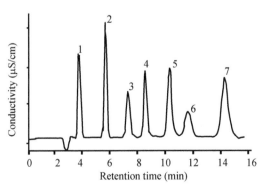

Basic Instrumentation: IC is a type of HPLC which separates and determines ions on columns packed with ion-exchange materials. Like conventional HPLC, an IC system typically consists of a sampler (manual or automatic), a high pressure pump, an analytical column, a detector and recorder (Figure 10-2). A **guard column** used to protect the analytical column is common in IC. A **suppressor** to reduce the back-ground signal is common in late model of IC instruments.

1. **IC column**: There are two types of ion-exchange packing, the **silica-based packing** and **polymer-based packing**. Silica-based packing has higher efficiency but has a limited pH range of stability and is incompatible with suppressor-based detector, while polymer-based packing has higher capacity and can be used over a broad pH range.

2. **IC detector**: The most common IC detector is conductivity detector, which is based on the fact that ions in solution can be detected by measuring the conductivity of the solution. However, in ion chromatography, the mobile phase contains ions that create a background conductivity. This problem can be greatly reduced by selectively removing the mobile phase ions after the analyte ion is eluted from the column. This is done by converting the mobile phase ions to a neutral form or removing them with an **eluent suppressor**, which consists of an ion exchange column or membrane (Figure 10-2).

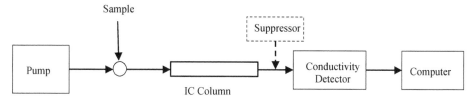

Figure 10-2 Components of a simple ion chromatograph.

C. Chemicals

1. Sodium fluoride (NaF, ACS grade, >99%).
2. Sodium chloride (NaCl, ACS grade, >99%).
3. Sodium bromide (NaBr, ACS grade, >99%).
4. Sodium phosphate (Na_2HPO_4, mono basic, ACS grade, >99%).
5. Sodium sulfate (Na_2SO_4, anhydrous, ACS grade, >99%).
6. Sodium bicarbonate ($NaHCO_3$, ACS reagent, >99.97%).
7. Sodium carbonate (Na_2CO_3, ACS reagent, >99.95%).

D. Apparatus

1. Basic IC system for anion analysis with or without suppressor.
2. Analytical balance.
3. Pipet, 100 µL, 1 mL, 5 mL.
4. Volumetric flask, 100, 1000 mL.

E. Procedure

1. Preparation of solutions

   a. *Preparation of 1000 mg/L individual anion stock standard solution*: The solid salts are dried at 105°C for 30 minutes, and let it cool to room temperature in a desiccator. To six 1 L volumetric flasks, weight 2.2100 g NaF, 1.6485 g NaCl, 1.2876 g NaBr, 1.4947 g Na_2HPO_4, 1.4786 g Na_2SO_4. Bring to mark with deionized water.

   b. *Preparation of 10 mg/L mixed mediate standard*: Pipet 1 mL of each stock standard into 100 mL volumetric flask. Dilute to mark with deionized water.

   c. *Preparation of calibration standards*: Pipet 1, 2, 5, 10, 20 mL of 10 mg/L mixed standard into 100 mL volumetric flasks. Bring to mark with deionized water. This yield mixed standards with 0.1, 0.2, 0.5, 1 and 2 mg/L of each anion.

   d. *Preparation of eluent solution*: Weigh 0.1428 g sodium bicarbonate ($NaHCO_3$) and 0.1908 g of sodium carbonate (Na_2CO_3) into 1 L volumetric flask. Bring to mark with deionized water.

2.   Preparation of instrument

   a.   IC condition
- Column: anion exchange column (Dionex AS4A column or similar).
- Anion suppressor device (optional).
- Detector: conductivity cell.
- Eluent solution: sodium bicarbonate 1.7 mM, sodium carbonate 1.8 mM.
- Flow rate: 0.5-1.0 mL/min.

   b.   Ion separation

- Run mixed standard to check separation of anions. Under normal conditions as specified in **2.a**, the elution order is F^-, Cl^-, Br^-, PO_4^{3-} and SO_4^{2-}. Confirm the identity of each peak with individual anion standard if necessary.
- If suppressor is equipped, run mixed standard with and without turning suppressor on. Compare chromatograms, and examine the impact of suppression on the IC signals.
- Save the IC conditions for quantitative analysis.

3.   Quantitative analysis

   a.   Run mixed calibration standards. Identify peak for each analyte anion at each concentration. Integrate each analyte peak, and record result in data table below.

   b.   Construct calibration curve for each analyte ion through linear regression analysis on a spreadsheet.

Standard		1	2	3	4	5	Calibration	
C (mg/L)		0.1	0.2	0.5	1	2	m	b
Integral area	F^-							
	Cl^-							
	Br^-							
	PO_4^{3-}							
	SO_4^{2-}							

4.   Sample analysis

   a.   Run sample (tap water, or any drinking waters). Identify each analyte anion peak based on retention time. Integrate each peak, and record result in data table below.

   b.   Calculate concentrations of analyte anions in unknown samples with calibration obtained.

Sample	1		2		3	
	Area	C (mg/L)	Area	C (mg/L)	Area	C (mg/L)
F^-						
Cl^-						
Br^-						
PO_4^{3-}						
SO_4^{2-}						

F. Result report

1.   Include one chromatogram of mixed standard to show separation and identification of anions.
2.   Construct external standard calibration with linear regression on a spreadsheet.
3.   Calculate concentration of anions present in your water samples.

G. Questions for discussion

1. Use F^-, Cl^-, Br^- as example to explain the elution order of anions in IC (hint: the retention of anion is determined by charge/size ratio).
2. Explain why pH has greater impact on retention time of PO_4^{3-} than other anions analyzed in this experiment.
3. UV/Vis detector can be connected directly with IC system. Discuss why UV/Vis detector is not common in IC analysis. Give an example in which UV/Vis detector is a good option for IC.

H. Reference

1. Skoog, D. A., F. J. Holler and S. R. Crouch, 2007. Principles of Instrumental Analysis. 6th ed. Thomson Brooks/Cole Publishing. Belmont, CA.
2. Bhattacharyya, L. and J. S. Rohrer, 2012. Applications of Ion Chromatography in the Analysis of Pharmaceutical and Biological Products. 1 Ed. Willey.
3. Seader, J. D., E. J. Henley and D. K. Roper, 2010. Separation Process Principles. 3rd Ed. Willey.
4. Sinniah, K. and K. Piers, 2001. Ion Chromatography: Analysis of Ions in Pond Waters. J. Chem. Educ. 78(3): 358.
5. USEPA Method 300.0, 1993. Determination of Inorganic Anions by Ion Chromatography. (Online access: **http://water.epa.gov/scitech/methods/cwa/bioindicators/upload/2007_07_10_methods_method_300_0.pdf)**

EXPERIMENT 10B: DETERMINATION OF MOLECULAR WEIGHT DISTRIBUTION OF POLYSACCHARIDES WITH SIZE EXCLUSION CHROMATOGRAPHY

A. Objectives

1. To learn basic principles and instrumentation of size exclusion chromatography.
2. To construct SEC calibration curve of molecular weight distribution analysis.
3. To determine the size distribution of polysaccharides.

B. Introduction

Basic principle: **Size-exclusion chromatography** (**SEC**) is a chromatographic method in which molecules in solution are separated by their size (or in more technical terms, their **hydrodynamic volume**), rather than their interaction with mobile/stationary phases. In SEC, the larger molecules elute earlier than the smaller molecules (Figure 10-3). When an aqueous solution is used to transport the sample through the column, the technique is known as **gel-filtration chromatography** (**GFC**); and it's called **gel permeation chromate-gramphy** (**GPC**) when an organic solvent is used as a mobile phase. SEC is a widely used polymer characteri-zation method because of its ability to provide **molecular weight distribu-tion** (**MWD**) analysis for polymers.

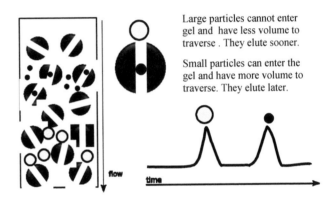

Large particles cannot enter gel and have less volume to traverse . They elute sooner.

Small particles can enter the gel and have more volume to traverse. They elute later.

Figure 10-3. Schematic representation of molecule separation in SEC based on size.

1. **Qualitative analysis**: Qualitative analyses in SEC are not common, as separation is governed by size, not composition. However, qualitative information about differences in molecular weight distributions (MWDs) may be derived from simple comparison of chromatograms of unknown samples.
2. **Quantitative analysis**: SEC is commonly used for determination of MWDs and molecular weight averages. MWDs are typically calculated and presented as the **cumulative weight fraction** MWD, or the **differential weight fraction** MWD. Most commercially available SEC software packages provide these options for plotting MWD data. Integrated SEC peak areas may also be used for determining the concentration of polymer in a matrix.

To use SEC for determination of molecular weight and MWD, it is necessary to establish structure/property relationships for polymers (calibration). Conversion of the retention time (volume) axis in SEC to a molecular weight axis can be accomplished in a number of ways including peak position (**conventional calibration**), **universal calibration**, broad standard (integral and linear), and determination of actual molecular weight.

In the **conventional calibration** method, a series of well characterized, narrow-fraction mole-cular weight standards of known peak molecular weight (*Mw*) are injected onto the SEC system and the retention times (volumes) determined. A plot of log(*Mw*) versus retention time (volume) is

136

constructed as shown in Figure 10-4. Depending on the type of SEC columns used, the calibration data points can be fit with either a linear or a third-order polynomial function

$$\log(Mw) = A + Br_T + Cr_T{}^2 + Dr_T{}^3 \qquad (10B-1)$$

where r_T is retention time. To eliminate the dependence on flow rate, retention volume (r_V) instead of retention time might be used

$$\log(Mw) = A + Br_V + Cr_V{}^2 + Dr_V{}^3 \qquad (10B-2)$$

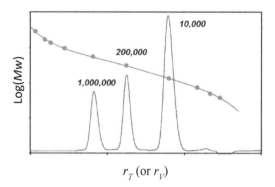

Figure 10-4 Conventional calibration of SEC.

Basic instrumentation: SEC is a specialized HPLC, thus, the basic theory and instrumentation are the same. The differences are the column and detector. Based on solvents used, SEC columns are classified to two categories: aqueous and organic.

1. **SEC column**: Unlike in other modes of HPLC, the separation efficiency comes only from the stationary phase, while the mobile phase should have no effect. The SEC packings are based on either **porous silica** or semirigid **organic gels** (e.g. styrene or divinylbenzene). In general, silica-based packings are more rugged than the organic packings.
2. **Detector**: Common spectroscopy detection techniques used in SEC are **refractive index** (RI) and **ultraviolet** (UV), which can determine the concentration of the particles in each fraction eluted. SEC detectors based on measurement of **laser light scattering** (LLS) and **viscosity** are also available.

C. Chemicals

1. Glacial acetic acid ($C_2H_4O_2$, reagent grade, >99%).
2. Sodium acetate, trihydrate ($CH_3COONa \cdot 3H_2O$, ACS grade, >99.5%).
3. Sodium hydroxide (NaOH, ACS grade, >97%).
4. Pullulan standard mixture with 8 molecular weight ranges (P-5, P-10, P-20, P-50, P-100, P-200, P-400, P-800) are available commercially.
5. Sample: chitsan, agar, starch.

D. Apparatus

1. Basic size exclusion chromatography.
2. Analytical balance.
3. Pipets, 1 mL.
4. Filtration equipment.
5. Beakers, 200-500 mL.
6. Electronic stirrer and heater.

E. Procedure

1. Preparation of standard and samples

    a. *Preparation of eluent*: Dilute 0.28 mL of concentrated glacial acetic acid in deionized water. Add 0.68 g sodium acetate trihydrate and dissolve thoroughly. Dilute to 1.0 L with deionized.

b. *Preparation of Pullulan standards mixture*: Dissolve 50 mg of pullulan standard fraction in eluent. Dilute to 100 mL with eluent. Do not stir or heat the solution. Let the pullulan particles hydrate overnight at 0 to 4 °C. Then carefully swirl the container to mix before injection.

c. *Preparation of polysaccharides sample*: Add 1 g sample (chitsan, agar and starch) to 100 mL of eluent. Stir overnight at room temperature. Dilute stock to 1/10 or 1/100, as appropriate. Heat might be applied to facilitate dissolution.

2. Preparation of instrument: The following instrumental conditions can be used for reference.

    a. Column: commercial SEC column (e.g. Zorbax BioPlus™ SE-250 or SE-450, or similar)
    b. Mobile Phase: 10 mM Acetate buffer (pH=7) as prepared in Step **1.c**; or 150 mM phosphate buffer (pH=7) if available.
    c. Flow Rate: 0.5-1.0 mL/min.
    d. Detection: RI (30 °C), and/or UV/Vis detector (200 nm).
    e. Injection Volume: 10-50 μL.

3. Molecular weight vs. retention time calibration

    a. Run the standard mixture. Assign each peak to molecular weight.
    b. Tabulate average molecular weight (Mw), log(Mw), retention time (r_T) and retention volume (r_V).

Standard	Mw (x1000)	log(Mw)	r_T (min)	r_V (mL)
P-5	5			
P-10	10			
P-20	20			
P-50	50			
P-100	100			
P-200	200			
P-400	400			
P-800	800			

    c. Plot log(Mw) versus r_T and r_V. Build a calibration curve with the standards (linear or polynomial). Show the equation and R^2.

4. Measurement of samples

    a. Run samples under the same condition. Identify elution time (or volume) for the peaks present in the unknown sample.
    b. Calculation of the molecular weight of your unknown using equation from the calibration.

Sample		Peak 1	Peak 2	Peak 3	Peak 4	Peak 5	Peak 6	Peak 7
chitsan	r_T (min)							
	Mw (x1000)							
agar	r_T (min)							
	Mw (x1000)							
starch	r_T (min)							
	Mw (x1000)							

5. Hardware shutdown and cleanup: Shut off main power of the instrument and the computer. There is hazardous waste generated.

F. Result report

1. Include a chromatogram of standard mixture to show the separation of weight standard.
2. Plot log(Mw) vs. retention time (r_T) and/or volume (r_V). Fit the plot with linear regression (if the plot is linear) or with a polynomial Eqn. (10B-1 and 10B-2).
3. Attach all sample chromatograms and identify peaks in the samples by comparing retention time of each peak present with the standard chromatogram. Calculate molecular weights of peaks present on the sample chromatograms with the calibration curve derived above.
4. (optional) Calculate weight ($\overline{M_w}$), number ($\overline{M_n}$) and z ($\overline{M_z}$) averages of samples if the software provides such functions.

G. Questions for discussion

1. Discuss why SEC is not a suitable technique for qualitative analysis.
2. Discuss the difference of the calibration methods between SEC and other chromatographic technique such as GC and HPLC.
3. Compare your result of the molecular weight distribution of chitsan, agar and starch with published data (Nguyen at al., 2009; Han et al., 2005).

H. Reference

1. Skoog, D. A., F. J. Holler and S. R. Crouch, 2007. Principles of Instrumental Analysis. 6th ed. Thomson Brooks/Cole Publishing. Belmont, CA.
2. Seader, J. D., E. J. Henley and D. K. Roper, 2010. Separation Process Principles. 3rd Ed. Willey.
3. Nguyen, S., S. Hisiger, M. Jolicoeur, F. M. Winnik and M. D. Buschmann, 2009. Fractionation and characterization of chitosan by analytical SEC and ^{1}H NMR after semi-preparative SEC. Carbohydrate Polymers. 75: 636–645.
4. Han, J-A., H. Lim and S.-T. Lim, 2005. Comparison between Size Exclusion Chromatography and Micro-Batch Analyses of Corn Starches in DMSO using Light Scattering Detector. Starch/Stärke. 57: 262–267.
5. Online introduction: **http://en.wikipedia.org/wiki/Size-exclusion_chromatography**

EXPERIMENT 10C: DETERMINATION OF LIGHT ABSORBING ANIONS IN ENVIRONMENTAL SAMPLES BY CAPILLARY ELECTROPHORESIS

A. Objectives

1. To learn the basic principles and instrumentation of capillary electrophoresis.
2. To determine the concentrations of UV absorbing anions in environmental samples.

B. Introduction

Basic principle: **Electrophoresis** is the motion of dispersed particles relative to a fluid under the influence of a spatially uniform electric field. For a given set of solution conditions, the velocity with which a particle moves divided by the magnitude of the electric field is called the **electrophoretic mobility**, which is directly proportional to the magnitude of the charge on the particle and inversely proportional to the size of the particle.

Electrophoretic separations are performed in two different formats: **slab electrophoresis** and **capillary electrophoresis**. Slab separation is carried out on a thin layer of porous semisolid gel containing aqueous buffer solution within its pores. Samples are introduced as spots or bands and a DC electric field is applied across the slab. Upon the completion of the separation, the separated species are visualized by staining in the way similar to thin layer chromatography (TLC).

In **capillary electrophoresis (CE)**, also called **capillary zone electrophoresis (CZE)**, the analytes are introduced into a capillary. The migration of the analytes is initiated by an electric field supplied to the electrodes by the high-voltage power supply between the source and destination vials. The analytes separate as they migrate due to their **electrophoretic mobility**, and are detected near the outlet end of the capillary.

Basic instrumentation: A basic capillary electrophoresis system is consisted of a **sample vial, source and destination vials**, a **capillary**, **electrodes**, a **high-voltage power supply**, a **detector**, and a **data output and handling device**.

The source vial, destination vial and capillary are filled with an **electrolyte** such as an aqueous buffer solution. To introduce the sample, the capillary inlet is placed into sample vial and then returned to the source vial. All ions, positive or negative, are pulled through the capillary in the same direction by electroosmotic flow. The different compounds separated by electrophoresis are generally detected during the run by a UV-visible absorbance detector or a fluorometer positioned at the cathode end of the capillary, and the signal is recorded and displayed as an **electropherogram**. Separated chemical compounds appear as peaks with different migration times in an electropherogram.

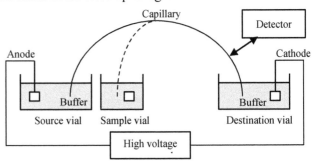

Figure 10-5 Capillary zone electrophoresis.

C. Chemicals

1. Sodium tetraborate decahydrate ($Na_2B_4O_7 \cdot 10H_2O$, ACS grade, >99.5%).
2. Methanol (CH_3OH, HPLC grade, >99.9%).
3. Sodium hydroxide (NaOH, ACS grade, >97%).
4. Sodium bromide (NaBr, ACS grade, >99%).
5. Sodium iodide (NaI, ACS grade, >99.5%).
6. Sodium nitrite ($NaNO_2$, ACS grade, >97%).
7. Sodium nitrate ($NaNO_3$, reagent grade, 99%).
8. Sodium thiosulfate ($Na_2S_2O_3$, reagent grade, >99%).
9. Potassium chromate (K_2CrO_4, ACS grade, >99%).
10. Potassium ferrocyanide ($K_4[Fe(CN)_6] \cdot 3H_2O$, ACS grade, >98.5%).

D. Apparatus

1. A capillary electrophoresis system with a fixed wavelength UV-Vis detector (200 nm).
2. Volumetric flasks: 100 mL, 1 L.
3. Pipet: 1-10 mL.

E. Procedure

1. Preparation of standard solution

    a. *Preparation of 1000 mg/L stock solution*: The solid salts are dried at 105°C for 30 minutes, and let it cool to room temperature in a desiccator. To seven 1 L flasks, weight 1.2876 g NaBr, 1.1811 g NaI, 1.4997 g $NaNO_2$, 1.4101 g $Na_2S_2O_3$, 1.6741 g K_2CrO_4, 1.3708 g $NaNO_3$, 1.9928 g $K_4[Fe(CN)_6] \cdot 3H_2O$. Bring to mark with deionized water.

    b. *Preparation of mixed stock standard*: Pipet 1 mL of each stock standard into 100 mL volumetric flask. Dilute to mark with deionized water. This gives a mixed standard of 10 mg/L of each anion.

    c. *Preparation of calibration standards*: Transfer 2, 5, 10, 20, 50 mL of mixed standard into 100 mL volumetric flasks. Bring to mark with deionized water. This yield mixed standards of 0.2, 0.5, 1, 2and 5 mg/L of each anion.

2. Preparation of electrolyte

    a. *Preparation of 100 mM sodium tetraborate stock solution*: Weigh 95.35 g sodium tetraborate into 1 L volumetric flask, add approximately 500 mL deionized water to dissolve the solid. Add 50 mL methanol, and bring to mark with deionized water.

    b. *Preparation of series of electrolyte solution*: Transfer 20, 30, 40, 50 mL of 100 mM sodium tetraborate stock solution into four 100 mL volumetric flasks. Bring to mark with 1/20 methanol/water. This gives electrolyte solution with 20, 30, 40, 50 mM of sodium tetraborate.

3. Preparation of instrument

    Adjust the instrument condition based on the system used. The following condition is based on HP CE capillary electrophoresis system, and only for reference or use as starting point.

    a. *Capillary column conditioning*: Pretreat the new capillary column with the following sequence: 1 M NaOH (10 min), 0.1 M NaOH (10 min), deionized water (30 min), and running electrolyte buffer (30 min). A 3-min capillary purge with carrier electrolyte solution was performed prior to each injection.

    b. *Separation conditions*: Capillary temperature was maintained at 25°C and separation voltage of -23 kV (current -150 μA). Samples and standards were injected by pressure of 20 s at 50 mbar. A 3-min capillary purge with carrier electrolyte solution was performed prior to each injection.

    c. Polyimide-coated fused-silica capillaries of 22 cm effective length or longer x50 μm I.D. The detection mode was UV direct, and the wavelength was 200 nm (or 254 nm).

5. Optimization of electrophoretic conditions

   a. First, a mixture of standards was separated and anions are identified. Standard of individual anion might be run to check mobility and assist identification of peaks. The same mixed standard solution is further tested to optimize the electrophoretic conditions as follow.

   b. *Influence of applied potential.*

      • Increase applied potential to increase the current from -100 to -175 μA.
      • Run mixed standard under same condition as in Step **5.a**. Watch the change in elution time of the last peak, and the separation of peaks.

   c. Influence of the concentration of electrolyte.

      • Run mixed standard under the same condition as in Step **5.a** for the electrolyte solutions with different concentrations of sodium tetraborate. Watch the change in elution time of the last peak, and the separation of peaks.

6. Once method is optimized, run standards and samples

   a. *Standard*: Run mixed calibration standards. Identify and integrate all analyte peaks. Record in the data table below. Construct standard calibration curve for each analyte.

Standard		1	2	3	4	5	Calibration	
C (mg/L)		0.2	0.5	1.0	2	5	m	b
Integral area	Br^-							
	I^-							
	NO_2^-							
	$S_2O_3^{2-}$							
	CrO_4^{2-}							
	NO_3^-							
	$Fe(CN)_6^{4-}$							

   b. *Samples*: Follow the same condition to run samples. Identify and integrate analyte peaks. Calculate analyte concentration in unknown sample with calibration curves established above.

Sample	1		2		3	
	Area	C (mg/L)	Area	C (mg/L)	Area	C (mg/L)
Br^-						
I^-						
NO_2^-						
$S_2O_3^{2-}$						
CrO_4^{2-}						
NO_3^-						
$Fe(CN)_6^{4-}$						

F. Result report

1. Include one electroferograms to show the separation of anions.
2. Tabulate the migration time, integral area for the standard solutions (data table in Step **6.a**) for each anion.

3. Construct calibration curve for each analyte by running linear regression analysis.
4. Tabulate the migration time, integral area for the standard solutions (data table in Step **6.b**) for each anion.
5. Calculate concentrations of analytes in unknown samples using the calibration obtained.

G. Questions for discussion

1. Both IC and CE can be used for separation of charged species. Compare differences between them.
2. Explain the impact of applied potential on the separation of ions based on the results from this experiment (Step **5.b**).
3. Explain the impact of concentration of electrolyte on the separation of ions based on the results from this experiment (Step **5.c**).

H.   Reference

1. Skoog, D. A., F. J. Holler and S. R. Crouch, 2007. Principles of Instrumental Analysis. 6th ed. Thomson Brooks/Cole Publishing. Belmont, CA.
2. Seader, J. D., E. J. Henley and D. K. Roper, 2010. Separation Process Principles. 3rd Ed. Willey.
3. García, D. C., K. Y. Chumbimuni-Torres and E. Carrilho. 2013. Capillary Electrophoresis and Microchip Capillary Electrophoresis: Principles, Applications, and Limitations. Wiley.
4. Janusa, A. M., L. J. Andermann, N. M. Kliebert and M. H. Nannie, 1998. Determination of Chloride Concentration Using Capillary Zone Electrophoresis: An Instrumental Analysis Chemistry Laboratory Experiment. J. Chem. Educ. 75(11): 1463.
5. Boyce, M., 1999. Separation and Quantification of Simple Ions by Capillary Zone Electrophoresis. A Modern Undergraduate Instrumentation Laboratory. J. Chem. Educ. 76(6): 815.
6. M.I. Turnes Carou, P. Lo´pez Mah´ıa, S. Muniategui Lorenzo, E. Ferna´ndez Ferna´ndez, D. Prada Rodr´ıguez, 2001. Capillary zone electrophoresis for the determination of light absorbing anions in environmental samples. J. Chromatogr. A. 918: 411–421.
7. Online introduction: **http://en.wikipedia.org/wiki/Capillary_electrophoresis**
8. Application note: Ion Analysis with Agilent Capillary Electrophoresis Systems (online access: **http://www.chem.agilent.com/library/applications/5990-5244en.pdf**).

CHAPTER 11

THERMAL ANALYSIS

Thermal analysis (TA) is a group of well-established techniques in which the property or physical quantity of a substance is measured as a function of temperature whilst the substance is subjected to a controlled temperature programme (IUPAC). They are widely used to obtain qualitative and quantitative information about the effects of various heat treatments on materials of all kinds, including plastics, ceramics, alloys, construction materials, minerals, foods and medicines etc. Heating is performed under strictly controlled conditions and can reveal changes in important properties of the material being studied. Such studies are of great practical importance in the use of materials. Table 11-1 is a list of thermoanalytical techniques and the properties/physical quantities measured in each technique. This chapter offers laboratory experiments for three most commonly used TA techniques, i.e. TGA, DTA and DSC. Details of the basic principles and instrumentation are introduced in each section.

Table 11-1 *Classification of thermoanalytical techniques (IUPAC).*

Property or Physical Quantity	Technique	Abbr.	Notes
Heat	Calorimetry		
Temperature	Thermometry		May also be described as heating or cooling curves.
Temperature Difference	Differential Thermal Analysis	**DTA**	A technique where the temperature difference between a sample and a reference material is measured.
Heat Flow Rate	Differential Scanning Calorimetry	**DSC**	A technique where the heat flow rate difference into a sample and a reference material is measured.
Mass	Thermogravimetry or	TG	The abbreviation TG has been used, but should be avoided, so that it is not confused with T_g (glass transition temperature).
	Thermogravimetric Analysis	**TGA**	
Dimensional and Mechanical Properties	Dynamic Mechanical Analysis	DMA	Moduli (storage/loss) are determined.
	Thermomechanical Analysis	TMA	Deformations are measured.
	Thermodilatometry	TD	Dimensions are measured.
Electrical Properties	Dielectric Thermal Analysis	DEA	Dielectric Constant/Dielectric Loss measured.
	Thermally Stimulated Current	TSC	Current measured.
Magnetic Properties	Thermomagnetometry		Often combined with TGA.
Gas flow	Evolved Gas Analysis	EGA	The nature and/or amount of gas / vapour is determined.
	Emanation Thermal Analysis	ETA	Trapped radioactive gas within the sample is released and measured.
Pressure	Thermomanometry		Evolution of gas is detected by pressure change.
	Thermobarometry		Pressure exerted by a dense sample on the walls of a constant volume cell is studied.

Optical Properties	Thermoptometry		A family of techniques in which an optical characteristic or property of a sample is studied.
	Thermoluminescence	TL	Emitted light measured
Property or Physical Quantity	**Technique**	**Abbr.**	**Notes**
Acoustic Properties	Thermosonimetry or Thermoacoustimetry		Techniques where the sound emitted (sonimetry) or absorbed (acoustimetry) by the sample is studied.
Structure	Thermodiffractometry		Techniques where the compositional or chemical nature of the sample are studied.
	Thermospectrometry		

General Reading

1. Skoog, D. A., F. J. Holler and S. R. Crouch, 2007. Principles of Instrumental Analysis. 6th ed. Thomson Brooks/Cole Publishing. Belmont, CA.
2. James W. R., E. M. Skelly Frame, G. M. Frame II, 2004. Undergraduate Instrumental Analysis, Sixth Edition, CRC Press.
3. IUPAC, 1998. Chapter 5, In: Compendium of Analytical Nomenclature (BS - IUPAC Chem Nomenclat). Wiley; 3rd edition.
4. Gabbott, P., 2007. Principles and Applications of Thermal Analysis. Wiley-Blackwell.
5. Menczel, J. D., and R. B. Prime, 2009. Thermal Analysis of Polymers, Fundamentals and Applications. Wiley.
6. Ehrenstein, G. W., G. Riedel, P. Trawiel, 2004. Thermal Analysis of Plastics: Theory and Practice. Hanser Gardner Pubns.

EXPERIMENT 11A: TGA ANALYSIS OF DEHYDRATION OF COPPER SULFATE PENTAHYDRATE

A. Objectives

1. To explain the basic principle and instrumentation of TGA.
2. To describe the dehydration reaction of hydrated compounds.
3. To interpret the analytical information from TGA curves.

B. Introduction

Basic principle of TGA: **Thermogravimetric analysis** (TGA) is a technique in which the mass of a substance is recorded as a function of temperature or time as the sample is subjected to a controlled temperature program in a controlled atmosphere. The plot of mass as function of temperature or time is called **thermogravimetric curve (thermogram)**. In a thermogravimetric curve, the abscissa (x-axis) can be displayed as temperature (or time) and the ordinate (y-axis) can be displayed as weight (mg) or weight percent (%).

Figure 11-1 shows a typical thermogravimetric curve of copper sulfate pentahydrate ($CuSO_4 \cdot 5H_2O$). The decrease in weight (mass) corresponds to losses of water at 63°C, 109°C and 220°C respectively. The amount of mass loss is proportional to number of waters lost at each stage (2:2:1).

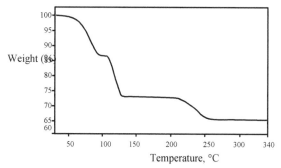

Figure 11-1 Thermogram of copper sulfate pentahydrate.

Basic instrumentation of TGA: TGA relies on a high degree of precision in three measurements: mass change, temperature, and temperature change. Therefore, a basic TGA instrument consists of a micro-balance (also called thermobalance), furnace, sample holder, temperature measurement and control unit, an enclosure for establishing the required atmosphere, and a recorder recording and displaying the data (Figure 11-2).

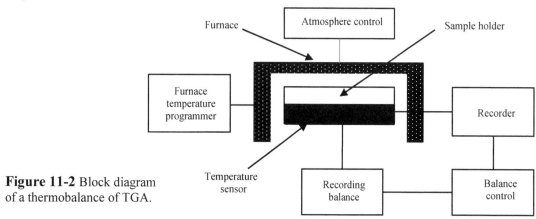

Figure 11-2 Block diagram of a thermobalance of TGA.

1. **Thermobalance**: A thermobalance is used for weighing a sample continuously while it is being heated or cooled. The basic requirements of an automatic recording thermobalance include accuracy, sensitivity, reproducibility, and capacity. Thermobalances are of two types, null point

and deflection type. Thermobalances used in TGA instruments usually have measuring range from 0.0001 mg to 1 g depending on sample container used.

Based on the configuration of thermobalance, TGA instruments can be divided into two general types: vertical and horizontal balance. Vertical balance instruments have a sample pan hanging from the balance or located above the balance on a sample stem. It is necessary to calibrate these instruments in order to compensate for buoyancy effects due to the variation in the density of the purge gas with temperature, as well as the type of gas. Vertical balance instruments generally do not have reference pan and are incapable of true DTA or DSC measurements. Horizontal balance instruments normally have two pans (sample and reference) and can perform DTA and DSC measurements.

2. **Furnace**: The temperature and control system must provide linear heating at over the whole working temperature range and is able to maintain any fixed temperature. A wide temperature range generally -150°C to 2000°C of furnaces is used in different instruments depending on the models. Nichrome furnace can be used up to 1300°C, whereas platinum and its alloy is employed for temperature up to 1750°C and tungsten or molybdenum (Mo) for higher range up to 2000°C. Subambient studies require a cooling accessory such as an ice-water bath, mechanical refrigeration, or liquid nitrogen cooling.

3. **Sample container**: Sample container materials commonly available include aluminum, platinum, silica, and alumina (Al_2O_3). The shape of sample containers ranges from flat plates to deep crucible of various capacities.

4. **Temperature measurement and control**: Temperature measurement is commonly done using thermocouples. Temperature may be controlled using a program controller with two thermo-couples, the signal from one actuates the control system whilst the second thermocouple is used to record the temperature.

5. **Recorder**: Graphic recorders are preferred to meter type recorders. X-Y recorders are commonly used as they plot weight directly against temperature. The present instruments facilitate micro-processor controlled operation and digital data acquisition/processing using personal computer.

6. **Atmosphere control for furnace and sample holder**: Inert (He, N_2) or reactive gas (O_2) can be used to circulate in the sample and reference chamber. Some systems also have the capability of operating at high and low pressure.

Application of TGA: TGA is commonly used to determine selected characteristics of materials that exhibit either mass loss or gain due to decomposition, oxidation, or loss of volatiles (such as moisture). The ability of TGA to generate fundamental quantitative data from almost any class of materials has led to its widespread use in every field of science and technology. Key application areas are listed below:

- **Thermal stability**: related materials can be compared at elevated temperatures under the required atmosphere. The TGA curve can help to elucidate decomposition mechanisms.
- **Kinetic studies**: a variety of methods exist for analyzing the kinetic features of all types of mass loss or gain, either with a view to predictive studies, or to understanding the controlling chemistry.
- **Material characterization**: TGA and DTG (derivative thermogravimetry) curves can be used to "fingerprint" materials for identification or quality control.
- **Corrosion studies**: TGA provides an excellent means of studying oxidation, or reaction with other reactive gases or vapors.
- **Simulation of industrial processes**: the thermobalance/furnace may be thought of as a mini-reactor, with the ability to mimic the conditions in some types of industrial reactor.
- **Compositional analysis**: by carefully selecting temperature program and gaseous environment, many complex materials or mixtures may be analyzed by selectively decomposing or removing

their components. This approach is regularly used to analyze composition of materials, e.g. filler content in polymers, carbon black in oils, ash and carbon in coals, and the moisture content of many substances.

Copper sulfate pentahydrate (cupric sulfate pentahydrate, $CuSO_4 \cdot 5H_2O$): the pentahydrate of copper sulfate ($CuSO_4$) is the most common salt form of $CuSO_4$. The anhydrous form of CuSO4 is a pale green or gray-white powder, whereas the pentahydrate is bright blue. The anhydrous form occurs in nature as a rare mineral known as chalcocyanite. The hydrated copper sulfate occurs in nature as chalcanthite (pentahydrate), and two more rare ones: bonattite (trihydrate) and boothite (heptahy-drate).

The blue hydrated copper sulfate has been used to demonstrate many thermal techniques. When heated, copper sulfate pentahydrate loses its hydration water. It first loses two molecules of water at a 63°C, followed by two more at 109°C and finally, the last water molecule is lost at 220°C. At a temperature of 650°C, copper sulfate gets decomposed into copper(II) oxide (CuO) and sulphur trioxide (SO_3). The following is the sequence of dehydration/decomposition reaction when $CuSO_4 \cdot 5H_2O$ is heated.

$$CuSO_4 \cdot 5H_2O \rightarrow CuSO_4 \cdot 3H_2O \rightarrow CuSO_4 \cdot H_2O \rightarrow CuSO_4 \rightarrow CuO + SO_3$$

C. Chemicals

1. Copper sulfate pentahydrate ($CuSO_4 \cdot 5H_2O$, ACS, $\geq 98\%$).

D. Apparatus

1. Analytical balance (0.0001 g).
2. Basic TGA system.
3. Aluminum sample pans.

E. Procedure

Depending on the specific instrument used, a detailed operational procedure should be prepared by the instructor. The following general procedures are for a basic TGA instruments, and might not be suitable for the specific instrument used.

> **Safety Precautions:**
> 1. The thermobalance in TGA instrument is delicate, use caution when loading/removing sample onto/from sample holder.
> 2. Avoid touching the sample container and inside of the TGA furnace with bare hand. Wear gloves and use forceps when preparing sample. Use a small tweezer to handle the sample container.
> 3. The TGA furnace can be very **HOT**. After running an experiment, allow the furnace to cool down before opening the furnace and removing sample from the sample holder.

1. Turn on the main power of the instrument. Turn on the computer and start the software program. Make sure the communication between instrument and computer is established.
2. Open the atmosphere gas (nitrogen or air) valve and the TGA release valve. Adjust flow rate if necessary.
3. Pre-weight 5-10 mg copper sulfate pentahydrate to sample container with an analytical balance.
4. Open the furnace assembly. Carefully place the sample to the sample holder. Close the furnace assembly.
5. Set up the experiment parameter as follow. Other parameters (such as gas flow rate) may be required for some TGA instruments.

Start Temp.	End Temp.	Heat Rate	Hold time	Gas
25°C	350°C	10°C/min	0	N_2 or air

6. Start the heating program.
7. After the run, save the TGA curve (thermogram) if a computer is used to record the result.

8. After the furnace is cooled, open the furnace and remove the sample container.
9. Repeat Step 3-8 for more samples.
10. After all experiments are conducted, close the purge gas and turn off TGA and computer.

F. Result report

1. Include your TGA curve(s) of copper sulfate pentahydrate in lab report.
2. If an X-Y recorder is used, measure the mass loss for each step. Fill in the blank in the following form. If a computer is used, use the software to calculate the mass loss (%) of each reaction step.
3. Calculate the theoretical mass loss (%) for each step based on the reactions listed below. Compare theoretical mass losses with the measured ones.

	Reaction	Theoretical mass loss (%)	Experimental mass loss (%)
1	$CuSO_4 \cdot 5H_2O = CuSO_4 \cdot 3H_2O + 2H_2O$		
2	$CuSO_4 \cdot 3H_2O = CuSO_4 \cdot H_2O + 2H_2O$		
3	$CuSO_4 \cdot H_2O = CuSO_4 + H_2O$		
4			
	Total loss (%)		

G. Questions for discussion

1. Discuss the main sources of uncertainties in TGA analysis.
2. Occasionally, TGA experiments cannot indicate "true" sample decomposition. Explain why this is the case.
3. Explain how sample mass, sample shape, and position of the sample on the sample pan can affect data in a TGA experiment.

H. Supplementary experiments

1. **Thermogravimetric (TGA) verification** -- Calcium oxalate monohydrate

   Calcium oxalate monohydrate ($CaC_2O_4 \cdot H_2O$) is a well characterized material that has three distinct weight loss events that occur during heating: H_2O, CO, CO_2 (Figure 11-3).

   $$CaC_2O_4 \cdot H_2O \rightarrow CaC_2O_4 \rightarrow CaCO_3 \rightarrow CaO + CO_2$$

   To verify the performance of a TGA instrument, following similar procedure in the main experiment to conduct an experiment using calcium oxalate monohydrate. Compare the mass loss measured from the TGA curve and the theoretical values (Figure 11-3).

2. **Derivative thermogravimetry** (DTG)

   Figure 11-3 also shows the derivative of the TGA curve (DTG). DTG is often useful in revealing extra detail, such as the small event around 400°C, which would not have been seen on the TGA curve itself. A DTG curve presents the rate of mass change (dm/dt) as a function of temperature, or time (t) when substance is heated at uniform rate. The DTG curve is sometimes used to determine inflection points on the TGA curve, to provide reference points for weight change measurements in systems where the mass losses are not completely resolved. Most commercial TGA software provides function to obtain DTG from the TGA curve.

3. **Hyphenated techniques** -- Calcium oxalate monohydrate

   TGA is inherently quantitative, but gives no qualitative information. The ability to analyze the volatile products during a mass loss is of great value. By coupling a thermogravimetric analyzer

(TGA) with a mass spectrometer (MS), gases evolving from the sample as it is heated in a TGA can be identified by the MS. Some TGA manufacturers provide MS as optional component of TGA instrument.

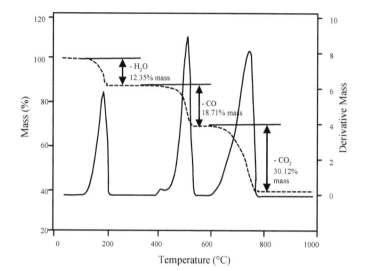

Figure 11-3 TGA thermogram and derivative thermogram of calcium oxalate monohydrate

I. Reference

1. Skoog, D. A., F. J. Holler and S. R. Crouch, 2007. Principles of Instrumental Analysis. 6th edition. Thomson Brooks/Cole Publishing. Belmont, CA.
2. James W. R., E. M. Skelly Frame, G. M. Frame II, 2004. Undergraduate Instrumental Analysis, 6th edition. CRC Press.
3. Brown, M. E., 2001. Introduction to Thermal Analysis. Kluwer Academic Publisher, London.
4. Gabbott, P., 2007. Principles and Applications of Thermal Analysis. Wiley-Blackwell.
5. D'Amico, T., C. J. Donahue and E. A. Rais, 2008. Thermal Analysis of Plastics. J. Chem. Educ. 85(3): 404-407.

EXPERIMENT 11B: DTA ANALYSIS OF THERMAL PROPERTIES OF BENZOIC ACID

A. Objectives

1. To explain the basic principle and basic instrumentation of DTA.
2. To obtain DTA thermogram of benzoic acid.
3. To interpret the analytical information from DTA therrmogram.

B. Introduction

Basic principle of DTA: In **differential thermal analysis** (DTA), the sample and an inert reference (such as Al_2O_3) are subjected to identical thermal cycles, while recording any temperature difference between them. This differential temperature (ΔT) is then plotted against time, or temperature (**thermogram**). Reactions occurring in the sample, either **exothermic** (heat released) or **endothermic** (heat absorbed), can be detected relative to the inert reference. Thus, a DTA curve provides information on the transformations that have occurred in sample, such as glass transitions, crystallization, melting and sublimation. The area under a DTA peak is the enthalpy change and is not affected by the heat capacity of the sample.

Usually, the temperature program is set in such a way that the temperature of the sample (T_s) increases linearly with the time. The difference in temperature (ΔT) between the sample (T_s) and reference (T_r) is monitored and plotted against sample temperature to give a differential thermogram (Figure 11-4). Exothermic (e.g. oxidation) process is plotted upwards, indicating that the temperature of the sample is greater than that of the reference. Endothermic process (e.g. melting) is plotted downwards, indicating that the temperature of the sample lags behind that of reference.

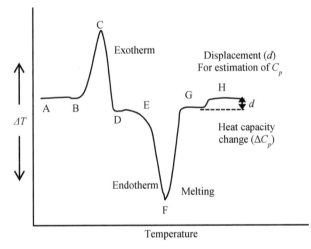

Figure 11-4 DTA thermogram showing exothermic and endothermic processes. Exothermic reaction starts and give rise to a peak BCD with a maximum at point C, corresponding to the temperature at which maximum rate of heat evolution. Area of the peak BCD is proportional to the amount of reacting material. For endothermic reaction, the peak EFG shows that the ΔT will be negative because heat is absorbed. Baseline shift from AB to DE and from G to H is due to change in heat capacity of the sample with temperature.

When no reaction occurs in the sample, the temperature of the sample (T_s) remains similar to that of reference substance (T_r), i.e. temperature difference ΔT will be near zero. When a reaction starts, a peak develops on the curve for the temperature difference ΔT against temperature of furnace or time. Note that the levels of base lines of extotherm curve, AB and DE are at different levels above x-axis. This is due to the fact that heat capacity of the sample has changed as a result of the exothermic process.

Peak areas depend upon sample mass (m), **enthalpy change** (ΔH) of the process and geometric and conductivity factors such as heating rate f and particle size. If latter two factors are expressed by a factor K called calibration factor, then peak area can be express as follows.

152

$$Peak\ area\ (A) = \pm\Delta H m K \qquad (11\text{B-}1)$$

K is also called calibration constant which is temperature dependent (the similar K value in DSC is not temperature dependent). It can be determined by calibrating DTA with some standard. Once the value of K at a particular temperature is known, the peak area can be to determine the mass of sample or energy (enthalpy changes) of a reaction. Usually, the sample peak area is compared with a standard (**e.g.** indium, melt point: 156.4°C, $\Delta H_{fusion} = 28.5$ J g^{-1}) undergoing an enthalpy change at a similar temperature T under the same conditions.

***B**asic instrumentation of DTA*: A typical DTA consists of sample and reference holders, a furnace assembly, a temperature programmer, a recording system and an enclosure for establishing the required atmosphere. The key feature is the existence of two thermocouples connected to a microvolt amplifier. One thermocouple is placed in reference holder, while the other is placed in the sample holder (Figure 11-5).

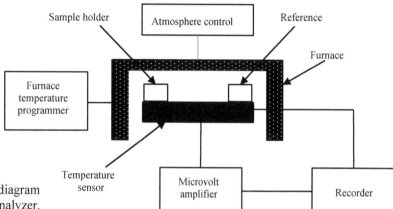

Figure 11-5 Schematic diagram of a differential thermal analyzer.

- **The furnace assembly**: like in TGA, the temperature and control system must provide linear heating at over the whole working temperature range and is able to maintain any fixed temperature.
- **Sample and reference holder with temperature detector**: designed to accommodate even a small quantity of material and to give maximum thermal effect. It can be of Pt, Ni, stainless steel, Ag and alloy such as Pt-Rh. Certain ceramic material such as sintered alumna, silica, quartz etc. have recommended as material for specimen holder.
- **Temperature programmer**: uniform rate of heating of the furnace is ensured through electronic temperature regulator.
- **Amplifier and recorder**: automatic pen and ink electronic recorder are still used in older models. Later models are commonly connected to a computer which controls the temperature program and record the signals.
- **Atmosphere control equipment for furnace and specimen holders**: purge gas compatible with the sample, sample container, and sample holder needs to be selected. Inert gases (e.g. Ar, N_2 or He) are commonly used for superambient operation while dry He is preferred for subambient operation. Purge gas flow rates on the order of 10 cm^3/min are generally used.

Application: The principal use of DTA is, and all the other uses of DTA are derived from, the measurement of transition temperature, transition enthalpy and heat capacity. Properties measured by DTA (and DSC) include phase changes, glass transition, melting, purity, evaporation, sublimation, crystallization, pyrolysis, heat capacity, polymerization, denaturation / aggregation, compatibility etc.

C. Chemicals

1. Benzoic acid (C_6H_5COOH, ACS grade, >99.5%).
2. Alumina (high purity synthetic sapphire, corundum, α-Al_2O_3).

D. Apparatus

1. Analytical balance (0.0001 g).
2. Basic DTA system.
3. Al_2O_3 crucibles used as sample and reference container.

E. Procedure

1. *Preparation of the instrument*: Depending on the instrument used, follow the users' manual or consult the instructor to prepare the instrument. Typical DTA instrument needs to be turned on and equilibrate before running any heating program.

> **Safety Precautions:**
> 1. The sample/reference holder area is fragile and easily damaged for typical DTA. If you have questions regarding loading/removing sample, ask your instructor or TA for assistance.
> 2. Avoid touching the sample container and inside of the DTA furnace with bare hand. Wear gloves and use forceps when preparing sample. Use a small tweezer to handle the sample/reference container.
> 3. The DTA furnace can be very **HOT**. After running an experiment, allow the furnace to cool down before opening the furnace and removing sample from the sample holder.

2. Procedure

   a. Open the atmosphere gas valve. It may be necessary to set the flow rate of the atmosphere gas.
   b. Switch on the instrument and wait for 10 minutes. Turn the computer to establish communication between DTA and computer.
   c. Set the heating program including range (start and end) temperature, rate of heating etc.

Start Temp.	Hold Time	End Temp.	Hold Time	Heating Rate	
Ambient	0	400°C	0	10-20°C/min	

   d. Load two empty Al_2O_3 crucibles onto sample and reference holders. Start the heating program.
   e. After the run is completed, save the thermogram as blank.
   f. Prepare the sample (benzoic acid) by powdering up to < 150 mesh in agate mortar to get a homogeneous sample.
   g. After the furnace has been cooled down, remove the sample crucible from DTA. At this point, leave the reference crucible in DTA.
   h. Weight small amount of benzoic acid (<10 mg) into the sample crucible.
   i. Load the sample crucible onto sample holders carefully.
   j. Start the heating program and record the DTA curve (thermogram). Save the thermogram as your sample.
   k. Repeat Step **d-i** for more samples.

3. Hardware shutdown

   a. After all samples are completed, wait for the furnace to be cooled down, remove the sample and reference containers from the furnace carefully.
   b. Turn off the instrument and computer. Shut off the purge gas.

F. Result report

1. Attach the thermogram(s) in your lab report.
2. Recognize the peak(s) on your thermograms. Are they exothermic or endothermic?

3. Identify the processes associated with the DTA peak(s). Look up the parameters (melting and boiling points) of the respective processes from literature, compare your result with the reported ones.

G. Questions for discussion

1. Discuss the main sources of uncertainties in DTA analysis.
2. Explain why it's useful to couple DTA with TGA and mass spectrometry.
3. The following diagrams are DTA curves obtained for the same sample at different heating rates. On the left, the differential temperature is plotted against temperature, and the DTA curves are broadened when heating rate increases. On the right, the differential temperature is plotted against time, and the DTA curves are broadened when heating rate decreases. Explain this phenomenon.

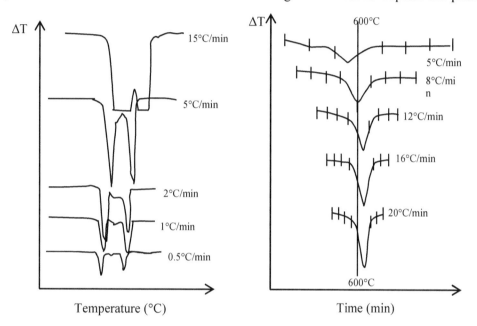

H. Supplementary experiments: Characterization of Polymeric Material with DTA

Introduction: DTA is a very useful technique for the characterization of polymeric materials. Figure 11-6 illustrates the types of physical and chemical changes in polymeric materials that can be studied by DTA. Four transitions can be recognized: glass transition, crystallization, melting and oxidation, abbreviated as T_g, T_c, T_m and T_d respectively.

Glass transition temperature (T_g) is the characteristic temperature at which glassy, amorphous polymer becomes flexible or rubberlike because onset of the concerted motion of large segments of the polymer molecules. There is a more detailed introduction on glass transition and how to determine T_g (page 163).

Crystallization of polymers, an exothermic process, is a process associated with partial alignment of their molecular chains. When polymer is heated to characteristic temperature (T_c), microcrystals begin to form, giving off heat. The enthalpy change of this process can be measured by compare the integral area of sample with a reference material with known enthalpy change at similar temperature (Eqn. 11B-1).

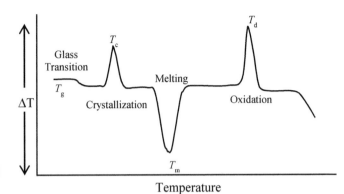

Figure 11-6 DTA curve of a typical
polymeric sample.

Polymers are not able form 100% crystals, and always have at least two phases, amorphous and crystalline. Therefore, it is not its glass transition, T_g, but its **crystallinity** that determines whether the material is a plastic or rubber. The crystals (hard phases) and rubbery (soft phases) make the polyethylene behave as a plastic with toughness, and not as a rubber. Both melting and crystallization cover a specific range of temperatures around the peak temperatures, T_m and T_c. The uncompleted crystallization process is responsible for the re-crystallization on heating. Hence, when the polymer is heated, re-crystallization will take place at temperatures before the melting temperature of the existing crystals.

The exothermic **oxidation** peak is only encountered when the sample is exposed to oxygen, and would be absent in inert atmosphere (N_2, He etc.).

Experiment: Follow the similar procedures illustrated in the main experiment, conduct the DTA experiments for polymer samples (LDPE, HDPE, Nylon etc.) with inert and/or oxidizing atmosphere. Determine T_c, T_m, T_d for the polymer material samples.

I. Reference

1. Skoog, D. A., F. J. Holler and S. R. Crouch, 2007. Principles of Instrumental Analysis. 6th ed. Thomson Brooks/Cole Publishing. Belmont, CA.
2. James W. R., E. M. Skelly Frame, G. M. Frame II, 2004. Undergraduate Instrumental Analysis, Sixth Edition, CRC Press.
3. Gabbott, P., 2007. Principles and Applications of Thermal Analysis. Wiley-Blackwell.
4. Menczel, J. D., R. B. Prime, 2009.Thermal Analysis of Polymers, Fundamentals and Applications. Wiley.
5. Wendlandt, W. W., 1961. Reaction kinetics by differential thermal analysis: A physical chemistry experiment. J. Chem. Educ. 38 (11): 571.

EXPERIMENT 11C: DETERMINATION OF SPECIFIC HEAT CAPACITY (C_p) OF MATERIALS BY DSC

A. Objectives

1. To explain the basic principle and basic instrumentation of DSC.
2. To determine specific heat capacity of organic compounds with DSC.
3. To interpret the analytical information from DSC thermogram.

B. Introduction

Basic principle of DSC: **Differential scanning calorimetry** (DSC) is a thermoanalytical **technique** in which the difference in energy inputs into a sample (and/or its reaction product(s)) and a reference is measured as a function of temperature whilst the sample and reference are subjected to a controlled temperature program (IUPAC). Both the sample and reference are maintained at nearly the same temperature throughout the experiment. Generally, the temperature program for a DSC analysis is designed such that the sample holder temperature increases linearly as a function of time. The reference should have a well-defined **heat capacity** over the range of temperatures to be scanned.

On a typical DSC curve (Figure 11-7), the x-axis is temperature and the y-axis is heat flow rate (Φ in W or J s^{-1}). Similar to DTA curve, the positive peak (C) and negative peak (F) represent **endothermic** and **exothermic** reactions respectively. The peak area in DSC is proportional to the amount of sample (m, g or mol), the **enthalpy change** (ΔH) and can be expressed as

$$Peak\ area (A) = \pm \Delta H m K \qquad (11C\text{-}1)$$

where K is a constant called calibration factor. With Eqn. 11C-1, enthalpy change for a reaction can be determined directly from peak area if the value of K is known. However, there is no guarantee that K is temperature independent for a specific instrument. Hence, standard calibration of K with reference material (e.g. indium, tin, zinc etc.) at the same temperature range of the process in study is necessary (Gatta et. Al, 2006).

Alternately, enthalpy change can be determined by comparing the ΔH of the sample with the known ΔH of the standard

$$\Delta H_s = \Delta H_r \times \frac{A_s}{A_r} \times \frac{m_r}{m_s} \qquad (11C\text{-}2)$$

where ΔH_s and ΔH_r are enthalpy changes, m_s and m_r are masses, and A_s and A_r are areas of peaks of sample and standard, respectively.

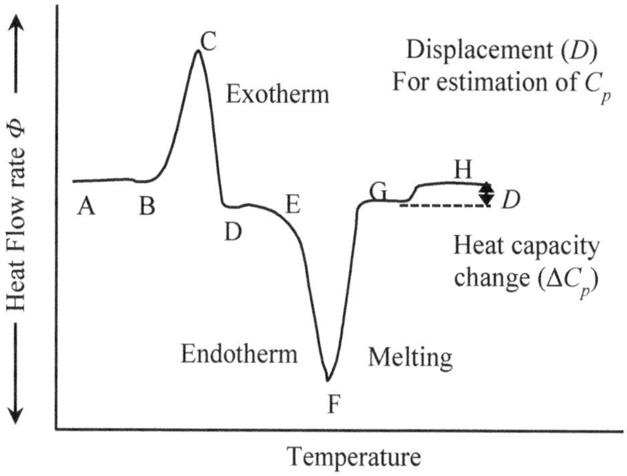

Figure 11-7 A DSC curve showing exothermic and endothermic processes.

DSC technique is not only sensitive for the determination of ΔH, it is also very sensitive for the determination of **heat capacities** (C_p). When a sample is subjected to a heating program in DSC, the rate of heat flow into the sample is proportional to its heat capacity. This is reflected by shift of the base line as illustrated in Figure 11-7. The value of C_p may be determined at a particular temperature by measuring this displacement (D):

$$C_p = k \times \frac{D}{\beta \times m} \qquad (11C\text{-}3)$$

where $D = dH/dt$ is heat flow to sample (J s^{-1} or mJ s^{-1}, corrected by blank) which is the displacement of sample on the DSC curve relative to the blank (Figure 11-7), β is heating rate (K s^{-1}), m (g or mol) is sample mass and k (dimensionless) is instrument calibration constant. On a DSC curve, D is the vertical distance between the sample and blank lines (Figure 11-8). The unit of C_p is determined by units of D, β and m.

In practice we normally measure the base line shift by reference to a base line obtained for empty sample and reference containers. To further minimize experimental error we usually determine heat capacity of the sample by comparing with the known heat capacity of the standard as

$$\frac{D_s}{D_r} = \frac{C_{ps} \times m_s}{C_{pr} \times m_r} \qquad (11C\text{-}4)$$

where D_s and D_r are displacements, C_{ps} and C_{pr} are heat capacities, m_s and m_r are mass of sample and standard, respectively. Since the heat capacity is temperature dependent, the displacements of sample and standard should be measured at the same temperature.

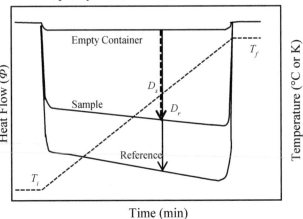

Figure 11-8 DSC curves for the determination of heat capacity. T_i and T_f are initial and final temperatures.

***B**asic instrumentation of DSC*: Two types of DSC instrument are commercially available: **heat flux** and **power compensation DSC**. Most DSC instruments are of the heat-flux design.

In heat-flux DSC, sample and reference are in the same chamber. Both of them are heated in the same rate, and the difference in temperature between them is recorded. In power-compensation DSC, sample and reference are not in same chamber. Both of them are heated until the final temperature is equal, and the supplied energies for the two samples are different, and the difference is recoded.

A typical heat flux DSC (Figure 11-9) comprises the sample and reference holders, the temperature control and recording system, the heat sink, the furnace and purge gas. Heat is supplied into the sample and the reference through heat sink and heat resistor. Heat flow is proportional to the heat difference of heat sink and holders. Heat sink has the enough heat capacity compared to the sample. In case an endothermic or exothermic reaction occurs in sample, the heat released or absorbed is compensated by heat sink. Thus the temperature difference between the sample and the reference is kept constant. The difference in the amount of heat supplied to the sample and the reference is proportional to the temperature difference of both holders. By calibrating with the standard material, the quantitative measurement of unknown sample is achievable.

The primary signals from the cell (mV for T, and μV for ΔT) are boosted with low noise high gain amplifiers. The control of the furnace, signal acquisition, and data storage and analysis are usually handled by a computer.

Temperature calibration is carried out by running standard materials, usually very pure metals (e.g. indium) with known melting points. Energy calibration may be carried out by using either known heats of fusion for metals, commonly indium, or known heat capacities. Synthetic sapphire (corundum, or aluminum oxide) is readily available as a heat capacity standard, and the values of heat capacity have been accurately determined over a wide temperature range (Appendix 11A).

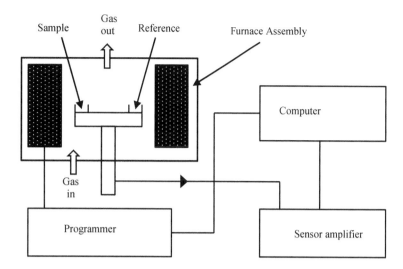

Figure 11-9 The block diagram of heat flux DSC

A variety of sample pans can be used for different purposes. The best quantitative results for polymers are obtained from thin samples crimped flat between the pan and a lid. Hermetically-sealed pans are used for liquids with high vapor pressure, or when it is necessary to retain volatiles. Very high-pressure can be achieved using O-ring or screw-threaded seals. For materials that react with aluminum, or for higher temperatures, pans may be made from stainless steel, Inconel (Ni-Cr alloy), gold, alumina, graphite, silica or platinum.

Typical purge gases are air and nitrogen, though helium is useful for efficient heat transfer and removal of volatiles. Argon is preferred as an inert purge when examining samples that can react with nitrogen. The experiment can also be carried out under vacuum or under high pressure if the instrument used provides such capability.

Applications: DSC can be used to measure a number of characteristic properties of a sample. With DSC, it is possible to observe fusion and crystallization events as well as glass transition temperatures T_g. DSC can also be used to study oxidation, as well as other chemical reactions. In this experiment, heat capacity of selected samples will be measured with standard reference material.

C. Material and Chemicals

1. Sapphire standard (α-Al_2O_3).
2. Silicone oil.
3. Low density polyethylene – LDPE.
4. Indium calibration standard (for temperature and heat flow calibration, >99.999%).

D. Apparatus

1. Analytical balance (0.0001 g).
2. Basic DSC system.
3. Aluminum pan or crucible used as sample and reference container.

E. Procedure

1. *Preparation of the instrument*: Depending on the instrument used, follow the users' manual or consult the instructor to prepare the instrument. Typical DSC instrument needs to be turned on and equilibrate before running any heating program. Most DSC instruments used today has computer to control the instrument, record signal and process data. Turn on the computer and the main power switch of DSC, make sure the communication between instrument and computer is established. Open purge gas.

2. *DSC calibration*: A useful test of a DSC system performance is to conduct a temperature and heat flow calibration with pure indium metal standard (melting point T_m = 156.6°C, heat of fusion H_f =

28.62 J/g). Indium is widely used as a DSC calibration standard. Consult the instructor for details of this calibration. The follow table lists some parameters which can be used to conduct temperature and heat flow calibration. A full scale calibration (Richardson and Charsley, 1998) for temperature and heat flow is not required for this experiment.

Calibration	Pan	Standard	Start Temp.	End Temp.	Heating Rate	Atmosphere
Temp./Heat flow	Aluminum	Indium	120°C	180°C	10°C/min	N$_2$, 50 cm^3/min

Safety Precautions:
1. The sample/reference holder area is fragile and easily damaged for typical DSC. If you have questions regarding loading/removing sample, ask your instructor or TA for assistance.
2. Avoid touching the sample container and inside of the DSC furnace with bare hand. Wear gloves and use forceps when preparing sample. Use a small tweezer to handle the sample/reference container.
3. The DSC furnace can be very **HOT**. After running an experiment, allow the furnace to cool down before opening the furnace and removing sample from the sample holder.

3. Experiment procedure

   a. *Set up DSC parameters*: Start the program software, set up the heating program and other instrument conditions. The following is recommended conditions for this experiment which may be modified for the instrument used.

Start Temp.	Isothermal	End Temp.	Ramp	Isothermal	Atmosphere
40.0 °C	5 min	200.0 °C	20.0 °C/min	5 min	N$_2$, 50 cm^3/min

   b. *Empty container*: Run heating program with both sample and reference containers empty to determine background heat flow to be subtracted from the standard and samples.

   c. *Determination of instrument calibration constant, k*

      i.   Tare the built-in microbalance with both sample and reference containers empty.
      ii. Pre-weigh the sapphire standard to sample container on an analytical balance.
      iii. Carefully load the sample container with sapphire standard to sample holder with the reference container empty.
      iv. Record the mass (m_r) of the standard. This mass will be used to calculate the instrument calibration constant, k.
      v.   Start the heating program. After the run is completed, display and save the thermogram as heat flow vs. time as shown in Figure 11-8.
      vi. Choose the temperature (e.g. 87 and 107°C) at which the heat capacity of sample is to be determined. Measure the vertical distance between the run of empty pan and the sapphire standard (D_r, unit is the same as the heat flow axis) at the temperatures of interest.
      vii. Calculate k at the temperatures of interest using Eqn. 11C-3. Specific heat capacity of sapphire (C_p) can be found in the table of Appendix 11A.

   d. *Measure C_p of silicone oil*

      i.   Follow the same procedure in Step **c** to obtain the thermogram for silicone oil sample.
      ii. Measure the vertical distance between the run of empty pan and the silicone oil (D_s) at the same temperature in Step **c**.
      iii. Calculate C_p of silicone oil (C_{ps}) with Eqn. 11C-3 using k value obtained in Step **c**.

iv. Alternately, use Eqn. 11C-4 to calculate C_{ps} of silicone oil. This should give the same result.

e. Follow the procedure above to measure C_p of LDPE at chosen temperature (e.g. 67°C).

f. After the furnace assemblies have cooled sufficiently, remove the sample. If you are running multiple DSC scans, you may use the same reference pan. If you are done with your testing, remove the reference pan.

g. *Hardware shutdown*: After the experiment is completed, turn off the nitrogen purge gas. Turn off the computer and the main power switch on the instrument.

F. Result report

1. Include the thermogram(s) of the empty pan, the standard and the samples.
2. Calculate C_p of samples used. Show following calculations in your lab report.

   a. Calculate instrument calibration constant k at selected temperatures (67, 87, 107°C) using Eqn. 11C-3.
   b. Calculate C_p of silicone oil at 87 and 107°C using Eqn. 11C-3 with k value derived from standard reference.
   c. Calculate C_p of LDPE polymer at 67°C using Eqn. 11C-3.
   d. Calculate C_p of silicone oil and LDPE at appropriate temperatures using Eqn. 11C-4.

G. Questions for Discussion

1. Discuss what are the main sources of uncertainties in your estimation of C_p of the samples?
2. Explain why it's useful to couple DSC with TGA and mass spectrometry.
3. What are the differences between DTA and DSC? What are the advantages and disadvantages of the two techniques?

H. Supplementary Experiment: Determination of Glass Transition Temperature of Polymer (T_g) with DSC

Introduction: The glass–liquid transition (or glass transition) is the reversible transition in amorphous materials (or in amorphous regions within semicrystalline materials) from a hard and relatively brittle state into a molten or rubber-like state. The glass transition temperature, T_g, is the characteristic temperature of this process.

In the DSC experiment, T_g is manifested by a change in the base line, indicating a change in the heat capacity of the polymer (Figure 11-10). No enthalpy is associated with the glass transition, so the glass transition is second order transition. The effect of glass transition on a DSC curve is slight and is observable only if the instrument is sufficiently sensitive.

Figure 11-10 The glass transition. If there are sloping baselines before and after the glass transition, the baseline before the transition is extrapolated forwards and the baseline after the transition is extrapolated backwards (as shown by dotted lines). The baseline shift is measured when the transition is about 50% complete (as shown by arrows).

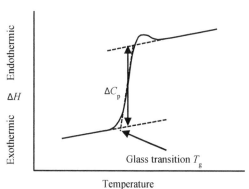

Experiment: Weigh 5-20 mg any type of plastic into sample container. Follow the similar program illustrated in the main experiment to obtain thermagram (heat flow vs. temperature). Determine T_g by extrapolating the baselines as shown in Figure 11-10.

I. Reference

1. McNaught, A. D. and A. Wilkinson, 1997. Compendium of Chemical Terminology, 2nd ed. (IUPAC, the "Gold Book"). Blackwell Scientific Publications, Oxford.
2. Harris J. D. and A. W. Rusch, 2013. Identifying Hydrated Salts Using Simultaneous Thermogravimetric Analysis and Differential Scanning Calorimetry. J. Chem. Educ. 90 (2): 235–238.
3. Richardson, M. J and E. L. Charsley, 1998. Chapter 13 Calibration and Standardisation in DSC, Original Research Article, Handbook of Thermal Analysis and Calorimetry, Volume 1, 1998, Pages 547-575.
4. D'Amico, T., C. J. Donahue and E. A. Rais, 2008. Thermal Analysis of Plastics. J. Chem. Educ. 85(3): 404-407.
5. Gatta, G. D., M. J. Richardson, S. M. Sarge and S. Stølen, 2006. Standards, Calibration, and Guidelines in Microcalorimetry, Part 2. Calibration Standards for Differential Scanning Calorimetry. Pure Appl. Chem. 78(7): 1455–1476.

J. Appendix 11A

Heat capacity data (literature values) for sapphire as a function of temperature. The values in the table were determined by Ginnings and Furukawa of the National Bureau of Standards on aluminum oxide in the form of synthetic sapphire (corundum). The sapphire pieces passed a #10 sieve but were retained by a #40 sieve, and had 99.98 to 99.99 % purity by weight.

Temperature		Heat Capacity	Temperature		Heat Capacity
T (°C)	T (K)	C_p (J/g°C)	T (°C)	T (K)	C_p (J/g°C)
6.85	280	0.7343	126.85	400	0.9423
16.85	290	0.7572	136.85	410	0.9545
26.85	300	0.7788	146.85	420	0.9660
36.85	310	0.7994	156.85	430	0.9770
46.85	320	0.8188	166.85	440	0.9875
56.85	330	0.8373	176.85	450	0.9975
66.85	340	0.8548	186.85	460	1.0070
76.85	350	0.8713	196.85	470	1.0161
86.85	360	0.8871	206.85	480	1.0247
96.85	370	0.9020	216.85	490	1.0330
106.85	380	0.9296	226.85	500	1.0409
116.85	390	0.9296	236.85	510	1.0484

Appendix A: International Atomic Masses (IUPAC 2009)

Name	Symbol	Atomic Number	Atomic Mass	Name	Symbol	Atomic Number	Atomic Mass
Actinium	Ac	89	[227]	Mendelevium	Md	101	[258]
Aluminium	Al	13	26.9815386(8)	Mercury	Hg	80	200.59(2)
Americium	Am	95	[243]	Molybdenum	Mo	42	95.96(2)
Antimony	Sb	51	121.760(1)	Neodymium	Nd	60	144.242(3)
Argon	Ar	18	39.948(1)	Neon	Ne	10	20.1797(6)
Arsenic	As	33	74.92160(2)	Neptunium	Np	93	[237]
Astatine	At	85	[210]	Nickel	Ni	28	58.6934(4)
Barium	Ba	56	137.327(7)	Niobium	Nb	41	92.90638(2)
Berkelium	Bk	97	[247]	Nitrogen	N	7	14.007
Beryllium	Be	4	9.012182(3)	Nobelium	No	102	[259]
Bismuth	Bi	83	208.98040(1)	Osmium	Os	76	190.23(3)
Bohrium	Bh	107	[270]	Oxygen	O	8	15.999
Boron	B	5	10.81	Palladium	Pd	46	106.42(1)
Bromine	Br	35	79.904(1)	Phosphorus	P	15	30.973762(2)
Cadmium	Cd	48	112.411(8)	Platinum	Pt	78	195.084(9)
Caesium	Cs	55	132.9054519(2)	Plutonium	Pu	94	[244]
Calcium	Ca	20	40.078(4)	Polonium	Po	84	[209]
Californium	Cf	98	[251]	Potassium	K	19	39.0983(1)
Carbon	C	6	12.011	Praseodymium	Pr	59	140.90765(2)
Cerium	Ce	58	140.116(1)	Promethium	Pm	61	[145]
Chlorine	Cl	17	35.45	Protactinium	Pa	91	231.03588(2)
Chromium	Cr	24	51.9961(6)	Radium	Ra	88	[226]
Cobalt	Co	27	58.933195(5)	Radon	Rn	86	[222]
Copernicium	Cn	112	[285]	Rhenium	Re	75	186.207(1)
Copper	Cu	29	63.546(3)	Rhodium	Rh	45	102.90550(2)
Curium	Cm	96	[247]	Roentgenium	Rg	111	[280]
Darmstadtium	Ds	110	[281]	Rubidium	Rb	37	85.4678(3)
Dubnium	Db	105	[268]	Ruthenium	Ru	44	101.07(2)
Dysprosium	Dy	66	162.500(1)	Rutherfordium	Rf	104	[265]
Einsteinium	Es	99	[252]	Samarium	Sm	62	150.36(2)
Erbium	Er	68	167.259(3)	Scandium	Sc	21	44.955912(6)
Europium	Eu	63	151.964(1)	Seaborgium	Sg	106	[271]
Fermium	Fm	100	[257]	Selenium	Se	34	78.96(3)
Flerovium	Fl	114	[289]	Silicon	Si	14	28.085
Fluorine	F	9	18.9984032(5)	Silver	Ag	47	107.8682(2)
Francium	Fr	87	[223]	Sodium	Na	11	22.98976928(2)
Gadolinium	Gd	64	157.25(3)	Strontium	Sr	38	87.62(1)
Gallium	Ga	31	69.723(1)	Sulfur	S	16	32.06
Germanium	Ge	32	72.63(1)	Tantalum	Ta	73	180.94788(2)
Gold	Au	79	196.966569(4)	Technetium	Tc	43	[98]
Hafnium	Hf	72	178.49(2)	Tellurium	Te	52	127.60(3)
Hassium	Hs	108	[277]	Terbium	Tb	65	158.92535(2)
Helium	He	2	4.002602(2)	Thallium	Tl	81	204.38
Holmium	Ho	67	164.93032(2)	Thorium	Th	90	232.03806(2)
Hydrogen	H	1	1.008	Thulium	Tm	69	168.93421(2)
Indium	In	49	114.818(3)	Tin	Sn	50	118.710(7)
Iodine	I	53	126.90447(3)	Titanium	Ti	22	47.867(1)
Iridium	Ir	77	192.217(3)	Tungsten	W	74	183.84(1)
Iron	Fe	26	55.845(2)	Ununoctium	Uuo	118	[294]
Krypton	Kr	36	83.798(2)	Ununpentium	Uup	115	[288]
Lanthanum	La	57	138.90547(7)	Ununseptium	Uus	117	[294]
Lawrencium	Lr	103	[262]	Ununtrium	Uut	113	[284]
Lead	Pb	82	207.2(1)	Uranium	U	92	238.02891(3)
Lithium	Li	3	6.94	Vanadium	V	23	50.9415(1)
Livermorium	Lv	116	[293]	Xenon	Xe	54	131.293(6)
Lutetium	Lu	71	174.9668(1)	Ytterbium	Yb	70	173.054(5)
Magnesium	Mg	12	24.3050(6)	Yttrium	Y	39	88.90585(2)
Manganese	Mn	25	54.938045(5)	Zinc	Zn	30	65.38(2)
Meitnerium	Mt	109	[276]	Zirconium	Zr	40	91.224(2)

Numbers in parentheses indicate the uncertainties in the blast digital of the atomic mass. Number in brackets indicates the mass number of the longest-lived isotope of the element.

Appendix B: SI Base Unit

Base quantity	Name	Symbol
Length	meter	m
Mass	kilogram	kg
Time	second	s
Electric current	ampere	A
Thermodynamic temperature	kelvin	K
Amount of substance	mole	mol
Luminous intensity	candela	cd

Appendix C: Derived Units

Derived quantity	Name	Symbol
Area	square meter	m^2
Volume	cubic meter	m^3
Speed, velocity	meter per second	m/s
Acceleration	meter per second squared	m/s^2
Wave number	reciprocal meter	m^{-1}
Mass density	kilogram per cubic meter	kg/m^3
Specific volume	cubic meter per kilogram	m^3/kg
Current density	ampere per square meter	A/m^2
Magnetic field strength	ampere per meter	A/m
Amount-of-substance concentration	mole per cubic meter	mol/m^3
Luminance	candela per square meter	cd/m^2
Mass fraction	kilogram per kilogram, which may be represented by the number 1	kg/kg = 1

Appendix D: Derived Units with Special Names and Symbols

Derived quantity	Name	Symbol	Expression in terms of other SI units	Expression in terms of SI base units
Frequency	hertz	Hz	-	s^{-1}
Force	newton	N	-	$m \cdot kg \cdot s^{-2}$
Pressure, stress	pascal	Pa	N/m^2	$m^{-1} \cdot kg \cdot s^{-2}$
Energy, work, quantity of heat	joule	J	$N \cdot m$	$m^2 \cdot kg \cdot s^{-2}$
Power, radiant flux	watt	W	J/s	$m^2 \cdot kg \cdot s^{-3}$
Electric charge, quantity of electricity	coulomb	C	-	$s \cdot A$
Electric potential difference	volt	V	W/A	$m^2 \cdot kg \cdot s^{-3} \cdot A^{-1}$
Capacitance	farad	F	C/V	$m^{-2} \cdot kg^{-1} \cdot s^4 \cdot A^2$
Electric resistance	ohm	Ω	V/A	$m^2 \cdot kg \cdot s^{-3} \cdot A^{-2}$
Electric conductance	siemens	S	A/V	$m^{-2} \cdot kg^{-1} \cdot s^3 \cdot A^2$
Magnetic flux	weber	Wb	$V \cdot s$	$m^2 \cdot kg \cdot s^{-2} \cdot A^{-1}$
magnetic flux density	tesla	T	Wb/m^2	$kg \cdot s^{-2} \cdot A^{-1}$
Inductance	henry	H	Wb/A	$m^2 \cdot kg \cdot s^{-2} \cdot A^{-2}$
Celsius temperature	degree Celsius	°C	-	K
Luminous flux	lumen	lm	$cd \cdot sr$ [c]	$m^2 \cdot m^{-2} \cdot cd = cd$
Illuminance	lux	lx	lm/m^2	$m^2 \cdot m^{-4} \cdot cd = m^{-2} \cdot cd$
Catalytic activity	katal	kat		$s^{-1} \cdot mol$

Appendix E: Important Physical Constants

Constant	Symbol	Value
Atomic mass unit	amu, m_u or u	1.66×10^{-27} kg
Avogadro's Number	N	6.022×10^{23} mol^{-1}
Bohr radius	a_0	0.529×10^{-10} m
Boltzmann constant	k	1.38×10^{-23} J K^{-1}
Faraday constant	F	9.649×10^4 C mol^{-1}
Gas constant	R	8.314 J mol^{-1} K^{-1}
Planck constant	h	6.626×10^{-34} J s
Speed of light in vacuum	C	2.9979×10^8 m/s

Appendix F Partial *t*-table

1-tailed	0.05	0.025	0.01	0.005	0.001
2-tailed	0.1	0.05	0.02	0.01	0.002
df					
1	6.314	12.706	31.821	63.657	318.310
2	2.920	4.303	6.965	9.925	22.326
3	2.353	3.182	4.541	5.841	10.213
4	2.132	2.776	3.747	4.604	7.173
5	2.015	2.571	3.365	4.032	5.893
6	1.943	2.447	3.143	3.707	5.208
7	1.895	2.365	2.998	3.499	4.785
8	1.86	2.306	2.896	3.355	4.501
9	1.833	2.262	2.821	3.250	4.297
10	1.812	2.228	2.764	3.169	4.144
11	1.796	2.201	2.718	3.106	4.025
12	1.782	2.179	2.681	3.055	3.930
13	1.771	2.160	2.650	3.012	3.852
14	1.761	2.145	2.624	2.977	3.787
15	1.753	2.131	2.602	2.947	3.733
16	1.746	2.120	2.583	2.921	3.686
17	1.74	2.110	2.567	2.898	3.646
18	1.734	2.101	2.552	2.878	3.610
19	1.729	2.093	2.539	2.861	3.579

CPSIA information can be obtained
at www.ICGtesting.com
Printed in the USA
LVHW061931040122
707835LV00009B/761